Therapy with Older Clients

A Norton Professional Book

Therapy with Older Clients

Key Strategies for Success

MARC E. AGRONIN

W. W. NORTON & COMPANY
New York • London

For information about permission to reproduce selections from this
book, write to Permissions, W. W. Norton & Company, Inc., 500 Fifth
Avenue, New York, NY 10110

For information about special discounts for bulk purchases, please
contact W. W. Norton Special Sales at specialsales@wwnorton.com or
800-233-4830

Manufacturing by Worldcolor, Fairfield Graphics
Production Manager: Leeann Graham

Library of Congress Cataloging-in-Publication Data

Agronin, Marc E.
    Therapy with older clients : key strategies for success / Marc E.
Agronin. — 1st ed.
        p.   ; cm.
    "A Norton professional book"—t.p. verso.
    Includes bibliographical references and index.
    ISBN 978-0-393-70583-6 (hardcover)
1. Geriatric psychiatry.   I. Title.
[DNLM: 1. Psychotherapy—methods.   2. Aged—psychology.
3. Aging—psychology.   4. Empathy.   5. Geriatric Psychiatry—
methods.   6. Professional-Patient Relations.   WT 150 A281t 2010]
RC451.4.A5A383   2010
618.97'689—dc22   2009054278

ISBN: 978-0-393-70583-6

W. W. Norton & Company, Inc., 500 Fifth Avenue,
New York, N.Y. 10110
www.wwnorton.com

W. W. Norton & Company Ltd., Castle House, 75/76 Wells St.,
London W1T 3QT
1   2   3   4   5   6   7   8   9   0

This book is dedicated to the humble older men and women—soldiers and survivors of the great and terrible war among them—who have come to my office as clients. They have graciously served as my teachers, guides, and sages and have taught me key lessons about hope.

With gratitude to my wife, Robin, and sons, Jacob, Max, and Sam, for their support, time, and necessary distractions, which allowed me to write this book.

Contents

Acknowledgments

I am indebted to Andrea Costella, my editor at W. W. Norton, for conceiving the idea for this book, seeking me out, and providing a wealth of guidance, support, and patience. I offer my gratitude as well to Associate Managing Editor Vani Kannan, who offered the best of comments and suggestions to shepherd the manuscript to its final form. The book that first inspired my interest in psychiatry so many years ago was published by W. W. Norton, and so it is truly a special honor for me to contribute to their catalog.

I would also like to acknowledge the influence of so many therapists who have served as my own teachers, supervisors, and colleagues over the years, indirectly enabling me to write this book. Herb Cohen and Leslie Cedar have been particularly exemplary role models.

I would like to thank the staff and residents of Miami Jewish Health Systems for supporting the role of a geriatric psychiatrist in their midst. In particular, several colleagues provided case material for the therapeutic approaches cited in the book: Victoria Barnett, Michele Fiorot, Shyla Ford, Rita

Gugel, Chrystine Kopscik, Mairelys Martinez, and Stephanie Willis.

Finally, though I cannot cite them individually, I profusely thank the countless older clients with whom I have worked over the years for allowing me that opportunity. This book is dedicated to them.

Therapy with Older Clients

Introduction

The ideal encounter with an aged individual is sometimes best reflected through the eyes of a child. I have learned this on the many Sunday afternoons when I have brought one or more of my three sons to the nursing home where I work as a geriatric psychiatrist. For a young boy or girl, it is an exciting place, as the expansive inner courtyard of this venerable Miami institution is shaded by the canopies of two massive 400-year-old Kapok trees that offer hiding places between the undulations of their lower trunks, which splay into equally massive roots. Children love to chase the brown- and gold-speckled wild chickens around the trellised gardens and run in and out of the courtyard's large wooden gazebo, which is surrounded by an impressive banyan tree and several tall fern-bearded date palms. As it usually turns out, an equally memorable part of the day for even the most rambunctious child is the journey onto the floors to visit the resident grandparents and other loved ones. As an adult, I am fascinated by how the residents gravitate toward the visiting children, holding out hands, smiling, and calling out greetings in English, Spanish, Creole, and Yiddish.

On one particular visit, I took my oldest son, who was then 6 years old, to meet our oldest resident, a 106-year-old woman named Gloria. My son was bursting with questions en route: "How old is she really? What is it like to be 106?" and "What does she do all day?" He wondered whether she would be like the Japanese super-centenarian Kamato Hongo, who at the age of 116 would sleep for 2 days and then remain awake for the subsequent 2. When we met up with Gloria, his questioning suddenly ceased, and the two eyes that just moments before had been darting about the white-tiled corridors now became like saucers. I beheld the scene of my young son and the elderly woman staring at each other in wonder at the 100 years between them. I saw in my son's face and in his entire demeanor a sense of awe and deep curiosity. We have had many visits to the facility since then, but he still remembers that ineffable moment.

If my only task were to offer up the single most important therapeutic tool for working as a mental health clinician with older clients, I would bottle up my young son's stance that day as the ultimate tonic. Innumerable clinical experiences with aged individuals have taught me the indelible lesson that a spirit of wonder is always the most effective therapeutic guide. I say this knowing that all the challenges we face with clients suffering from mental distress are amplified in later life, and can easily overwhelm the patience and care that we aspire to bring to each encounter. The mission of this book, then, is to provide clinicians with several key tools to guide them through the reality of working with older clients while preserving the basic values that inspire our best work. But at the outset of this journey, let me emphasize three key interrelated virtues that underlie all successful therapeutic work.

Curiosity

Curiosity has many definitions but perhaps is best illustrated by the words of one of its keenest practitioners. "Experience has taught me," wrote the great American psychiatrist Henry Murray, "to believe in no fixation of beliefs, but in the exciting process of perpetually reconstructing them in order to encompass new facts, experiences, and conditions" (1954/1981, p. 613). Such a pervasive spirit of curiosity allows the clinician to delve into the complexity of the older client with interest, openness, and patience. It brings us requisite knowledge for the clinical assessment as well as enjoyment in learning about an individual's long life and in the process helps to forge a caring relationship. The mastery of one's curiosity with the older client—meaning the ability to bring it appropriately to the service of the client, not simply satiating one's own intellectual or emotional impulses—is a key component to maturation as a therapist.

Curiosity also helps us understand and cope with certain paradoxes of aging without becoming overwhelmed or despairing. The importance of wrestling with a similar clinical dialectic was illustrated in a fascinating essay titled "The Productive Paradoxes of William James," written by the social psychologist Gordon Allport (1943). In this essay, Allport spoke of several key "riddles" that each psychologist encounters in his or her work, including the psychophysical riddle ("How is the mind related to the body?") and the riddle of the self ("How do you explain the unity of the human personality?"). Allport described how William James had a particularly successful way of exploring all aspects of each riddle without insisting on an answer. This ability may have stemmed, in part, from James's own developmental encounters with coexisting states of deep depression and great hope. Like Murray, Allport spoke to the nobility of curiosity: "Narrow consistency can neither bring salvation to your science, nor help to mankind. Let your approaches be diverse. . . . If you find yourselves tangled in paradoxes, what of that?" (1943, p. 119).

My first instruction to the reader is thus to allow your curiosity to explore what I am calling the "productive paradoxes of aging," for they are recurrent themes throughout the book. Like the internal workings of each cell in the human body, each of these paradoxes of aging deals with the simultaneous building up and breaking down of the products of life. The goal of this book is to strongly emphasize the positive elements that are often overlooked, with the therapist's and client's curiosity serving as the key to their discovery. These paradoxes include the following.

The Paradox of Body Versus Mind

In Chapter 1 I explore a definition of aging and several major theories of the life cycle. Most striking in this discussion is the tension between the absolute decline of the aging body set against the distinct possibility of mental growth and maturation. We sometimes assume that bodily decay brings inevitable mental decay, but this is a limited view of the aging process, as it does not balance the measurable continuity of cellular aging with the qualitative discontinuities seen in late-life psychological development.

The Paradox of Growth Versus Decline

It can be dizzying to inventory all the age-related changes in the social and psychological lives of older clients, especially as they struggle with the drive to preserve or even expand certain core habits, relationships, and activities at the same time they face enormous losses in these domains. Chapter 2 explores the roles of the therapist in dealing with these seemingly opposing forces with varying client types and in different settings and focuses on how we react to and cope with our own internal fears and prejudices toward aging. Chapter 3 reviews how the evaluation of the older client can best identify most of these important age-related elements, and Chapter 4 discusses the roles and reactions of caregivers.

The Paradox of Eros Versus Thanatos

The proximity of Thanatos, or death, in late life grows ever greater even as individuals pursue Eros, represented by loving and life-affirming relationships and activities. The common age-related clinical issues discussed in Chapters 5 through 8 represent the discontinuities in the pursuit of Eros, such as those due to physical illness, pain, depression, cognitive impairment, or the loss of loved ones, and the submission to Thanatos as some individuals withdraw from life in despair. By reviewing major diagnoses and therapeutic modalities, the four central chapters of this text present some of the most effective techniques to balance out these forces.

The Paradox of Renewal Versus Cessation

In the final stage of life, there may be a cessation of certain activities and relationships that are seen as inaccessible or just too difficult to maintain. Sometimes even therapists come to silently conspire with clients to accept the futility of certain pursuits, especially in the context of dementia. As a counterpoint to this, Chapter 9 discusses how the renewal of vital skills and endeavors in the last days of an individual's life can bring transcendent pleasure and meaning. The therapist's own creativity and passion for working with aged clients can sometimes bring a spectacular transformation to even the most debilitated individuals.

Ultimately, curiosity plays a life-giving role in the therapeutic dyad. For the therapist, it drives age-specific therapeutic modalities such as reminiscence or life review therapy and problem-solving therapy. In the client it is a trait associated with positive emotions, enhanced intelligence and decision making, and even lower mortality rates (Peterson & Seligman, 2004; Swan & Carmelli, 1996). When engaged, it allows us to momentarily suspend the need for certainty and paves the way for new discoveries that serve, in turn, as the very substrates of hope.

Caring

Older individuals come into therapy for reasons that are both age-specific and timeless. Regardless, the facticity of aging imposes a sense of existential vulnerability on most individuals that increases the risk of despair, disgust, and disintegration in response to ongoing losses. One critical antidote to these forces is the therapist's ability to care for the client with a spirit of several closely related virtues, including kindness, compassion, and generosity. This stance seems obvious but can actually be quite challenging, especially in work with individuals who are losing the intellectual ability to articulate their thoughts and engage in a mutual relationship.

A fundamental skill inherent to caring is empathy, defined

by Howard Book as the ability to creatively imagine what another individual is thinking and feeling and to mentally "oscillate from being observer to being participant to being observer" (1988, p. 421). The current psychological literature distinguishes between a passive, receptive form of empathy and one that is more active and projective (Halpern, 2001; Hoffman, 2000). The great American poet and small-town physician William Carlos Williams described the former approach in his day-to-day practice:

> I lost myself in the very properties of their minds: for the moment at least I actually became them, whoever they should be, so that when I detached myself from them at the end of a half-hour of intense concentration over some illness which was affecting them, it was as though I was reawakening from a sleep. For the moment I myself did not exist, nothing of myself affected me. As a consequence I came back to myself, as from any other sleep, rested. (1958/1984, p. 119)

Such a sublime connection with his patients was well reflected in William Carlos Williams's poetry and short stories. We must bear in mind, however, that in contrast to a small-town family practitioner such as Williams, therapists must be able to limit their engrossment in the client's story. The psychiatrist and philosopher Jodi Halpern has argued that in a more ideal form of empathy, the "empathizer is able to resonate emotionally with, yet stay aware of, what is distinct about the patient's experience" (2001, p. 85). The ability to put this balanced approach into action with older clients is described throughout the book.

Courage

The third pillar of clinical work with aged individuals is courage, a multifaceted virtue that involves persistent and honest action in the face of great challenges. With older clients, these challenges involve simultaneous medical, psychiatric, and social impairments set against the ever-approaching horizon of an individual's life span. At the same time, both psychopharmacological and psychotherapeutic treatments can take longer to work in late life, defying our initial expectations for recovery. In the face of this uphill struggle with the older client, we may come to view therapy as futile, and this viewpoint quickly percolates out to clients and their caregivers. Somehow we must be able to persist in our efforts by retooling our approaches, shoring up our patience, and realizing that our very presence as a caring listener can make a difference over time.

At the core of therapeutic work with older clients is the singular challenge of dealing with our own fears of aging, disability, and death that loom over every encounter. Without the ongoing cultivation and reevaluation of the three interrelated virtues emphasized here, our clinical work risks becoming heartless and frustrating. These risks are even greater when we are working with clients living with forms of cognitive or physical impairment who are limited in their abilities to interact with us, and who may not notice or be able to defend themselves against attitudes or actions that are discriminatory, disrespectful, or intrusive. But if we are able to stand in front of our older clients with a sense of wonder and awe for the true gifts that aging has given them, our work with them will flow naturally and be imbued with energy and hope. On that basis, all the therapeutic tools I describe in this volume will prove useful.

A Few Words on the Book

This book differs from other professional material on therapy with older clients in its very practical case-based approach that focuses as much on the *how* of therapy as on the *what*. Such an approach derives from the fact that an understanding of aging alone is not sufficient to make one an effective therapist, but it must be coupled with a genuine interest and rapport with the client. To a large extent, these unique interpersonal aspects of working with older clients can only be learned through experience. I have tried, however, to provide both the form and the feel of therapy in order to approximate such hands-on learning.

Some readers might be wondering why I use the term *client* in this book as opposed to *patient*. The term *patient* seems more in line with the prevailing medical model of mental health care, whereas *client* seems to imply more of a business relationship. There is a reason for this. Historically speaking, this usage derives from the client-centered therapy pioneered by Carl Rogers and other therapists starting in the 1950s. A major tenet of the philosophy behind this approach was that the individual in therapy—the *client*—has the inner strengths necessary to recover. It is the job of the therapist to provide a comfortable and supportive environment for these strengths to emerge. When we undertake therapy with older individuals, we must recognize the existence of these strengths even in the most seemingly debilitated person. Because this philosophy permeates the book, the term *client* seems most appropriate.

It is my sincerest hope that this book will help readers feel inspired and energized in their work with older clients. As the number of aged individuals booms over the coming decades, the clinical mission to which this book is dedicated will become even more in demand, and there must be a dedicated pool of clinicians ready to support their mental health needs. To this end, I welcome readers to share with me their comments and suggestions on the material.

Marc E. Agronin, MD
Magronin@mjhha.org

1

PERSPECTIVES ON THE OLDER CLIENT

What do we mean when we refer to a client as *old*? What happens to a person over time that makes him or her old? And what fundamental aspects of being old are most relevant to psychotherapy? These are the central questions of this chapter. The terms *older* and *aged* are used interchangeably throughout the text, both monikers generally referring to individuals who are at least 65 years old and are dealing to a greater or lesser extent with psychotherapeutic issues shaped by age-associated factors. The starting point of 65 years is certainly not a magic number, as there are no specific watershed physical or psychological events at this age that automatically confer "oldness" on a person. Nonetheless, the scientific literature uses the age of 65 as the most widely recognized designation of oldness, perhaps inspired by the fact that it is the age at which individuals in the United States become eligible for Medicare benefits. Over the last several decades, however, the age of 65 has come to seem increasingly young, especially because the fastest-growing age group is actually those 85 years and above, centenarians being the single fastest-growing age (U.S. Census Bureau, 1999). Moreover, for therapists working with elderly individuals, it is common for the majority of their clients to be in their 80s and 90s. On the flip side, some individuals slightly younger than 65 years old present with age-related diseases or other disabilities that pose many of the same problems seen in older individuals. Fortunately, the information dispensed in this book is less dependent on exact chronological age and more on the age-associated issues at hand.

What Is Old?

An essential tool in every therapeutic setting is the clock. The perpetual passing of its hands not only measures the time spent with the client but sets the schedule for the work at hand, determines the requisite fees, and creates the history that we eventually weave into a formulation and treatment plan. And yet despite the inescapable uniformity of each minute and hour that we spend with the client, the experience of time is quite malleable. Therapy time seems short or long, routine or momentous, and strikes us as distant or absorbing, depending upon the events of the hour. We cannot truly turn back time, but the history discussed during the therapy session and its impact on life events may jump all over time, resurrecting distant memories and emotions that defy the notion of a past.

The concept of aging that we apply to our work with older clients holds similar properties. Current theories of biological aging, or senescence, postulate a form of a molecular clock in our DNA that keeps track of time and is associated with changes in the human body and brain. This cellular clock was discovered in the early 1960s by the eminent biologist Leonard Hayflick, who observed that cultured human cells undergo a finite number of divisions and then die. Known as the Hayflick limit, this phenomenon may be determined on a molecular level by the shortening of a region of repetitive DNA at the end of each chromosome (known as the telomere) with each cell division (Hayflick, 1994). At the same time, human cells slowly accumulate damage to their DNA and other structures from the buildup of toxic agents such as highly reactive oxygen molecules known as free radicals. Cellular metabolism and function are further eroded by the cumulative deleterious effects of abnormal binding between sugars and proteins in processes such as glycation and cross-linking, by declining levels of stimulatory growth factors and other hormones, and by excess levels of stress hormones known as glucocorticoids (Butler, 2008; Sapolsky, Krey, & McEwen, 1986).

The direct results of cellular senescence at the level of bodily tissues and organs include declining functions across the board: decreased clearance of toxins in the blood by the liver and kidneys; decreased strength and resilience of muscle, bone, and connective tissues; decreased respiratory capacity and cardiac output; decreased sensory acuity; and in the brain the slowing of mental processing and the increased risk of cognitive disorders (Leventhal & Burns, 2004; Rupert, Loewenstein, & Eisdorfer, 2004). Put together, this entire process of aging is defined by Arking as the "time-dependent series of cumulative, progressive, intrinsic, and deleterious functional and structural changes that usually begin to manifest themselves at reproductive maturity and eventually culminate in death" (2006, p. 11). Along the way, we do have a certain degree of control over the events that either facilitate or retard the process of biological aging, and increasingly we are seeing what James Fries (1980) has described as a compression of disease and disability into a much later and shorter period of time for those living up to and beyond 100 years.

The *experience* of aging, however, is a different process entirely, measured less by the movement of the hands of the clock or the strands of the chromosomal telomeres and more by moments of joy or disappointment, solitude or intimacy, and the vital involvements or routines that fill our lives. It is exactly at these points of friction between the aging body and mind where the therapist enters the scene. The ensuing therapeutic process, regardless of its form, is shaped by several core elements, including the state of the aging brain, the individual's adaptation to aging, social and historical forces, and the psychological strengths and weaknesses conferred by the individual's personality and its ongoing development across the life cycle.

The Aging Brain

The paradoxes of aging described in the introduction to this book all stem from contradictions between the aging of brain structures (and its associated impact on discrete neuropsychological functions) and a larger view of the human experience in later life. These opposing elements will soon become clear.

At the moment of birth, the human brain has already eliminated half of its original stock of 200 billion brain cells, or neurons. This illustrates the fact that from the time of its very formation, the brain is actively remodeling itself to maximize the availability and connectivity of critical centers while pruning back on other components. A tremendous amount of neuronal development occurs from childhood through young adulthood, resulting in a peak of well over 100 trillion connections or synapses between neurons. With aging beyond middle adulthood, however, this trend reverses, with increasing neuronal loss throughout the brain brought on by all the factors inherent to cellular senescence as well as by variable extrinsic pathological factors such as microvascular damage due to atherosclerosis and hypertension, direct trauma, toxic exposures, stroke, and neurodegenerative brain disorders such as Alzheimer's disease and other forms of dementia.

Under normal conditions, it is estimated that from the age of 65 through 90 years old, the brain loses anywhere from 10% to 80% of the neurons in various regions, hitting hard subcortical centers such as the hippocampus, the nucleus basalis of Meynert, and the locus ceruleus, which are critical to memory function and emotional regulation, respectively (Timiras, 1994; Victoroff, 2005). This cumulative neuronal damage and loss leads to decreases in the synthesis, release, and overall synaptic transmission of key neurotransmitters such as norepinephrine, acetylcholine, dopamine, and GABA (Rupert et al., 2004; Victoroff, 2005), often setting the stage for the disturbances in personality, mood, and behavior that bring clients into therapy. Look at any aged brain and you will see generalized atrophy, widening of the fluid-filled ventricles, and the presence of microscopic pathology such as extracellular amyloid-filled plaques and intracellular proteinaceous neurofibrillary tangles—the same features seen in much greater magnitude in Alzheimer's disease (Pickholtz & Malamut, 2008).

So what is the impact of these normal anatomical changes on actual brain function? The answer is not clear, as normal neuronal loss in the older brain in the absence of dementia is quite variable and has not been demonstrated to correlate with specific impairments. We do know, however, that aging is associated with mild but predictable decreases in immediate, short-term, and working memory functions; cognitive processing speed; selective and divided attention; complex visuospatial skills; speech comprehension; verbal/word fluency; the ability to name objects; psychomotor performance; numeric ability; and sensory perception (Mahncke, Bronstone, & Merzenich, 2006; Rupert et al., 2004; Schaie & Willis, 1993; Sugar & McDowd, 1992). The typical patterns of decline from the 20s to 80s, as observed in the Seattle Longitudinal Study (Schaie, 2005; Siegler et al., 2009), are illustrated in Figure 1.1. As can be seen in the figure, skills such as numeric ability and word fluency peak early and then decline mildly starting in the early 50s, whereas skills such as inductive reasoning, verbal ability, and spatial orientation peak in the 30s to 60s and then begin to decline in the late 60s and early 70s. By the 80s, all cognitive skills studied in the Seattle study demonstrate considerable decline.

Other longitudinal research has emphasized, however, that several cognitive skills remain remarkably stable with aging, including sustained attention, vocabulary, verbal expression,

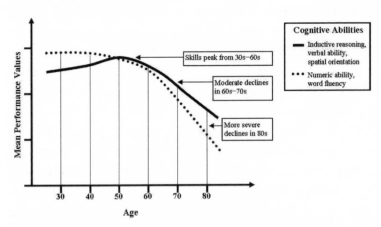

Figure 1.1. Longitudinal changes in cognitive abilities. Adapted from the results of the Seattle Longitudinal Study presented by Schaie (2005) and Siegler et al. (2009).

general knowledge or semantic memory, long-term memory, and the ability of the brain to organize and abstract, known as executive function (Dunkin & Amano, 2005; Pickholtz & Malamut, 2008). Mean performance scores across all cognitive skills have generally increased with successive cohorts over the past century (Schaie, 2005). In addition, we know from studies such as the Advanced Cognitive Training for Independent and Vital Elderly or ACTIVE trial that cognitive training programs can lead over time to sustained improvements across a variety of cognitive and functional skills (Ball et al., 2002; Willis et al., 2006).

Amid all the focus on the potential for cognitive stability in some areas at best, and decline in most other areas as the rule, there is a bright spot. General knowledge does increase with time, as does the experience that comes with age. A number of researchers have proposed that a person's cognitive style has the potential to mature with age in ways that go beyond Piaget's concept of formal operations—a stage that occurs by young adulthood and is characterized by the ability to formulate and test hypotheses and thus deal with variability (Agronin, 1994). Postformal thinking has been given many labels in the literature, including structural analytic thought (Commons & Richards, 1984), dialectical thinking (Basseches, 1984), and intersystemic thought (LaBouvie-Vief, 1982), and is described as the maturing ability to think relatively and to appreciate the tensions between competing sets of relationships or systems. Stevens-Long summarized how older thinkers can "integrate logic and the irrational aspect of experience. . . . [They] see not only how truth can be a product of a particular system, but also how the thinker participates in creating the truth" (1990, p. 133). Extrapolating into late life, we can presume that these changes may allow an individual to think less logically but

17

more pragmatically, finding solutions that are socially adequate to his or her needs (Agronin, 1994).

A bolder and more popular term that also captures the concept of postformal thinking is *wisdom*. As the neuropsychologist Elkhonon Goldberg has described it, wisdom springs from a maturing brain that has, over the years, developed well-worn neural pathways—also referred to as cognitive templates—that facilitate the recognition of familial patterns of experience. Goldberg has noted that with age, decision making "takes the form of pattern recognition rather than problem solving," and that "a growing number of future cognitive challenges is likely to be readily covered by a pre-existing template, or will require only a slight modification of a previously formed mental template" (2005, p. 20). Thus, it is not simply knowledge that accumulates with age, but also a method of using that knowledge to solve problems in a more efficient and harmonious manner.

There is an important lesson here for the therapist: Older clients may approach problem solving in ways that confuse younger therapists, who lack the perspective of age. Although we imagine that wise decision making by an older person should strike us as immediately correct and even prescient, that is not always the case. As a form of postformal thinking, wise decision making is likely to be less ideological and more practical from the point of view of the client than might be recommended by the therapist. Consequentially, a common mistake for therapists engaged in problem-solving therapy with older clients is falling into the trap of what William James (1890) described as the *psychologist's fallacy*, erroneously believing that we know what someone else is thinking or feeling—and then basing treatment decisions on those wrong assumptions.

Aging and Dementia

Terms such as *benign senescent forgetfulness* and *age-associated memory impairment* (AAMI) have been used over the years to describe individuals with subjective memory complaints but without serious illness (Crook et al., 1986; Kral, 1962). Neither term has gained wide usage because of the difficulty of actually distinguishing each condition in a clinically meaningful way. For many aging individuals, cognitive impairment is a more serious problem. At one end of the spectrum is *mild cognitive impairment*, or MCI, a syndrome involving objective declines in a discrete cognitive ability such as short-term memory, but not affecting general cognitive abilities and daily function. Individuals with MCI bear close monitoring, as approximately 10% to 15% per year progress to an actual dementia (Geda, Negash, & Peterson, 2006). This progression from normal memory to dementia over time, with AAMI representing a state equivalent to or slightly worse than normal and MCI representing a pathological bridge to dementia, is illustrated in Figure 1.2. This progression is not inevitable with age, and when it occurs, it does not always unfold in such a

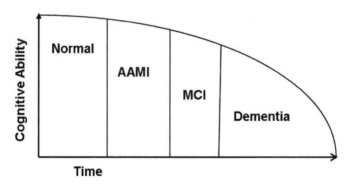

Figure 1.2. Potential progressive loss of cognitive ability with age.

direct curve. Still, it is important to realize that there are always opportunities to intervene at each stage to either slow the progression or mitigate exacerbating factors.

Dementia is defined under various schemes as a brain disease with memory impairment for new or previously learned information at its core but also involving one or more of the following areas of impairment: aphasia, or language disturbance; apraxia, or impaired ability to carry out skilled motor activities (despite intact motor function); agnosia, or disturbances in recognition of familiar people, places, or items despite intact sensory function; and executive dysfunction, involving the ability to plan, initiate, organize, and abstract (Agronin, 2008; American Psychiatric Association, 2000). The diagnostic evaluation involves reviewing the course of the cognitive impairment, taking a thorough medical and psychiatric history, and analyzing data from a brain MRI or CT scan, relevant laboratory tests, and a mental status examination that might include detailed neuropsychological testing. Because of the lack of highly specific diagnostic tests for most types of dementia, clinicians are forced to make educated guesses that, fortunately, gain currency over time as the clinical picture unfolds.

Alzheimer's disease is the most common form of dementia, representing 60% to 70% of all cases, and involving progressive global impairment that evolves over eight to 12 years or longer. Alzheimer's typically begins quite subtly with deficits in delayed verbal recall and progresses to involve all the aforementioned impairments, culminating in a state of profound loss of function and total dependency on external caregivers. Alzheimer's disease, like other dementias, commonly involves a host of associated psychiatric problems, including behavioral disturbances (e.g., agitation, impulsivity), depression, psychosis, sexual dysfunction, sleep disorders, and vulnerability to delirium. The main risk factor for Alzheimer's and most other types of dementia is age. For example, the rate of Alzheimer's in individuals living in the community between the ages of 65 and 75 years old is in the range of 3% to 5%, but this increases to nearly 20% in individuals 75 to 85 years old and almost 50% in individuals older than 85 (Knopman, 2006). Other forms of dementia and their major characteristics are summarized in Table 1.1.

The presence of dementia, regardless of type, is a central challenge for all therapists and requires adaptations in technique and expectations that have not been well captured in research or treatment algorithms. It is often up to the creativity and persistence of the therapist to effect change, which can be slow in coming and must be measured in more subtle ways than those used to measure cognitively intact elders. Suggested therapeutic tools are discussed in Chapter 6.

Adaptation to Aging

In his famous essay "On Old Age" written in 44 BCE, the Roman philosopher Cicero wrote that "the reasons why old age is regarded as unhappy are four: one, it withdraws us from active employments; another, it impairs physical vigor; the third, it deprives us of nearly all sensual pleasures; and four, it is the verge of death" (trans. 1951). The balance of these four inevitable forces would seem, in the end, to still be the determinants of the experience of aging. We do, however, need to update Cicero's scheme by adding in factors of medical or psychiatric illness with associated pain and disability, as well as all the unique losses that older individuals face in terms of physical beauty and strength, key relationships with loved ones and

Table 1.1. Major Types of Dementia

Dementia Type	Characteristics
Mild cognitive impairment	• Mild memory complaints with objective memory impairment for age, but without functional decline or dementia. • Seen in 3% to 19% of individuals in the community over 65 years. • Annual 12% to 20% conversion rate to actual dementia (Geda et al., 2006).
Alzheimer's disease	• Progressive global cognitive impairment over 10 to 12 years until death. • The most common form of dementia, accounting for over 60% of all cases.
Vascular dementia	• Dementia resulting from embolic or hemorrhagic stroke in cortical or subcortical regions of the brain. • Symptoms determined by stroke location. • Accounts for up to 25% of all dementias and often seen comorbidly with Alzheimer's disease.
Dementia with Lewy bodies	• Progressive global dementia involving triad of fluctuating symptomatic course, especially with attention and alertness; Parkinsonism (muscle rigidity and slowed gait); and prominent, detailed visual hallucinations. Many individuals are sensitive to antipsychotic medications, resulting in delirium. • May affect 15% to 25% of all individuals with dementia.
Frontotemporal dementia	• Disproportionate degeneration of frontal and temporal lobes, resulting in the early onset of prominent language disturbances and often bizarre behavioral problems. • More common in younger individuals ages 40 to 60 years, and accounts for 12% to 22% of dementias in that age range but only 1% to 5% of dementias overall.
Dementia due to medical illness or injury	• A wide spectrum of dementias due to conditions such as traumatic brain injury, infectious encephalopathy (e.g., AIDS, syphilis), toxic exposure (e.g., lead poisoning, alcohol), normal pressure hydrocephalus, and neurodegenerative disease (e.g., Huntington's disease, multiple sclerosis).

Note. Adapted from Agronin (2008).

friends, and defining social and vocational roles (Cullum et al., 2000; Pickholtz & Malamut, 2008). How do older people cope with these profound changes?

On the one hand, aged individuals sometimes lack adequate social supports, financial resources, or physical abilities to cope. Lifelong intrapsychic conflicts may limit their range of coping mechanisms, leaving them unable to draw upon former constructive strengths, relationships, positive values, and other sources of self-esteem (Jacobowitz & Newton, 1990). The presence of a personality disorder or other severe psychiatric illness may further restrict their behavioral repertoire. Sooner or later, these limited individuals hit a wall at which point they cannot avoid critical stressors or situations that prove overwhelming. In response, we see states of depression, anxiety, panic, psychosis, or the exaggeration of pain and other somatic complaints. Not surprisingly, suicide rates are greatest among older adults, especially older white men coping poorly with their own or their spouses' health problems (Centers for Disease Control and Prevention, 2005).

Despite all the predictable changes in the anatomy and functioning of the aging brain and the aforementioned expected losses of aging, the actual experience of aging still varies greatly for each individual. But once we inventory all the age-related blows and losses of each older client, why don't we have a clear blueprint of what aging is like? The answer lies in what is missing from the equation—all the positive forces of adaptation and personality that must be weighed on the scales. Herein lies one of the most powerful and practical perspectives on aging that can be drawn upon in therapy.

George Vaillant (2002) has written extensively about adaptation to aging based on his leadership of the seminal Study of Adult Development at Harvard, the longest longitudinal study in history, which has followed three cohorts of over 800 individuals since the 1920s and 1930s. He describes adaptation as the process of altering oneself or the surrounding world in order to continue living with the inexorable changes in life (Vaillant, 1977). Successful adaptation, translated into successful aging for Vaillant, is not "just numbers of years lived with a perfect Mini–Mental State Exam" but is about "the sustained capacity for joy" (2007, p. 181). This joy for Vaillant entails vital activities such as loving and playing with others, working on interesting or meaningful tasks, and learning new things. These ideas stem from the predictors of successful adaptation that emerged from his longitudinal research:

- Good relationships facilitate happiness more than events do.
- Key personal strengths that facilitate good relationships are forgiveness, gratitude, and loving-kindness.
- A good marriage at 50 years old predicts positive aging at 80.
- Healthy ego defense mechanisms include humor, altruism, sublimation, and suppression.
- Alcohol abuse is predictive of unsuccessful aging.
- Friendship, play, and creativity after retirement facilitate enjoyment more than income.
- Subjective good physical health is a better predictor than objective health.

Another key determinant of adaptation lies in the aging personality. Henry Murray defined personality as "the organizing or governing agent of the individual," which for the aged individual "is not a series of biographical facts but something more general and enduring ... which, from birth to death, is ceaselessly engaged in transformative functional operations" (quoted in Hall & Lindzey, 1958, p. 164). Murray's contemporary Gordon Allport described personality as "the dynamic organization within the individual of those psychophysical systems that determine his unique adjustments to his environment" (1937, p. 48). Put together, these definitions portray personality as a unique conglomeration of mental and physical elements that act together and give us a consistent and hence predictable motion through life. And how do we get to know the personality of an older client? We rely on as much past history that the clients and their informants can provide, but we also have to observe them over time. As Henry Murray so aptly described it, "the history of the personality is the personality" (Murray & Kluckhohn, 1953, p. 8).

As a positive force used to deal with the stresses of aging, an individual's personality does a remarkable thing: Its core features remain stable, like the hull and mast of a sailboat in a storm, whereas its behavioral styles, like the mainsail and jib in the wind, are flexible and change widely to accommodate age-related stresses. Vaillant captured this duality perfectly when he wrote that "If one defines personality by traits measured with pencil and paper—intelligence, extroversion, even self-esteem, for example—then over time little changes. . . . If one defines personality by an individual's adaptive style . . . then over time personality changes profoundly" (2002, p. 284).

Most longitudinal studies on personality have focused on measurable personality traits, defined by McCrae and Costa as "dimensions of individual differences in tendencies to show consistent patterns of thoughts, feelings, and actions" (1990, p. 23)—a definition that parallels general descriptions of personality. The most widely studied traits are the "big five":

neuroticism, extraversion, openness to experience, agreeableness, and conscientiousness (Costa & McCrae, 1994). These
traits are described in Table 1.2. Both cross-sectional and longitudinal studies of these traits have found remarkable stability with aging, with some minor changes from the age of 30 to
80, including small declines in neuroticism, extraversion, and
openness to experience and small increases in agreeableness
and conscientiousness (Costa & McCrae, 1994).

Translating this knowledge of personality stability versus
change into practical clinical pearls is challenging, because
each individual has his or her own story that must be regarded
unto itself. However, the use of several theories of adult development across the life cycle and into later life can be extremely useful in providing a scaffold for these traits.

Aging and the Life Cycle

In thinking about the development of an individual across the
life span, we can again begin with the wisdom of Cicero from
his essay "On Old Age," in which he wrote: "Life has its fixed
course, and nature one unvarying way; to each is allotted its
appropriate quality, so that the fickleness of boyhood, the im-
petuosity of youth, the sobriety of middle life, and the ripeness
of age all have something of nature's yield which must be gar-
nered in its own season" (trans. 1951). Like Cicero, the great
developmental theorists of our time speak of successive "sea-
sons" or stages of life that confer specific tasks, require necessary dispositions, and hopefully yield gifts of experiences and
personal strengths that guide us into the next stage. For example, consider the first and most fundamental stage of life. In
order to stay alive, the infant must have a bond with a parent
who provides nutritional support and social nurturance, and

Table 1.2. The Five-Factor Model of Personality

Trait	Description
Neuroticism	Neuroticism describes an individual's level of "emotional adjustment versus instability" (Costa & Widiger, 1994, p. 3). Subscales measure anxiety, angry hostility, depression, self-consciousness, impulsiveness, and vulnerability.
Extraversion	Extraversion describes an individual's preferred degree of "interpersonal interactions, activity level, need for stimulation, and capacity for joy" (Costa & Widiger, 1994, p. 3). Subscales measure warmth, gregariousness, assertiveness, activity, excitement seeking, and positive emotions.
Openness to experience	Openness to experience involves an individual's "active seeking and appreciation of experiences for their own sake" (Costa & Widiger, 1994, p. 3). Subscales measure fantasy, appreciation for art and beauty, receptivity to inner feelings, willingness to try new activities, intellectual curiosity, and readiness to reexamine values.
Agreeableness	Agreeableness describes the "kinds of interactions a person prefers along a continuum from compassion to antagonism" (Costa & Widiger, 1994, p. 3). Subscales measure trust, straightforwardness, altruism, reactions to conflict, modesty, and sympathy for others.
Conscientiousness	Conscientiousness describes an individual's degree of "organization, persistence, control, and motivation in goal-directed behavior" (Costa & Widiger, 1994, p. 3). Subscales measure sense of one's own competence, neatness and organization, dutifulness, ambition, self-discipline, and deliberation.

Note. Adapted from Costa and McCrae (1992).

the infant must, in turn, both elicit and acquiesce to the efforts of the parent. The physical capabilities of the infant and the hormonal environment of the nursing mother enable this connection, and the clearly observed mutuality between infant and parent sets the mold for future stages.

In classic psychoanalytic theory, Freud focused on the infant's oral connection to the mother's breast as the primal attachment in the first stage, whereas later object relations theorists such as Melanie Klein and W. R. D. Fairbairn emphasized the psychic internalization of this attachment (Gabbard, 2005). Both of these psychodynamic approaches carry development through childhood and into young adulthood but provide little guidance after that except to rely upon a reading of the childhood psyche. The concept of psychological development in later life was untouchable for Freud, as he wrote in his 1905 essay "On Psychotherapy":

> Near or above the age of fifty the elasticity of the mental processes, on which the treatment depends, is as a rule lacking—old people are no longer educable—and, on the other hand, the mass of material to be dealt with would prolong the duration of the treatment indefinitely. (1905/1964b, p. 264)

Although the life span around the time Freud wrote his essay was close to 50 years, he and others certainly had experiences with clients in old age—a state that he himself would attain several decades later. Fortunately, psychodynamic perspectives on adult development have evolved since then to encompass adult development beyond the age of 50 and are well captured in several hypotheses formulated by Robert Nemiroff and Calvin Colarusso (1990):

- Adult development is an ongoing, dynamic process.
- Whereas psychic structures are forming in childhood, they are evolving in adulthood.
- There is a continual and vital interaction between childhood and adult themes.
- Physical processes affect psychological expression.
- Growing awareness of death is an age-specific theme.

These hypotheses move us away from the idea of the child as being the only "father" of man, to paraphrase the poet William Wordsworth, but they provide little detail on the novelty of adult development. For this we turn to several seminal students of the life cycle.

Erikson's Eight Stages of Development

Erik Erikson was a child psychoanalyst who was schooled in orthodox psychoanalytic theory (having been analyzed by Anna Freud) but whose writings on the life cycle broke through many rigid notions of how we develop as we age. In his influential work *Childhood and Society*, Erikson (1950/1985) proposed a relatively invariant sequence of eight stages of development that unfold within the structure of physical development (e.g., feeding during infancy, development of sphincter control by toddlers) but are shaped by a dialectic of psychological and social forces. As he wrote in his last book, *The Life Cycle Completed*, "The stages of life remain throughout 'linked' to somatic processes, even as they remain dependent on the psychic processes of personality development and on the ethical power of the social process" (Erikson & Erikson, 1997, p. 113). Within each stage an individual must navigate between interdependent ego-syntonic and ego-dystonic forces and find a healthy balance that yields, in turn, certain enduring strengths. As illustrated in Figure 1.3, these stages appear to form a series of steps, yet with each new stage an individual carries with him or her the experiences, knowledge, struggles, strengths, deficits, and fixations from previous stages. By the time one reaches adulthood, issues of trust versus mistrust, autonomy versus shame or doubt, initiative versus guilt, industry versus inferiority, identity versus role confusion, and intimacy versus isolation are all still important to personality and present residual tensions but no longer serve as central developmental tasks (Agronin, 1994).

Adulthood and old age present several challenges for Erikson. Unlike earlier stages, neither involves predictable age-specific physical changes to herald a life transition other than the highly variable process of aging (in contrast to the very discrete and predictable physical changes that occur from birth through puberty). Thus, take ten 40- to 70-year-old adults, and you will find 10 different physical specimens whose anatomy and physiology have little impact on the central tasks of living unless there are significant issues of physical illness, pain, or disability (which play more common and profound roles in the last stage of life). Instead, the stage of generativity versus stagnation and self-absorption in adulthood is largely a psychological and social stage during which an individual is focusing on family, career, and community involvement. Generativity itself "encompasses procreativity, productivity, and creativity, and thus the generation of new beings as well as of new products and ideas, including a kind of self-generation concerned with further identity development" (Erikson & Erikson, 1997, p. 67). Along the way, adults struggle with failures to engage in mutual relationships with others, for which

	INFANCY	EARLY CHILDHOOD	PLAY AGE	SCHOOL AGE	ADOLESCENCE	YOUNG ADULTHOOD	ADULTHOOD	OLD AGE
	Basic Trust vs. Basic Mistrust							
		Autonomy vs. Shame, Doubt						
			Initiative vs. Guilt					
				Industry vs. Inferiority				
					Identity vs. Confusion			
						Intimacy vs. Isolation		
							Generativity vs. Stagnation	
								Integrity vs. Despair, Disgust
	HOPE	WILL	PURPOSE	COMPETENCE	FIDELITY	LOVE	CARE	WISDOM

Figure 1.3. Erikson's eight stages of the life cycle. Adapted from Erikson (1950/1985), Erikson et al. (1986), and Erikson and Erikson (1997).

31

self-absorption acts as both a cause and effect, or they stagnate when personal involvements prove frustrating or unfulfilling. But it is exactly at those moments of tension when the adult is best able to learn about him- or herself and have the drive and ideas to renew or seek out alternative avenues. Successful navigation of adulthood holds the promise of yielding a true sense of caring for the world.

Old age, not defined per se by Erikson but clearly representing the 80s and 90s, brings the closing off of many relationships and activities as a result of physical changes and the death of spouses and peers. There is a new context, however, in which an individual gathers in and beholds a lifetime of memories that either stabilize the pathway or leave one feeling bereft in the final years. Erikson characterizes the ego-syntonic sense of integrity as the ability to bring together and harmonize both the conscious and unconscious aspects of one's life that have guided all previous stages—including the current and "legitimate feelings of cynicism and hopelessness" that characterize the opposing ego-dystonic sense of despair (Erikson, Erikson, & Kivnick, 1986). Perhaps best illustrated at this point is how the ego-syntonic and dystonic forces exist not in an "either/or" but rather in an "and" fashion throughout each stage; indeed, one cannot exist without the other.

There is the enduring hope that even in the final stage of life, individuals may find a measure of intellectual peace known as wisdom and defined by Erikson as a "detached concern with life itself in the face of death itself. It maintains and learns to convey the integrity of experience, in spite of the decline of bodily and mental functions" (Erikson et al., 1986, pp. 37–38). This definition is different in several respects from the earlier characterization of wisdom as a form of postformal thinking, as Erikson emphasizes both the practicality and the propinquity of decision making to one's final station of life but leaves out broader consideration of other related systems. Such a definition is perhaps informed by the Eriksons' own sense that despair becomes the dominant force in late life, carrying with it the risk that a feeling of disdain or disgust will reign as "a reaction to feeling (and seeing others) in an increasing state of being finished, confused, and helpless" (Erikson & Erikson, 1997, p. 61). A ninth stage proposed by Erik and Joan Erikson is discussed in Chapter 9.

Vaillant's Developmental Tasks

George Vaillant, like most theorists of adult development, is deeply schooled in Erikson's scheme, but his extensive empirical research as director of the Study of Adult Development at Harvard has brought about necessary revision. On the one hand, he has written:

> Like Erikson I have concluded that one way to conceptualize the sequential nature of adult social development may lie in appreciating that it reflects each adult's widening radius over time. Imagine a stone dropped into a pond; it produces ever-expanding ripples, each older one encompassing, but not obliterating, the circle emanating from the next ripple. Adult development is rather like that. (Vaillant, 2002, p. 44)

On the other hand, having observed and studied so many aging individuals, Vaillant has moved his focus on adult development away from stages and more toward the developmental tasks of late life that are typically but not always sequential. Drawing upon his image of ripples in a pond, an illustration of Vaillant's developmental tasks is presented in Figure 1.4.

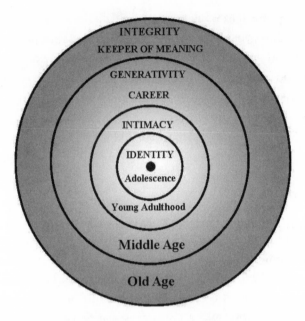

Figure 1.4. Vaillant's developmental tasks. Based on Vaillant (2002).

For both Vaillant and Erikson, an adolescent's main task is establishing an identity separate from his or her parents, whereas young adulthood brings the task of learning to sustain a mutual, committed relationship. Vaillant has highlighted the role of career consolidation in both young and middle adulthood, in which the individual is able to work at his or her chosen vocational tasks with appropriate sociability and a sense of satisfaction. Generativity grows out of one's career and represents an expansion of purpose to be a leader for the next generation. Vaillant (2002) found in his longitudinal studies that successful generativity triples the chances that an individual will experience more joy than despair in his or her 70s.

Vaillant's fifth development task, labeled "Keeper of the

Meaning," bridges many of the tasks Erikson assigned to both generativity and integrity and involves a focus "on conservation and preservation of the collective products of mankind—the culture in which one lives and its institutions—rather than on just the development of its children" (Vaillant, 2002, p. 48).

Like the adult in the postformal stage, the Keeper of the Meaning tends to have a less ideological worldview than earlier years because there is a widening and less selective circle of concern. At the same time, one's efforts and energies may be less creative and forward thinking than those of younger and more generative adults, but they often allow for more meaningful intergenerational relationships because they tap into the enduring foundations of culture and history.

Vaillant's last developmental stage of integrity echoes that of Erikson, indicating the necessary task of accepting and finding some meaning for and ownership over what has come before in life, without succumbing to despair over the narrowing possibilities of age.

Cohen's Human Potential Phases

Although Vaillant has emphasized that no one stage is more important than another, both he and Erikson end up with the last task in life involving a sort of wrapping up and an associated risk of dissolution, without emphasizing the possibility of growth. In contrast, Gene Cohen has based his work on the potential in late life for both neuronal and psychological growth, the latter coming through postformal thinking that allows us to "energize our creativity and jump-start our efforts to explore new ideas or make desired change" (2005, p. 7). On this basis, Cohen proposed a series of human potential phases that "reflect evolving mental maturity, ongoing human development, and psychological growth as we age" (p. 7). These are charted in Figure 1.5.

Cohen's scheme begins with the midlife reevaluation phase, starting in the mid- to late 30s and continuing through the mid-60s, and involving newfound motivation to reevaluate one's life and make positive changes through what Cohen has described as "quest energy." He gave the example of the author Alex Haley, who at the age of 55 published the best-selling book *Roots*, which represented the culmination of 12 years of research into his African American family history. The liberation phase occurs in the mid-60s to mid-70s and allows individuals to take advantage of new personal freedom and creativity conferred in part by retirement. One may have a sense of needing to act now, and to engage in experimental or innovative activities that one would not have considered in the

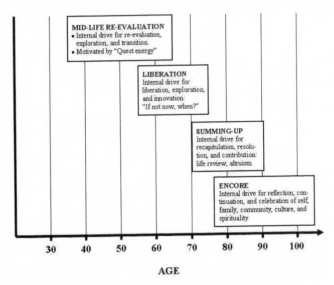

Figure 1.5. Cohen's human potential phases. Based on G. D. Cohen (2005).

past. One of Cohen's examples is former Senator Jim Jeffords of Vermont, who at the age of 68 switched political parties and thus shifted control of the Senate (G. D. Cohen, 2005).

In the summing-up phase, which occurs in the late 60s to 90s, there is a search for a larger meaning in life, facilitated in part by life review, and fostering both a sense of wisdom and a desire to contribute to the world. Cohen cited the example of the famous dancer Martha Graham, who, after retiring at the age of 75, put her energies into the choreography of major new ballets and revivals up to her death at the age of 96. The encore phase occurs in the late 70s to the end of life and involves a drive for personal reflection and associated endeavors to restate, reaffirm, and celebrate the major themes in one's life. The potential for even this last stage to be vital and energetic is illustrated by Cohen's example of sisters Bessie and Sadie Delaney, who at the ages of 101 and 102, respectively, coauthored a best-selling story of their lives together (G. D. Cohen, 2000).

The goal of Cohen's work is to provide a new paradigm of aging that emphasizes the potential for positive growth, regardless of the earlier vicissitudes of life. It is likely that with an increasing span of healthier aging and the advent of aging cohorts who have devoted their lives to their physical and mental well-being, this paradigm will begin to transform the very nature of the older client.

Putting It All Together

This chapter has presented a complete overview of the aging process, including the respective roles of the brain, intellect, personality, and entire life history. The ultimate hope is that these forces can be directed in such a way as to guarantee a relatively active and contented old age that is free of most age-related decline. Such a state has been labeled "successful aging" by John Rowe and Robert Kahn (1998) in their seminal work based upon the MacArthur Foundation Study of Aging in America. Robert Hill (2005) has proposed the idea of "positive aging" to describe a process of decision making that allows an individual not simply to live longer but to make the experience of aging meaningful and worthwhile. The active and optimistic focus of both successful and positive aging bases its technology on many of the lessons learned from the life histories of individuals spread across the developmental rubrics of Erikson, Vaillant, and Cohen.

The average older client who comes into therapy, however, is often not the paragon of success, optimism, or ego-syntonicity that might be produced by a life well lived. When one is faced with these individuals, it becomes quite clear that all the aspects of aging presented so far represent only a scaffold upon which we might begin to formulate their dilemmas, and an insufficient one at that. Numerous life events, personal idiosyncrasies, and pressing physical or social problems occupy each level of the scaffold, filling out the walls, furnishings, and window coverings that actually make up the whole of the person who seeks our help. And those details and dilemmas only emerge and allow for therapeutic engagement within the clinical relationship—a topic covered throughout this book.

I would, nonetheless, offer a way of thinking about each client that compresses the material from this chapter into the following heuristic equation:

$$\frac{\text{Physiological aging process (intellect + personality)}}{\times \text{ Life history (adaptation + maturation)}}$$
$$= \text{Products of aging}$$

In this equation, the products of aging, meaning the strengths, weaknesses, circumstances, and therapeutic problems brought to us by an aging client, result from the interactions between two functions: the impact of physiological aging on the relatively enduring phenotypes of intellect and personality, and the manner in which an individual, through his or her ability to adapt in the short run and manage developmental tasks in the long run (termed *maturation* here), has dealt with events in his or her personal and cultural life history. It is not that the therapist needs to or should be able to simultaneously hold all these factors under mental consideration. Rather, it is critically important for the therapist to move among the components of this equation when formulating the case and developing a sound treatment plan.

One missing element to this equation must be entered, and that is the role of the therapist. In any work with older clients, there is great risk that the therapist will be overwhelmed by the complexity inherent to the products of aging and in response will select a defensive approach to the client. Such approaches are common pitfalls of work with older clients and are characterized by attitudes that lack empathy, are overly paternalistic, and are limited by unwarranted fatalism. It is to the exploration of both the possibilities and risks of the therapist's role with the older client that I turn in Chapter 2.

2

THERAPEUTIC CHALLENGES AND COUNTERTRANSFERENCE

In Jonathan Swift's classic satiric novel *Gulliver's Travels*, the protagonist, Lemuel Gulliver, recounts his voyage to the kingdom of Luggnagg, where he learns of a group of immortal individuals called Struldbruggs who live among the Luggnuggian people. Gulliver speaks ecstatically about the possibility of living such a long life:

> Happy Nation where every Child hath at least a Chance for being immortal! Happy people who enjoy so many living Examples of ancient Virtue, and have Masters ready to instruct them in the Wisdom of all former Ages! But, happiest beyond all Comparison are those excellent Struldbruggs, who born exempt from that universal Calamity of human Nature, have their Minds free and disengaged, without the Weight and Depression of Spirits caused by the continual Apprehension of Death. (Swift, 1735/2003, p. 209)

He goes on to imagine how glorious his own life would be were he an immortal elder, devoted to endless intellectual pursuits and eventually becoming an "Oracle of the Nation."

Gulliver's naive imaginings are, however, harshly countered by his Luggnuggian guides, who describe how in reality the incessantly aging Struldbruggs eventually become "Opinionative, Peevish, Covetous, Morose, Vain, Talkative, but incapable of Friendship, and dead to natural Affection," and how "Envy and impotent desires are their prevailing Passions" (Swift, 1735/2003, p. 210). By the time they age beyond several hundred years, the poor Struldbruggs are entirely decrepit wards of the kingdom.

Perhaps like Gulliver, we begin our own voyages as therapists for elderly individuals with many misconceptions—starry-eyed and overly sentimental notions of wise and peaceful sages versus terrifying projections of miserable, pain-wracked, and disabled individuals who are waiting to die. These are obviously two extreme views, but they represent the poles of our own conscious and unconscious reactions to aging in general, and to older clients in particular. The therapist must come to terms with these personal reactions while simultaneously dealing with a variety of clinical problems across an incredible array of settings, from private offices and public clinics to nursing homes, assisted living facilities, and even private residences. Growing into one's role as a therapist for older clients requires an exploration of the unique challenges to therapist-client relationships in late life, as well as a clear description of the clinical tools that can help. To begin, consider the following vignette.

Joy was an 87-year-old single woman who was referred for psychotherapy by her caseworker from a community social services organization. According to the caseworker, Joy was having difficulty adjusting to life in an assisted living facility and seemed depressed. The initial meeting with the therapist, Ms. A., went very well. Joy showed up on time, acted in a friendly and gracious manner, and seemed quite interested in the therapist even as she denied feeling depressed. "It's my eyes that are the real problem," Joy explained and then asked emphatically, "If I can't see, how can anything be worthwhile?"

Ms. A. was quite taken by Joy's dramatic persona, and fascinated by her history. Joy had grown up in Russia in the 1920s and at the age of 12 journeyed with her younger brother to the United States to meet up with her father, who had left years earlier. En route she came down with typhus and had to stay with an uncle in Warsaw for several months. Once she arrived in New York, her father took her in but was not a very loving or attentive parent. Joy gravitated toward the performing arts and became an actress, appearing in several off-Broadway productions. At the age of 20, she married and had a son, but her husband was tragically killed in a train accident when her son was only 2 years old. To make ends meet, she began singing in nightclubs, often leaving her son in the care of friends during the long nights that she worked. Despite all the losses she had faced in her life, as well as an estranged relationship with her son, Joy's one true love remained singing, and toward the end of the 50-minute session she broke out in song for the therapist.

Ms. A. was impressed, if not a little embarrassed, by Joy's spontaneous concert and scheduled another appointment. She felt that she had established good rapport with Joy and envisioned that Joy's strengths, such as her independent spirit and expressiveness, would help her cope with several recent stressors. The following month proved otherwise. Joy rarely showed up for sessions, and when she did, she often arrived an hour early or at the end of the hour, begging to be seen. Ms. A. began receiving phone calls from staff at the assisted living facility worried that Joy was increasingly depressed and even suicidal. They also reported that she was forgetful of her medication regimen and seemed overly sedated on certain days. When questioned, Joy would deny these problems and launch into repetitive, dramatic discussions about how her poor eyesight was the root of all her problems. She also described the assisted living facility as worse than the slums in New York where she once lived.

Joy was referred to an ophthalmologist by her primary care physician, but refused to take any eye drops, complaining that none of them helped. She also refused to take any medication other than an occasional Valium. She agreed to see a psychiatrist but refused to sign any paperwork, fearing that he would commit her to the hospital. After 6 months of struggle, Ms. A. came to loathe working with Joy and viewed her as a hateful, resistant, demented, and personality-disordered old woman. She resented the frequent phone calls from the case manager and assisted living facility and eventually decided to refer Joy to another colleague.

Therapeutic Challenges

Joy might seem at first glance to represent an extremely complex and challenging individual who is not the norm for most referrals. In reality, her case is fairly typical and represents a microcosm of all that can go wrong in work with older clients. First, the therapist started off with unrealistic expectations, thinking that Joy's background would inoculate her against the stresses of aging. Second, she didn't act aggressively enough to reports of memory lapses and depression, attributing them to the normal vagaries of aging. Third, once things went awry,

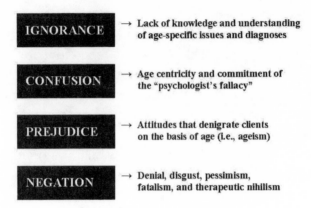

Figure 2.1. Four common therapeutic failures with older clients.

the therapist became tired of working with Joy and began to think that she would never get better. Finally, she gave up the case, sending a very powerful message to Joy that therapists are powerless to help. What started off as a promising relationship with an older client failed miserably, in part because of four major causes of failure that can arise with any client: ignorance, confusion, prejudice, and negation. These are portrayed in Figure 2.1 and are described in detail throughout the chapter.

Ignorance

When facing older clients, the therapist may be torn between wanting to normalize the encounter—viewing them as he or she would any other client—versus seeing them as unique by virtue of age. It is important to be able to oscillate between the two stances, but such an ability requires an understanding of relevant age-specific issues and diagnoses. The lack of this knowledge can produce blind spots in evaluation and treatment and lead to the other potential therapeutic failures discussed in this chapter.

In the psychosocial world of the older client, five common life-changing events are retirement, widowhood, loss of close friends and relatives, the assumption of a caregiving role or the need for a caregiver, and relocation to a congregate living setting, such as an independent or assisted living facility or a nursing home. In each case there may be seismic shifts in terms of roles, activities, finances, and available relationships, and these shifts may lead, in turn, to a variety of adjustment reactions (Lantz, 2006). Therapists may be unaware of the significance of such events and not realize the possibility of underlying vulnerabilities such as complicated bereavement (Rosenzweig, Prigerson, Miller, & Reynolds, 1997), increased morbidity and mortality (Schulz & Beach, 1999; Schulz, O'Brien, Bookwala, & Fleissner, 1995), neglect and abuse (Schonfeld, 2007), poverty (Himes, 2001), and social isolation. When present, these issues must be explored in the initial evaluation.

Therapeutic failures can also occur when the therapist does not understand enough about specific medical or psychiatric diagnoses or neglects to ask about them and integrate this knowledge into the therapy. At the same time, it is possible that these omissions may be due less to ignorance and more to the therapist's anxiety over working in unfamiliar territory or with frightening or terminal diagnoses (Knight, 1996). Issues that have the greatest impact include chronic pain; visual or hearing loss; physical disability; and cognitive impairment, which may result from a spectrum of diagnoses, such postoperative states, severe anemia, sleep apnea, major depression, and medication effects, or may be part of an actual dementia, typically Alzheimer's disease.

Confusion

In his groundbreaking work *The Principles of Psychology*, the great American psychologist and philosopher William James warned against the *psychologist's fallacy*, describing it as a clinician's "confusion of his own standpoint with that of the mental fact about which he is making his report" (1890/1988, p. 196). In practical terms, this mistake involves the hubris of assuming to know what someone else is thinking or feeling based on one's own state of mind. Of course we use empathy to try to bridge the gap—but how accurate can we be? This fallacy is rooted in our own age centricity, captured well by the social gerontologist Lars Tornstam:

> Many of us have a tendency to define the present time of life as the best one and as normative for how the rest of life should be. . . .
>
> Not surprisingly there are severe mismatches between the nuisances and miseries we tend to project onto old age and what those who have reached advanced age tell themselves. (2005, pp. 1–2)

This gap between what a therapist may be experiencing or imagining and the reality of the client's world is a fundamental issue in every therapeutic relationship but may be greatly amplified by differences in age and personal history. Consider the following case.

> Benny was an 82-year-old Native American man and war veteran with a history of major depression and post-traumatic stress disorder (PTSD). For many years he resisted seeing a mental health clinician, despite severe symptoms of anxiety and depression, preferring instead to visit the medicine man at his reservation. Though he found the ritual of the sweat

lodge calming and meaningful, it wasn't sufficient to treat his symptoms. Finally he agreed to meet with a psychotherapist at the veterans' hospital. He spent most of the initial sessions explaining his cultural history and rituals as well as his war experiences. The therapist tried his best to understand Benny, but it was difficult and even painful to hear about traumatic battles. After several months of treatment, Benny returned to the reservation, feeling that his symptoms were getting worse.

The therapist was facing several major hurdles in developing rapport with Benny: a 50-year difference in age, a lack of experience in the military during wartime, aversion to the very thought of having to kill enemy soldiers and witness the deaths of close buddies in battle, and little understanding of Native American culture and history. The therapist felt overwhelmed by the need to learn so much about the client and was confused and unnerved by the differences in technique between himself and the medicine man. Without knowing it, the therapist projected his own anxiety, lack of confidence, and even aversion to the client's violent past during sessions. As a result of the therapist's distorted construction of the client's inner emotions, he failed to sufficiently engage and assist the client. Although empathy can be a critical tool for bridging the experiential gaps between client and therapist, regardless of differences in age and personal history, it must be informed and modulated appropriately to avoid the potential failures of ignorance and prejudice.

Prejudice

One of the most pervasive and damaging causes of therapeutic failure is the stigma of aging, especially because its presence can be subtle and wholly unconscious. Stigma has been defined by Dobbs and colleagues as "the assignment of negative worth on the basis of devalued group or individual characteristics" (2008, p. 517). Robert Butler coined the term "ageism" to describe stigma based on age: "Ageism can be seen as a process of systematic stereotyping of and discrimination against people because they are old" (1975, p. 12). Some of the most common negative stereotypes of older individuals are that they are senile and incompetent, inflexible, unproductive, lonely, disengaged, old fashioned, disabled, and diseased. These stereotypes are associated, in turn, with many negative terms: old codger, biddy, old-timer, hag, fossil, old man, little old lady, old bat, geezer, grumpy old man, old fart, and so forth.

Stigma is the product of dominant cultural beliefs that label certain individuals in a negative way, resulting in loss of status and discrimination (Dobbs et al., 2008). When applied to older clients, it may begin to permeate their personal identities and increase their risk of depression, functional decline, loss of self-esteem, and social withdrawal (Blum, 1991; Hausdorf Levy, & Wei, 1999).

Therapists with unrecognized ageist views may infantilize and depersonalize clients by talking down to them, using cutesy language in what is called "elderspeak," ignoring care needs and pleas for help, adopting an overly paternalistic stance, or avoiding the client altogether. Such behaviors often unfold unconsciously and may reinforce a client's underlying feelings of inadequacy and decrepitude from aging. Consider the following vignette.

Evelyn was a 72-year-old retired teacher who had been living with the neurodegenerative disease of multiple sclerosis for 30 years. She used to love hiking and traveling but had to give up both interests after her worsening motor function left her unable to walk safely. She also began experiencing urinary incontinence, and as her care needs became overwhelming, she was forced to move into an assisted living facility. Nursing staff noticed that Evelyn's appetite was poor and she was frequently tearful, and they referred her to a psychologist named Dr. M. for counseling. The early morning appointment did not allow sufficient time for Evelyn to bathe, and so she arrived at the appointment somewhat unkempt and malodorous. Although she was a pleasant, intelligent, and articulate client, Dr. M. was preoccupied with Evelyn's appearance and odor and had a difficult time concentrating during the session. She imagined that Evelyn's appearance indicated that she was actually demented and unable to attend to her own hygiene. Instead of looking to Evelyn for suggestions, Dr. M. prescribed a treatment plan for her that included therapeutic activities with cognitively impaired individuals. Evelyn felt hurt and offended and refused to return for any further assistance.

When clients are viewed as senile, disabled, and decrepit simply because of their age and appearance and regardless of predisposing circumstances, we lose opportunities for connection with them and miss important areas of treatment. In this example, the therapist had already begun viewing the client as cognitively impaired before truly getting to know her.

Negation

In some clinical circumstances the facticity of aging is so troublesome to the therapist that it is simply blotted out of the equation. The denial of aging may take the form of ignoring age-associated changes (including the inevitability of physical decline and death) and either treating older clients as if they were much younger or lapsing into the excessive sentimentalism that regards old age as the golden years of life. Either way, the unique features of aging, whether positive or negative, are unwittingly factored out of therapy. Consider the following case vignette.

> Jenny was a 78-year-old widowed woman with a history of depression who was referred to Dr. B. for counseling as the result of a recent diagnosis of late-stage lymphoma. Jenny's energetic demeanor reminded Dr. B. of one of her beloved aunts, whom she used to treat like a sister, even though they were separated by many years. Jenny loved the friendly banter with Dr. B. in the counseling sessions, and the therapeutic relationship developed quite well. In the sessions, Dr. B. focused on Jenny's past romantic relationships and her current attempts to look good and attract a man. Several months into therapy, her condition suddenly deteriorated, and Jenny was hospitalized. Within 2 weeks she was placed in hospice, and Dr. B. could not bring herself to visit Jenny during that time. She died shortly thereafter.

In this case the therapist was so enamored by Jenny's youthful spirit that she began conducting therapy sessions more like gossip sessions between two friends. There was never any discussion of Jenny's serious medical condition or her anxiety about her impending death. When the reality of terminal illness and death finally became impossible to ignore, Dr. B. withdrew, unable to face the emotions associated with the loss of a beloved client. Ironically, what started off as a very close bond between Dr. B. and Jenny ended up an abandonment. The therapy itself was enjoyable but ended up robbing both therapist and client of the opportunity to say good-bye.

Negation of aging in the therapeutic setting can evolve into more insidious expressions of disgust for characteristics of the older client or pessimism regarding the possibility for any meaningful improvement. Some therapists too eagerly adopt a hospice approach to therapy, seeing their role as a means to provide some measure of comfort but no real cognitive or emotional change. This attitude, although caring and well intentioned, leads quickly to a fatalism over the client's condition (e.g., "She will only get worse, so let's forgo any heroic measures") or therapeutic nihilism (e.g., "Nothing will work at this point, so let nature take its course"). In either case, the therapeutic approach becomes overly passive, and the results can be catastrophic.

Harold was an 82-year-old man who had demonstrated rapid cognitive decline over a 4-month period of time. His primary care physician (PCP) diagnosed him with Alzheimer's disease and depression and sent him to a psychiatrist for evaluation. The PCP informed the psychiatrist of the diagnosis and refused to consider any further evaluation or treatment, viewing it as both unnecessary and futile. The psychiatrist agreed and recommended as the only course of action starting Harold on antidepressant medication. He also tried to convince the family to move Harold into a nursing home. The family was not convinced and took Harold to seek a second opinion. The other physician noted Harold's abnormal gait and rapid loss of language function and argued with his PCP and health insurance carrier for a more thorough evaluation. A brain scan revealed a large brain tumor to be the cause of Harold's symptoms. He underwent surgery, and the tumor, which turned out to be entirely benign, was successfully removed. Within 6 weeks Harold was back to his old self—walking, talking, and perfectly cognitively intact.

It is unfortunately common for older clients to be denied appropriate therapeutic services because they are viewed as too impaired or recalcitrant. In those circumstances, it is critical to consider whether the attitude of the therapist or other professionals is as much a barrier to improvement as the actual mental or physical condition.

Countertransference

The term *countertransference* stems from the concept of transference, the unconsciously motivated relationship that the client establishes with the therapist that is reminiscent of a past important relationship (Gabbard, 2009). Freud and others postulated countertransference as the therapist's own response to the transference relationship, again with a focus on unconscious motivation based on past relationships (Freud, 1912/1964a; Kernberg, 1965). The definition of countertransference has broadened over time, and it is described well by Maltsberger and Buie as comprised of "the therapist's emotional response to his patient's way of relating to him, and to transference which the therapist may form in relation to his patient" (1974, p. 625).

The most natural countertransferential reaction is for the younger therapist to view the older client as a parent or grandparent. The quality of his or her earlier or current relationships may then play a role in positive and negative ways, both unconsciously and intentionally. For example, a therapist who has been actively involved as a caregiver for an ill or disabled older loved one might find assuming a similarly active role with the client irresistible. Similarly, a therapist who is estranged from a parent because of past conflicts might find some of his or her emotional distance, impatience, or anger creeping into the therapy. Another interesting form of countertransference occurs when the therapist views the client as an aged form of him- or herself. In this case, personal views and anxieties about aging, illness, and death may arise in the relationship.

These examples are two poles on the spectrum of possibilities but illustrate how the complicated and sometimes burdensome issues associated with older clients, especially those living with chronic pain or dementia, can elicit very strong reactions on the part of the therapist. More important than the emotions associated with countertranference is how the therapist responds to them. And the more they are kept out of conscious awareness, the greater the risk for defensive postures, including inattention, anger, boredom, anxiety, disgust, aversion, and even hatred. Aversion and hatred are certainly the most antitherapeutic stances and may lead to abandonment of the goals of treatment or the clients themselves.

Boundary Issues

Establishing appropriate therapeutic boundaries in psychotherapy is a critical task, as it sets limits on physical contact, personal disclosure on the part of the therapist, gift giving, and contacts extraneous to the therapeutic process or outside of the therapy session. The goals of such boundaries are to allow for a focus on the psychological needs of clients (and avoid burdening them with the therapist's needs) and to prevent exploitation and abuse. Therapists can and should be friendly and caring, as boundaries do not prescribe that one be overly reserved or distant (Gutheil & Gabbard, 1998). The ultimate goal is a structured partnership that promotes a mutually trusting alliance between therapist and client (Dyer, 1988).

Older clients bring unique demands to therapy that challenge several of these boundaries and require necessary modifications of both style and content. These include the following:

- Greater dependency due to physical and cognitive disabilities.
- Greater need for assistance with physical mobility and transportation to appointments.
- Greater need to compensate for sensory impairment.
- More frequent interruptions due to medical problems.
- Greater proximity to existential issues of death.
- Necessary involvement of informants and caregivers with cognitively impaired clients.
- Greater interface with PCPs and other medical and mental health specialists.
- Greater interface with case managers, long-term care staff, personal aides, and other individuals with roles in day-to-day care needs.

Evident from this list is the fact that the therapist often has to play what Knight (1996) described as a caseworker role with many clients to ensure that they are able to get to appointments, provide adequate history, receive assistance with medications and daily care, and have access to life-sustaining services. Often, many of the stresses and vulnerabilities that clients bring to therapy relate directly to these factors and may continue unabated without direct assistance.

Other boundary issues arise with cohorts of older clients who grew up in an era when doctor-patient relationships were much closer and long standing and encompassed mental health care. To these individuals, the idea of a psychotherapeutic relationship may be quite unfamiliar, and they expect it to be similar to relationships with other doctors, in which there is a more mutual relationship with greater self-disclosure on the part of the clinician and a comfort level with social banter and even gift giving. Consider the following case vignette.

Boris was an 85-year-old Russian immigrant who brought his wife to see Dr. G. for routine psychiatric follow-up. Boris had survived War World II and spent most of his adult life in Soviet-era Russia, where it was common to use gifts and bribes to secure better medical care. He always insisted on bringing Dr. G. a small token of gratitude, ranging from boxes of candy to key chains and, on one occasion, a jug of brandy. When Dr. G. told him he could not accept the brandy, Boris became greatly upset, fearing that the doctor would no longer provide the wonderful care for his wife that he had "secured" with gifts.

The dilemma for the doctor is whether to graciously accept gifts or turn them down. A firm statement of a no-gifts policy at the outset would have been the recommended course in theory, but in practice it would have been difficult and awkward to implement with Boris—as with other similar clients. Similarly, older clients may sometimes ask for favors unrelated to the therapy (e.g., help with a medical or financial issue), want to give hugs or kisses in gratitude, or want to know about the therapist's family and background.

Addressing Therapeutic Challenges

The role of the therapist for older clients is distinguished first and foremost by the unique age-specific challenges outlined previously that must be navigated in any form of therapy. These challenges, however, force a fundamental shift in priorities with older clients such that therapy is as much about being with and doing for them as it is about talking with them. In many cases, clients are living with serious and sometimes terminal illnesses, including dementia, in which the therapist's presence is the most important factor. In those circumstances knowledge of clients' backgrounds and ways to connect nonverbally with them may be key. This approach requires both education (and sometimes a crash course) on the history and culture of the client or regarding a medical disease, as well as mindfulness about one's own blind spots and prejudices that may be driving a negative countertransference.

Such mindfulness might be prompted by the following questions:

- How do I feel about my own parents? Grandparents? Other aged individuals?
- How do I envision my own aging? What are my greatest fears about aging?
- What are my attitudes about death and dying?
- Is life worth living with a severe illness or dementia?

The answers to these questions can help the therapist gauge the impact of his or her own underlying attitudes on the client. More negative views in general about aging or specific to a client need to be acknowledged and perhaps discussed with a supervisor so that they do not corrupt therapy. These views are inevitable given the great uncertainty and fear that most people have about aging but can be effectively dispelled if one is honest with oneself, seeks counsel or supervision with colleagues, and gets to know the fascinating world of the client.

The last comment certainly betrays a degree of sentimentality for the aged and hearkens back to my suggestion in the introduction that the therapist should approach the older client with a sense of wonder and the willingness to be curious, empathic, and courageous. There is both theory and strategy, however, to back up these virtues, which set the foundation for one's role as a therapist with older clients. What Helen Kivnick and many others have called a "strength-based approach" (Kivnick, 1993; Tice & Perkins, 1996), and what Robert Hill (2005) referred to as "positive aging," encompasses a philosophy that identifies and promotes the abilities and resources of aging individuals that facilitate adaptation to stress as well as cultivation of physical and emotional well-being. The inherent optimism to this philosophy boosts both therapist and client in their mutual endeavors and serves as an antidote to the challenges identified in this chapter.

3

AGE-GUIDED EVALUATION

When my grandfather began practicing medicine in the 1940s, diagnosis relied heavily upon the physician's possession of a keen eye, a patient ear, and a firm touch, which together enabled the doctor to sense and palpate most aspects of the patient's anatomy. To know what was happening with a patient's heart, for example, the doctor had to rely upon listening to the gallops and cadence of the heartbeat, observing the jugular waves in the neck, and palpating pulses throughout the body, as there were no echocardiograms or cardiac catheterizations to provide the graphic images we have today. But even the best doctor could not rely on his or her senses alone to apprehend a disease, for requisite knowledge and sound clinical judgment also relied upon the doctor's knowledge of the patient's lifetime history as well as daily habits, diet, and behaviors. According to the 1936 edition of my grandfather's first medical textbook, Meakins's *Practice of Medicine*, the doctor "who 'knew the case' from birth had a perspective to which no one else might possibly attain" and he or she "must be a combination of a confessor, a judge, a counselor and, above all, a friend" (p. 1). Such a vantage point allows the doctor, or any clinician for that matter, to follow the dictum of Sir William Osler that "It is much more important to know what sort of a patient has a disease than what sort of a disease a patient has" (1919).

When evaluating the older client, the clinician must, like the old-time doctor, be willing to look, listen, and get involved in a deeper manner than might otherwise be expected at a time when diagnosis seems to drive therapy. There are three reasons for this stance. First, older clients have a lot more history that has to be gathered and factored into the equation. Second, the problems of older clients have a more complex interplay between mind and body, which influences the clinical picture, forcing us to determine the relative contributions of medical illness, psychological dynamics, and social stresses. Third, a significant percentage of older clients have cognitive deficits such as language impairment or behavioral disturbances such as apathy that limit their ability to provide history or even participate in the evaluation. This chapter explores numerous clinical tools that facilitate communication among the therapist, older client, and informants, thus enhancing the gathering of a truly comprehensive history.

Laying the Groundwork

In an ideal setting, a client makes an appointment, shows up on time, and is able to tell the therapist what the problem is along with his or her history, medical problems, and medications. In contrast, many older clients have underlying physical and cognitive impairments and a lack of social supports, which create fundamental roadblocks to this ideal approach. And these roadblocks affect not necessarily the therapy itself but the very act of getting to appointments promptly and being able to sit comfortably and provide necessary information. A great disincentive for many clients is having to run the gauntlet of making an appointment, gathering medication lists or bottles for review, setting up transportation, and engaging the assistance of family or other caregivers. Arriving at an appointment tired, harried, or without necessary information can impair rapport with the therapist and slow down the process of evaluation. Consider the following case vignette.

> Victoria was a 93-year-old widowed woman brought to an appointment by her son to be evaluated for behavioral disturbances. It had taken the son 4 weeks to get in for an appointment, and he had to take off time from work and miss a crucial meeting in order to be with her. At the appointment, however, Victoria's severe hearing loss made it nearly impossible for her to hear any questions posed by the doctor. Without a list of her medications, the therapist could not fully assess the effectiveness or potential adverse effects of her psychotropic regimen. Victoria's memory impairment made it impossible for the therapist to gather information about previous therapy in the absence of Victoria's medical records. Victoria and her son left after an hour without a completed evaluation and without a coherent treatment plan as a result of these deficiencies.

The lesson in Victoria's case is that the process of evaluation must begin prior to the appointment, with the therapist or his or her office staff communicating with clients and their caregivers to lay the groundwork for a successful visit. Key issues to be addressed prior to the appointment and suggestions on how to remedy them are listed in Table 3.1.

In my experience as a therapist for individuals who are an average age of 85 years old, many of whom suffer from cogni-

Table 3.1. Laying the Groundwork for the Clinical Evaluation

Issue	*Remedy*
Severe sensory impairment	• Request that hearing aids and glasses be worn to the interview. • Suggest evaluation to clean ears, adjust eyeglasses, or obtain/repair hearing aids prior to the appointment. • Have large-print forms and amplifying devices (with headphones) available for clients to use. • Ensure adequate lighting and acoustics and absence of ambient noise in the exam room.
Physical disability	• Determine need for wheelchairs and physical assistance to get into office, especially if the parking lot is far away. • Provide adequate space in evaluation room for wheelchairs. • Have training and contingency planning for potential falls.
Memory impairment	• Insist that informants/caregivers attend the evaluation to provide history and assistance. • Request that a list of medications (or all pill bottles) be brought to the appointment. • Request that medical records be sent prior to or brought to the appointment. • For long-term care residents, arrange for nursing reports and medication lists to be sent.
Transportation	• Determine how the client will get to the appointment and then get home afterward. • Provide directions or maps of the location of the office and where to check in and wait for the therapist. • Ensure availability of handicapped parking spaces. • Ensure availability of staff to recognize and check in clients. • Have an available list of public transportation options, municipal transportation services (e.g., STS), and taxi services to assist clients and caregivers. • Plan appointment times so that clients or caregivers do not have to drive in heavy traffic, darkness, or other situations that might be difficult.

(continued)

Table 3.1. Continued

Issue	Remedy
Care needs	• Ensure availability of handicapped bathrooms and assistance (via a caregiver) for individuals with hygiene or incontinence problems. • Have clients attend to toileting and hygiene issues before leaving for the appointment. • Determine whether there are preexisting behavioral problems (such as verbal or physical agitation) that might require extra assistance. • Inquire as to the time of day when client is most alert and least affected by symptoms such as pain or shortness of breath that might compromise history taking.
Legal/ethical issues	• For clients under guardianship, the legal guardian must either attend the appointment or send a designated caregiver and supply copies of guardianship papers. • Clients who come to the appointment at the request, urging, or insistence of a family member or other caregiver must be informed of the reason for the appointment and the type of therapist being seen.
Scheduling	• Ensure that staff are trained in understanding and communicating with clients who may have sensory and memory deficits. • Send out written reminders (in large print) and call to confirm appointments and arrangements several days before the appointment. • Have a flexible schedule that can accommodate unexpected late arrivals, phone interventions, and emergencies.

tive impairment, appointments are frequently missed, incomplete, or disappointing because one or more of the issues in Table 3.1 were not addressed prior to the appointment. The most common problem is the lack of information necessary to conduct a thorough assessment; this situation then requires that extra time be taken to track down informants, request medical records, and even phone pharmacies to piece together an accurate medication list. The best antidote is having well-trained staff to anticipate all these issues and resolve them before the client even shows up. Therapists must also have flexibility built into their schedules. This allows a client who shows up late because of one of many unexpected but preventable problems (e.g., transportation being late, inability to find the office, excessive time required to ambulate from the parking lot to the office, a need to use the restroom upon arrival) to be accommodated—especially because he or she may have had to wait weeks for an appointment. Although it is common practice with younger clients in these circumstances to simply reschedule, keep in mind that for an older, debilitated client, rescheduling might mean the difference between being able to intervene in a timely manner and letting the client languish for days to weeks—and often never seeing him or her again. The reasons behind missed or late appointments should be investigated and resolved before it is ever assumed that they have some underlying dynamic meaning (i.e., a transference reaction).

Building Rapport

One key goal of the initial interview with an older client is to build rapport that will serve as the basis for a therapeutic relationship. For many in the current cohort of older clients, a visit to a mental health specialist carries a stigma of insanity or the need to be "put away." Others cannot fully appreciate the meaning of the meeting, either as a result of cognitive impairment or the fact that they were brought to the appointment and did not initiate it themselves. Meeting a friendly, respectful therapist who orients them to the session is reassuring and builds immediate comfort and trust. Formal introductions, including the therapist's name and specialty, are necessary regardless of the state of the client and should be followed by an open query to the client as to why he or she is there and what the therapist can do to help. Very quickly the therapist will see how willing and able the client is to engage in the interview. Thus, even before much has transpired in the interview, it is important for the therapist to size up the cognitive and functional level of the client. Consider the following situation.

> Margaret was an 82-year-old woman who was brought to the appointment with Dr. F. by her sister Ann. After an introduction from the therapist, Ann jumped in and began speaking for Margaret, who sat quietly, and with a somewhat bewildered look on her face. When Dr. F. asked Margaret why she was at the appointment, she shrugged her shoulders and looked at Ann with an embarrassed smile.

At this point in the interview the actual client has been eclipsed, and we don't yet know why. Is she cognitively impaired and unable to understand and respond because of aphasia? Does she speak a different language? Is she so dependent on her sister that she always defers to her? The therapist needs to know right away so as to modulate the interview in order to interact with Margaret in the most appropriate manner.

> Dr. F. suggested that she meet alone with Margaret first and politely asked Ann to wait outside. Once alone, Margaret looked uncomfortable and began speaking in broken English. Dr. F. responded in Spanish, and Margaret's eyes lit up. Suddenly she began conversing in her native language in more detail and with greater animation. However, it was

clear that she did not understand why she was at the appointment and was not able to offer much information. Still, Margaret formed an immediate bond with Dr. F. and insisted on kissing her cheek at the end of the appointment.

Rapport building, as is evident in the case of Margaret, depends upon the therapist's ability to form both verbal and nonverbal connections with the client. The therapist might establish verbal connections by speaking in the client's native language or through the demonstrated understanding or use of culture-bound terms. Hearing a little bit about the client's background may also allow some commonalities to emerge, such as shared places of origin, interests, or history, as in the following case vignette.

Edgar was an 89-year-old World War II veteran who came to an evaluation for symptoms of depression. He had never seen a therapist before and was quite reluctant. "I'm not crazy" were the first words out of his mouth. Instead of jumping into his problems, the therapist asked him about his background. Edgar spoke proudly of his role during World War II as a tank commander in the Battle of the Bulge. The therapist was well versed in the history of the war and asked Edgar if he served under General Patton. "My God, you know your history!" Edgar exclaimed. From that point on, Edgar felt an immediate sense that he was understood by the doctor and was eager to talk about his feelings of depression.

Not every moment with the client will be so magical, but an undeniable truth of working with many older clients is that they place tremendous value on rapport with the doctor, often idealizing a more classical view of the doctor-patient relationship. Keep in mind, however, that in more formal therapy (especially with a psychodynamic bent) with cognitively intact older clients, the therapist may need to be more circumspect.

History Taking

During a visit to the National World War II Museum in New Orleans, I was walking through one of the exhibits when a small plaque on the wall caught my eye. The brief paragraph engraved on the plaque contained the eyewitness account of a young infantryman preparing for battle on the deck of a transport ship on the eve of D-Day. He detailed the mundane thoughts and activities of his buddies as they approached what would turn out to be one of the defining moments in 20th-century history. As I read the last sentence, the soldier's name appeared and I stood stunned—he had been one of my clients at the VA hospital where I had worked as a therapist! Suddenly the entire history of the museum was condensed to one person—an incredibly warm but very troubled veteran who had sought my help. And in a moment I was able to understand the crucible of wartime experiences that shaped his mental distress and the entire lifetime that followed.

One of the joys of working with older clients is the richness of their histories. Current cohorts of older clients have witnessed and participated in the most extraordinary historical events, including the Great Depression, World War II, the birth of television, the Cold War, the feminist and sexual revolutions, the civil rights movement, Vietnam, Watergate, and more recently the advent of personal computers and the Internet. Clients who, as children, had only the radio to listen to and spent most of their lives living within a small geographic radius of home now surf the Web and travel around the world.

Keeping this in mind will fire the curiosity of the therapist and help promote a thorough collection of personal history that goes beyond merely asking about the current problem.

The components of the history include the current problem and its recent course, medical history, psychiatric history, current medications, relevant past medications, allergies, social history, family history, functional status, a review of systems, an environmental assessment, and caregiver status. These components can be rearranged into many different schemes at the discretion of the therapist. Elements of the history that are specific to the older client are detailed in Table 3.2.

Mental Status Examination

The mental status examination (MSE) begins the moment a client walks into the office and begins to reveal his or her emotional state, ability to communicate, and willingness to participate in the interview. In this respect there are many observational aspects to the MSE that become even more important with clients who suffer from cognitive impairment, speech or language impairment, or behavioral disturbances such as apathy or agitation. This fact illustrates how the mental state of the older client is more often influenced by brain pathology than is that of younger cohorts.

The appearance of the older client does not always betray his or her chronological age, as physiological aging is quite variable and is influenced by many lifestyle issues. Neurological impairment is obvious from features such as a tremor, a slowed walk, paralysis, or the use of a walker or wheelchair. It is important to know the cause of the impairment in order to probe other areas of deficit. For example, a client with weakness and a limp on the right side of the body probably suffered

Table 3.2. An Age-Adjusted History

Component	Geriatric Characteristics
Current problem and its recent course	• Seek information from client and from informant (with client's permission). • Establish the baseline of cognitive abilities. • Look for recent changes in cognition and ask about antecedents. • For cognitive disorders, the time course may extend back for several years.
Medical history	• A complete list is essential in order to understand the impact of disease on the brain. • It is important to ask about associated features of pain, disability, and confusion. • The most common chronic disorders are cardiac disease, high blood pressure (hypertension), diabetes, gastroesophageal reflux, arthritis, osteoporosis, high cholesterol, thyroid disorders, cancer, stroke, respiratory disease, prostate enlargement (in men), hearing loss, anemia, and macular degeneration. • Important acute disorders are pneumonia, urinary tract infection, delirium, and bone fracture secondary to a fall or other trauma. • Disorders that most affect mood and cognition are stroke, Parkinson's disease, severe anemia, slow heart rate (bradycardia), and hypothyroidism.
Psychiatric history	• If present, specify the type of dementia, if known (e.g., Alzheimer's disease versus vascular dementia). • For dementia history, ask about associated symptoms of depression, agitation, psychosis, and apathy. • Qualify history of depression by asking about age at the time of diagnosis, types and number of episodes, any hospitalizations, and suicidality. • Qualify history of anxiety by asking about presence of panic, phobias, trauma history, obsessions, and compulsive behaviors.

Table 3.2. Continued

Component	Geriatric Characteristics
	• Inquire about potential somatization (i.e., chronic or diffuse debilitating physical symptoms without clear medical cause).
	• Look for clues as to the presence of personality disorders: family estrangement, never marrying or having children, history of criminal behaviors, interpersonal relationships that are exceptionally sparse or extremely erratic.
	• Inquire about potential sleep disorders, especially insomnia and sleep apnea.
	• The most common sexual disorders in late life are erectile dysfunction in men and low desire in women.
Substance use	• Inquire about past and current use of alcohol, prescription drugs (especially those being used for pain, sleep, stimulation, and anxiety), tobacco products, caffeine, and illicit drugs (marijuana, cocaine, heroin, methamphetamine, and hallucinogens).
	• Individuals often minimize current use; sometimes verbally overestimating use may prompt a more accurate response.
	• For alcohol, the CAGE screen is useful: Have you ever (1) felt that you should *cut* down use, (2) been *annoyed* by criticism of your use, (3) felt *guilty* about use, or (4) taken an *eye-opener* in the morning to treat a hangover?
	• Always inquire about family history of substance use.
	• Follow up with questions about potential health consequences of substance use, including bouts of withdrawal, blackouts, seizures, frequent falls or other unexplained injuries, legal problems, family conflicts or estrangement, and medical and neurologic diseases (see Chapter 5 and Table 5.7 for more details).

(continued)

Table 3.2. Continued

Component	Geriatric Characteristics
Current medications and relevant past medications	• Inventory all prescription and over-the-counter medications. • Inquire about use of over-the-counter sleeping pills. • Inquire about the use of vitamins, herbal supplements, and home remedies and obtain an ingredient list. Look for excessive and potentially toxic use of vitamin supplements. • Obtain current doses and schedule for all psychotropic medications, including antipsychotics, antidepressants, anxiolytics, stimulants, sleeping pills, mood stabilizers, and cognitive-enhancing agents (see Table 7.9 for a complete list of psychotropic medications). • Get specific information on daily or intermittent use of medications for anxiety known as benzodiazepines, which have the potential to cause oversedation, dizziness, unsteadiness and falls, and memory impairment. • Medications that commonly impair cognition are benzodiazepines, antihistamines, painkillers (with opioid ingredients), anti-Parkinson's agents, anticholinergics, and chemotherapeutics. • Medications that commonly affect mood are corticosteroids and stimulants. • Obtain a description of past use and response to all psychotropic medications.
Allergies	• List all medications, foods, and environmental allergens that have caused both classic allergic symptoms (rash, hives, swelling, numbness in mouth, wheezing or difficulty breathing, or anaphylaxis) and acute changes in mood, behavior, or orientation. • The most common drug allergies are from penicillin, codeine and other narcotic painkillers, and aspirin.

Table 3.2. Continued

Component	Geriatric Characteristics
Social history	• Ask about exposure to significant historical events, especially ones that involved traumatic experiences. • Determine quality of relationships with spouse, children, and caregivers and specify who the main contact is. • Make an inventory of strengths: hobbies, interests, close relationships, spiritual or religious involvements, ethnic/cultural connections, and favorite foods and activities.
Family history	• Ask about a history of depression, suicide, dementia, substance abuse, and other psychiatric illnesses in birth parents, siblings, and biological children. • Creating a small genogram for the family can be helpful for recalling intergenerational relationships (see Figure 7.1). • For psychiatric illnesses that run in the family, ask about medication response in other affected members.
Functional status	• Inquire about ability to manage basic activities of daily living, including bathing, dressing, eating, toileting, and transferring, as well as instrumental activities of daily living such as cooking, cleaning, and managing money.
Review of systems	• Important symptoms to document are physical pain, appetite loss, insomnia, immobility, sensory loss or acute changes, shortness of breath, incontinence, constipation, dizziness, faintness, and chest discomfort. • Always ask about previous transient ischemic attacks, which can be harbingers of stroke, manifested by brief episodes of any of the following symptoms: one-sided weakness or numbness, garbled speech, visual loss, confusion, and dizziness.

(continued)

Table 3.2. Continued

Component	Geriatric Characteristics
Environmental assessment	• Is the living environment clean and safe? • Are there physical assists for those with disabilities (e.g., wheelchair ramps, tub or shower seats)? • Are there adequate stimulating activities? • Does the individual have access to transportation? • Is there assistance with activities of daily living (e.g., bathing, shopping, cooking, cleaning), if needed? • Can the individual manage his or her own medications? • Is there exposure to unsafe situations? • Is the individual driving, using appliances, or caring for others but lacking the mental capacity to do these activities safely? • Is there evidence of physical neglect or abuse or financial exploitation?
Caregiver status	• Who is the main caregiver? • Does the caregiver show signs of burden, such as irritability, depression, increased somatic symptoms, insomnia, loss of appetite or weight, or anger directed toward the client? • Does the caregiver have adequate help? • Has the caregiver ever had suicidal or homicidal thoughts? Impulses?

a left-brain stroke, which is often associated with language impairment, or aphasia. Strokes in the left frontal and temporal regions of the brain are also highly associated with depression (Robinson, Starr, Kubos, & Price, 1983). In this case a neuropsychological profile and a depression screening need to be key parts of the evaluation and will inform the eventual psychotherapeutic treatment.

Speech and language deficits may have several sources. Aging itself should not produce any significant changes aside from a lowering of tone and possibly volume. Loud and pressured speech may be present in manic or psychotic states, whereas a reduced tone and emotional range (i.e., prosody) may be seen in states of severe depression and apathy. A client who has difficulty articulating words and sounds may have dysarthria, a condition in which there is disturbed muscular control over speech mechanisms (vocal cords, tongue, lips) because of peripheral nerve damage. The dysarthric client may well understand what is being said and know how to speak, but oral communication is difficult. Aphasia, on the other hand, involves disturbances in the comprehension or expression of language as a result of damage to key brain regions, particularly Broca's area and Wernicke's area in the left frontotemporal lobes of the brain (most individuals are left-brain dominant, but the language centers can be on the corresponding right-hand side in some). Aphasia is a ubiquitous symptom in the middle to late stages of Alzheimer's disease but presents much earlier on in frontotemporal dementia. Word-finding difficulty, stuttering, and other speech and language disturbances occur long before any memory disturbances manifest in frontotemporal dementia.

Affect refers to the observed emotional state of an individual, whereas *mood* refers to the client's own descriptions of his or her emotions. In theory affect tends to be more transitory, whereas mood is more enduring; this difference can be compared to the fluctuating weather of a location versus its characteristic climate. Comparisons between the affect, mood, and thought process and content of a client is important, and incongruities (e.g., an individual who is crying but stating that his or her mood is good) may reveal communication deficits, organic impairment (e.g., *pseudobulbar palsy*, or emotional incontinence in which spontaneous laughter or crying is due to central nervous system disinhibition) or *alexithymia* (inability to accurately describe one's emotions). Neutral affect in the presence of complaints or signs of physical pain or disability can sometimes indicate underlying somatization.

Disturbances in thought process and content are most pronounced in dementia, mania, and psychosis. With the older client, it is critical to determine the baseline cognitive status to know whether disturbances in cognition (such as disorientation and short-term memory deficits) reflect acute brain impairment, as in delirium, or a permanent dementia. Individuals with chronic schizophrenia are usually fully oriented and have grossly intact memory function but demonstrate disturbances in the organization and content of thought. However, as they age, individuals with schizophrenia have more pronounced deficits in cognitive abilities along with a diminution in the psychotic symptoms such as delusions and hallucinations that characterized their thoughts and perceptions throughout their illness. The residual type of schizophrenia is defined by the increased presence of negative symptoms (e.g., apathy, social withdrawal, impoverishment of speech) and even prominent cerebral atrophy (Heaton et al., 2001; Karim & Burns, 2006).

Suicidal ideation must always be assessed during the MSE. Caucasian men 85 years and older have the highest rate of suicide across the life span, over 7 times higher than seen in similarly aged women. In 2005, for example, there were 45.23 suicides per 100,000 men age 85 and above, compared to 17.7 per 100,000 for men of all ages (American Association of Suicidology, 2009). Suicide rates among African American men and women were significantly lower. Whether the therapist asks a direct question about suicidal ideation or leads up to it with more innocuous questions (e.g., "Do you sometimes feel life is not worth living?"), many older clients might deny any such thinking because of the stigma of being labeled crazy.

As a result, there are many associated factors of suicidality that must be explored, such as thoughts of hopelessness and helplessness. Risk factors for late-life suicide that need to be collected from the history include past suicide attempts, a family history of suicide, depression, substance abuse, widowhood, physical illness, pain, and disability (Conwell, Duberstein, & Caine, 2002; Duberstein, Heisel, & Conwell, 2006). Homicidal ideation is less common but might be seen within the context of an elderly caregiver for a spouse with dementia or terminal illness. Observation and informant reports about recent behaviors, medical status, and weight are critical with all clients in order to rule out more indirect and passive suicidality. For example, a client who is refusing life-sustaining nutrition, tests (e.g., blood sugar level), or treatments (e.g., insulin shots, high blood pressure medication) might be doing so because he or she wants to die but does not have the ability or will to do something more drastic.

The assessment of insight and judgment takes on great significance with many older clients because there are multiple factors that can impair both, including dementia, stroke, brain tumors, delirium, and medication side effects. Insight and judgment are most commonly impaired by damage to the frontal or temporal lobes of the brain or to the numerous neural tracks connecting them to subcortical regions. Clinical clues pointing to such damage include the presence of either sustained apathy or episodes of disinhibited behaviors, such as agitation or inappropriate displays of emotion. Lack of insight into the presence of illness is known as *anosognosia* and has been associated with right parietal cerebral damage.

In order to assess insight and judgment, the clinician needs to know whether the client understands the details of a situation, appreciates the fact that there are choices, realizes the various consequences of each choice, and then is able to express a preference. The differentiation among these elements can be challenging.

> Daniel was a 72-year-old widowed man who suffered brain damage due to loss of oxygen when his heart stopped during a heart attack. After being resuscitated, he was noted to be more impulsive and irritable. He refused to take any antidepressant medications, stating that they were poisoning him. His family respected his wishes and didn't question his judgment. When the clinician asked about his condition, Daniel had no memory of his heart attack and denied having any problems with his thinking. He clearly stated his intention not to take any "mind pills." Although his expression of this decision sounded reasonable, more in-depth probing indicated that Daniel believed that the doctor prescribing the medication was part of a plot to kill him. In addition, Daniel was not able to explain to the therapist the purpose of the medication, even after repeated reminders.

On the one hand, Daniel was able to clearly articulate a decision, and it sounded reasonable at first. However, it became clear that he had a poor understanding of his medical condition and was delusional about the reasons for being prescribed a certain pill. In this state he was unable to appreciate his choices, and he could not explain the potential risks and benefits. Clearly his insight and judgment were severely impaired—a fact that colored most of his decisions.

When conducting a more formal evaluation of an individual's decision-making capacity, one must keep two key principles in mind. First, decision making is always evaluated with respect to specific issues, such as financial affairs, medical treatment, relationships, or living situations. Thus, an individual like Daniel might be able to reasonably decide where he wants to live, but not able to make good medical decisions. Lack of capacity in one area does not always generalize to all other areas. Second, the only role of the clinician is to decide on the mental *capacity* of the client, whereas *competency* to make decisions is a legal state determined by a judge.

A final step in every MSE for older clients is a cognitive screening conducted to determine the presence of impairment. The cognitive screen should include questions concerning orientation, attention, short-term memory (usually verbal recall), general knowledge, reasoning (abstraction), mathematical ability, and visuospatial ability. The purpose of the cognitive screen is to identity a problem, not necessarily to make a diagnosis. When a memory disorder is suspected, more formal and detailed neuropsychological testing should be obtained.

Although the MSE itself provides much of the data of the cognitive screen, it is best to use a brief instrument that yields a score that can be tracked over time. The Mini–Mental State Examination (Folstein, Folstein, & McHugh, 1975) is one of the most popular instruments, but there are many others, including the Mini-Cog (Borson, Scanlan, Brush, Vitaliano, & Dokmak, 2000), the Montreal Cognitive Assessment (Nasreddine et al., 2004), and the St. Louis University Mental Status (Tariq, Tumosa, Chibnall, Perry, & Morley, 2006).

One of quickest and most useful cognitive screens for dementia is the Mini-Cog, which takes less than 5 minutes to administer and yields a wealth of data (Borson et al., 2000). It begins by asking the client to repeat and then memorize three words. The client is then given a sheet of paper and asked to draw a clock, including the numbers and the hands, that reads

10 minutes past 11. Once the client completes the drawing, he or she is asked to recall the three words. Scoring is straightforward: Recall of zero words indicates the presence of dementia, and recall of all three words suggests no dementia. If one or two words are recalled, the clock drawing is then reviewed. If the clock is drawn perfectly, a dementia is less likely to be present. Any mistakes in the clock drawing (in combination with forgetting one or two words) suggest the presence of a dementia. Although this decision tree might sound too rudimentary, it has actually been shown to be quite accurate in identifying the presence of an underlying dementia. The three-item recall measures impairment in delayed verbal recall, which is one of the most sensitive indicators of Alzheimer's disease. The clock drawing test measures an incredible array of cognitive skills, including attention, short-term recall, abstract thinking, mathematical ability, and right- and left-sided visuospatial skills. In the case of the clock drawing test, a picture does indeed paint a thousand words.

Physical and Neurological Examination

The average clinician will not be conducting a physical or neurological examination, nor will he or she be ordering brain scans or blood tests. Still, there are several important elements of the physical evaluation of older clients that all clinicians must be able to conduct and interpret.

In terms of physical appearance, there are several neurological terms that warrant definition. *Gait* is a formal term for a client's walk, and its quality is a reflection of muscle tone and strength, balance, vision, bone strength, joint integrity, and peripheral and central nerve function. Many older clients use assistive devices such as canes or walkers to compensate for poor balance or the loss of strength and coordination in the back, hips, or lower extremities. Individuals with Parkinson's disease have a characteristic slow and shuffling or festinating gait. Individuals with Alzheimer's disease develop gait instability and eventually lose their ability to walk in later stages. Many older clients in wheelchairs have suffered a fall or illness that left them bed-bound for weeks or months, which led in turn to muscle weakening or deconditioning and the inability to walk safely. Because ambulation is so central to being and feeling independent, many issues in psychotherapy revolve around either fear of falling and being injured or grief over the loss of the ability to walk.

Older individuals may also demonstrate tremors or shakes in their hands, arms, or head that result from aging itself (e.g., benign essential tremor), neurological illnesses such as Parkinson's disease or peripheral neuropathy, or side effects of medications. These movements may be a source of embarrassment and anxiety and a reason for social withdrawal due to an individual's appearance and difficulty writing or feeding him- or herself. The appearance of a tremor should always warrant referral to one's PCP, especially because it may be a completely reversible side effect of a medication.

Muscle rigidity (seen in slow, stiff movements), repetitive twisting or jerking of body parts (such as a chewing movement), and restlessness (constant movements, especially in the legs) may all represent *extrapyramidal symptoms*, which sometimes result from the use of antipsychotic medications. These movements may be uncomfortable and unsightly and reflect either an adverse reaction to the medication or too high a dose. *Akathisia* refers to a state of motor restlessness—particularly felt in the legs—that can be a side effect of all antipsychotic medications and some antidepressants. It is quite uncomfortable and often mistaken for anxiety (sometimes leading to *more* of the offending medication being administered!) but can be readily treated through either the discontinuation of the medication or the addition of an antidote. A more concerning syndrome called *tardive dyskinesia* refers to abnormal, involuntary movements in the hands, face, arms, or trunk that are sometimes a permanent effect of antipsychotics. Any such movements should be noted and reported to both the treating psychiatrist and the PCP. A list of antipsychotic medications that can produce these side effects can be found in Table 7.9.

Individuals who demonstrate difficulty staying awake during sessions may be overly sedated from medications, intoxicated from substance abuse, or suffering from a sleep disorder or a disorder of wakefulness known as narcolepsy. On the flip side, clients who are hyperactive during sessions may be manic, suffering from akathisia, in a hyperthyroid state, or overstimulated from certain medications (e.g., antidepressants, stimulants, caffeine, anti-Parkinson's medications, or steroids). Such potential findings emphasize again the importance of knowing what one's clients are ingesting.

The results of brain scans should always be noted in the evaluation, especially when there is evidence of a stroke, tumor, or bleed. Computerized tomography, or CT, scans use radiation to image the brain and are faster and cheaper to obtain but do not have the resolution of slightly more expensive and time-consuming magnetic resonance imaging, or MRI, scans, which use magnetic fields to produce images. It is common in older individuals to see shrinkage or atrophy of the brain as well as small spots of nerve-tract degeneration and damage. This atrophy may be more pronounced in individuals with Alzheimer's disease, especially in the memory-processing center known as the hippocampus. At the same time, the CT and MRI scans of individuals with Alzheimer's disease are relatively benign because the actual disease pathology cannot be visualized. When there is any evidence of cognitive impairment or rapid onset of psychiatric symptoms, clinicians should always inquire as to whether clients have had a medical evaluation by their PCP or other specialist that included a brain scan.

4

WORKING WITH FAMILIES AND CAREGIVERS

Several years ago I received a phone call from the daughter of a 98-year-old resident at the nursing home where I work. At the time, I was treating her mother for moderate to severe Alzheimer's disease and associated depression. The daughter expressed deep concern over her mother's advancing dementia, telling me that "She is no longer the mother I remember." She had cut back on her visits to the facility, uncertain of what to do when she saw her mother, and was discouraging her own children and grandchildren from visiting as well. We had a long talk about the course of Alzheimer's disease, and I encouraged her to rediscover her mother as she was in the present, and to find new ways to connect with her. I urged her to bring her children and grandchildren for regular visits, and I suggested a number of meaningful activities that they could do with their ailing matriarch. She seemed comforted by the conversation and agreed to pursue my suggestions.

Six months later, on a Saturday evening, I was driving our 16-year-old babysitter home when she noticed my ID badge from work in the car. "Oh, you work at the nursing home where my great-grandmother lives," she told me. She went on to describe how much she valued the time she spent visiting her great-grandmother—even though she was so impaired. I suddenly realized that our babysitter was the granddaughter of the woman who had called me in despair earlier that year. Upon hearing about her experiences, I felt incredibly gratified to have worked directly and indirectly with four generations of a family. As I got to know each generation over the ensuing year, I was able to gain tremendous insight into the character, history, and family dynamics of my 98-year-old client.

This experience illustrates a fundamental way in which working with older clients is unique, as clinicians have, by necessity, to work with family members and other caregivers, and this work can have a profoundly positive impact on a much wider web of intergenerational relationships. At the same time, this widening of contacts poses several specific challenges and responsibilities. First, there are legal and ethical regulations that guide and limit the type of contact that the therapist may have with these individuals. Second, such contact might add an additional layer of clients who face incredible burdens as caregivers and often need clinical attention themselves. And third, there are relationship dynamics between the client and his or her family and caregivers that involve the therapist in ways that must be understood and managed.

Rules of Contact

It is a ritual during all initial meetings with clients to ask them for their written permission to provide treatment, and to share health information with designated family and caregivers, insurers, and other health care specialists. Much of the current approach to obtaining permission to release health care information comes from the Privacy Rule of the Health Information Portability and Accountability Act, known simply as HIPAA. HIPAA regulations were developed to be applicable to health care providers who use electronic transmission of personal health information, but nearly all clinicians have adopted them as the most prudent safeguards for clients. Although many clinicians and their offices have adopted extremely stringent boundaries for contact with family, friends, and other caregivers (sometimes insisting on written permission before any information can be shared), HIPAA regulations simply state that in order to share health information, clinicians must seek the verbal permission or acquiescence of the client and exercise their professional judgment in situations when the client is unable to do so (U.S. Department of Health & Human Services, 2009).

Keeping health information private, however, is not only a legal obligation of the therapist as stipulated by HIPAA guidelines but also an ethical responsibility and a professional virtue. A client's trust in the therapist depends in part upon the knowledge that personal information will be safeguarded and only disclosed with permission and the utmost discretion. Therapists who regularly talk about clients to others not involved in their care or who regale colleagues with unnecessary and often embarrassing stories about clients engender a looseness and lack of respect that risks creeping into therapeutic interactions.

At the same time, many older clients are dependent upon family members and other caregivers for assistance with day-to-day life, or they have cognitive impairment that limits their capacity to make informed decisions about who should know about their health status. In these frequent situations, the therapist must be able to obtain information from and provide information on diagnosis and treatment to designated caregivers. Successful implementation of the entire treatment plan might rely upon these caregivers. In these situations, where should the clinician begin?

The first step is to determine the client's mental capacity to make decisions about health care. This capacity is not always obvious, and so the clinician should always spend the initial part of any evaluation alone with the client to conduct an MSE to assess orientation, attention, memory, reasoning, and the ability to understand and communicate (see Chapter 3). Formal evaluations of decision-making capacity should be specific to an issue (e.g., for health care or estate planning and gifts, or for selection of living situation).

A second step in work with all older clients is to determine the main point of contact (typically the next of kin) and to delineate a web of individuals who are close to the client and involved in his or her care. For individuals with impaired mental capacity, a legally authorized representative (as defined by state law) who will provide consent for evaluation and client history must be identified. The legally authorized representative and selected family members or caregivers in the web of contacts should be consulted regarding any safety concerns, and engaged in implementation of the treatment plan.

A third step is for the therapist to delineate the roles of family members and other caregivers and then assess the quality of the relationships between them and the client, especially because the clinical problem at hand may stem from conflicts within these relationships. Understanding these dynamics might also help the therapist avoid certain pitfalls, such as communicating with an estranged child, precipitating a fight among family members, or speaking to someone about issues out of his or her purview (e.g., speaking to an aide about care issues when there is a legal guardian who must make the decision under the auspices of a judge). Consider what makes this understanding so critical.

> Maria was an 83-year-old widowed woman who was referred to a social worker named Ms. K. for an evaluation of severe depression. Prior to the appointment, Maria's daughter Vickie called Ms. K. and insisted that her mother should not be referred to any dieticians or psychiatrists because she was providing her mother with homeopathic medications and organic foods. However, when Maria arrived at the appointment, she was accompanied by her son Jack, who insisted that Vickie was only meddling and should not be listened to. Maria was quite withdrawn and passive during the appointment and was not able to specify any preference for a main contact. Jack insisted that his mother start therapy with the social worker and see a psychiatrist to get started on medications. He also asked Ms. K. to order supplemental nutritional shakes for his mom.

In the case of Maria, the therapist had an immediate dilemma, because there were two children with equal involvement with their mom but diametrically opposed demands on the therapist, and the client was unable to clearly indicate whose views she most supported. It may be impossible for the social worker to provide care in this case without meeting with both siblings and coming to an agreement.

During the course of work with clients, the therapist should periodically review the list of designated caregivers and family members to keep their information and roles current. Sometimes the most helpful way to document and then review this network is through the use of a genogram. A genogram is a graphic display of family members (and others) and their relationships over several generations. There are many formats for genograms, and the type of information that can be included ranges from basic family demographics to more complex medical and psychiatric history, emotional relationships, and family narratives (McGoldrick et al., 2008). A sample genogram can be found in Figure 7.1.

The relationship that the clinician establishes with family members and caregivers should stem from the needs of the client. For example, if the client has physical limitations that may prevent him or her from getting to appointments or managing medications, the clinician may only need to engage the individuals who assist with those tasks, with the only exchange of information being relative to their facilitation. When there is cognitive impairment, there must be ongoing exchange of information with the legally authorized representative for consent to treat and with respect to all mental health decision making. Even in the latter situation, the clinician's interactions with the caregiver should be guided by clinical issues (e.g., how the client is responding to treatment), not extraneous matters such as business or social dealings. Otherwise there is a risk that the needs of the caregiver, which may run counter to or bear no relationship to those of the client, may corrupt the therapist-client relationship.

There are many instances, however, when caregivers have problems that directly affect the care of the client and warrant their own therapeutic interventions. In many such circumstances, it is impractical and potentially threatening to the therapeutic alliance for the therapist to simply refer the caregiver to outside services or colleagues. It is also unethical and sometimes even illegal not to intervene when abuse or neglect is suspected. The therapist should obtain basic information on the caregiver's problems, perhaps in a brief evaluation, and then either implement treatment or refer the caregiver to a colleague or community resource that can help—all the while maintaining a supportive and involved presence. This does not rule out a therapist working with caregivers or multiple generations in a family (as will be discussed in Chapter 7), but there must be clear lines of separation. Consider how these lines may become blurred.

> Mrs. V. was brought to a therapist by her husband because she was depressed and refusing to seek help. Throughout several months of therapy, Mr. V. would hover near the therapy room and often joined sessions to provide progress reports. Once Mrs. V. improved, she requested private sessions to speak about her marital woes. Mr. V. sought his own private sessions with the therapist as well as joint sessions. One of their daughters began phoning the therapist to report her own concerns, and all three individuals demanded to know what the others had said about them. On one occasion Mr. V. became enraged at the therapist and accused her of revealing his confidentially disclosed feelings to his wife without his permission.

In this case, the lines of communication became so enmeshed and confused that the therapist did indeed have a difficult time managing all the information. Clearly it would have been better to keep Mrs. V. as a client, set stricter limits on Mr. V.'s participation, and either involve a colleague for conjoint sessions or refer the couple to a therapist outside the practice.

The Burden of Caregiving

Referring to someone as a caregiver of a client means that he or she is more than simply a family member, loved one, or friend. It implies a direct role in supervision or hands-on assistance with daily activities, ranging from the most basic aspects of care (e.g., dressing, bathing, feeding) to complex management of finances, household chores, and transportation. Sometimes caregivers must also spend time watching clients to keep them safe and act on their behalf to make everyday decisions. Caregivers often have to manage medical issues and medications as well as symptoms of depression (e.g., social withdrawal, apathy, insomnia, loss of appetite), anxiety and panic, psychosis, and behavioral disturbances. These tasks can be extremely taxing and sometimes overwhelming, especially given the fact that the majority of caregivers are elderly spouses and are experiencing their own maladies. Being a caregiver is not a job for the faint of heart! Consider the case of Art.

Art describes his current life with Beverly as similar to a small boat slowly sinking into the depths. For 6 years now, Beverly has had Alzheimer's disease, and with each birthday, Art takes stock of the rising level of difficulty of caring for her. At 72 years old, Beverly is still relatively healthy and mobile, but she cannot be left alone. A year ago she walked out of the house and spent half a day wandering aimlessly around the neighborhood until the police found her and returned her to a frantic Art. Her short-term memory is nonexistent, and she is steadily losing the ability to recognize even her closest friends. Sometimes she'll get up at 4 AM, dress herself, and wake up Art, insisting that he make breakfast for her. She frequently wets or soils her pants and then fights

Art when he tries to clean her. Their sex life ended over a year ago, and Art mourns the loss of both the physical and emotional intimacy. Art had always committed himself to being with Beverly "till death do us part," but he is not so sure he can take it much longer. On top of this burden, Art has begun experiencing his own health problems, including severe esophageal reflux (Agronin, 2007a).

Art is what could be described as an informal caregiver because he takes on this role as an obligation rather than for pay or as part of a profession. It has been estimated that 70% to 80% of all individuals with dementia are cared for at home, with most care provided by family members—typically an elderly wife (Parks, 2000). On average, the home caregiver spends up to 70 hours a week assisting an individual with moderate to severe dementia. Informal caregivers often employ other individuals on a full- or part-time basis to help out with caregiving, especially when they either have to work or do not have the physical capacity to carry out tasks such as bathing or dressing the client.

The term *caregiver burden* has been used widely to describe the resulting physical, emotional, and financial toll. Caregivers for individuals with severe physical disabilities or various forms of dementia are in particularly difficult circumstances, as they have to spend significant time providing hands-on care, sometimes in the face of behavioral resistance. Even after a client is placed in a long-term care institution, the caregiver still plays an important role in daily care and still has to deal with feelings of guilt, sadness, and depression and the ongoing struggle of watching a loved one succumb to a tragic illness (Agronin, 2008).

The physical and emotional toll of this burden is troublesome. Caregivers experience higher rates of medical illness and have slower recovery times and poorer immune function than non-caregivers (Connell, Janevic, & Gallant, 2001; Schulz et al., 1995). Compared to non-caregivers, caregivers have 46% more physician visits, use 70% more prescription drugs, and have a higher mortality rate (Ernst & Hay, 1994; Schulz & Beach, 1999; Thompson, Spira, Depp, McGee, & Gallagher-Thompson, 2006). Caregivers also have increased rates of depression, anxiety, exhaustion, and sleep and appetite problems, along with greater use of psychotropic medications (Clipp & George, 1990). An estimated 20% to 50% of caregivers have depression, reflecting a risk 2 to 3 times greater than that of the general population (Harwood et al., 1998). Depression tends to amplify burden and decrease quality of life for caregivers, contributing to a vicious cycle. Of all types of caregivers, spouses may be at greatest risk of depression. Adding insult to injury is the fact that this burden has been associated with increased behavioral problems in the cognitively impaired individual, and with a greater likelihood of eventual long-term care placement (Dunkin & Anderson-Hanley, 1998).

All caregivers should be questioned about how they are coping with their loved one's illness, and the presence of any of the 10 key warning signs should prompt more in-depth investigation. These are:

- Denial of the disease and its effects.
- Anger directed toward the individual with dementia and others.
- Social withdrawal and isolation.
- Strong feelings of anxiety and of being overwhelmed.

- Feelings of depression, resignation.
- Feeling too exhausted to engage in caregiving and other activities.
- Impaired sleep.
- Irritability, negative attitudes.
- Poor concentration, forgetfulness, appearing harried.
- Increased health problems (Agronin, 2008; Alzheimer's Association, 2008).

A brief burden interview, as outlined in Table 4.1, can also be used for this purpose.

It is sometimes better to interview caregivers alone, or to conduct a telephone screen. This allows them to be open without worrying about upsetting, offending, or frightening their

Table 4.1. A Brief Burden Interview

Perceptions and Experience of Burden
1. Do you feel under significant stress? If yes, describe.
2. Do you feel depressed? Anxious? To what degree?
3. Have you had difficulty sleeping? Eating?
4. Do you have more medical problems than before?
5. Do you constantly feel exhausted?
6. Have you ever felt that life isn't worth living? Suicidal?
7. Have you ever felt like hitting or even ending the life of your loved one with dementia?

Potential Causes of Burden
8. Do you need more visitors? More assistance? More time for yourself?
9. Does your loved one have behavioral problems? Paranoia?
10. Is he or she depressed? Apathetic?

The greater the number of yes responses, the greater the likelihood of increased burden and the need for active intervention.

Note. From *Alzheimer disease and other dementias* (2nd ed., p. 329), by M. E. Agronin, 2008, Philadelphia, PA: Lippincott Williams & Wilkins. Copyright 2008 by Lippincott Williams & Wilkins. Reprinted with permission.

loved one. If they endorse feelings of depression, being overwhelmed, hopelessness, or helplessness, always inquire about suicidal and homicidal thoughts. Ask them to enumerate existing and potential supports. Sometimes there are adequate supports, but the caregiver either rejects them or doesn't appreciate their presence. A mentally stable caregiver with lots of respite time, family visitors, and social supports may still perceive his or her situation as quite bleak. Perceived burden is ultimately the most important factor (Agronin, 2007a).

When working with caregivers in addition to the client, the clinician needs to be part therapist and part social worker. Sometimes it is possible to reduce burden by simply pointing out the obvious stressors to caregivers and then being available to talk. But it is equally important to be able to steer them toward invaluable supports and resources.

Keep in mind the tremendous shift in roles, responsibilities, and family dynamics that might be taking place for both clients and caregivers. For example, caregivers who are caring for their spouses may find themselves assuming responsibilities for the client that are reminiscent of parenting duties that they performed when they had young children, such as toileting, feeding, bathing, and constant monitoring. Traditional gender roles can reverse, as when a husband or wife has to assume unfamiliar tasks once taken care of by his or her spouse, such as managing household finances, routine cleaning and maintenance of the home and yard, or grocery shopping. A spouse may lose his or her main source of communication and support. In addition, patterns of affection and sexuality often decline and eventually cease, leaving the caregiver without a partner to fulfill his or her intimate needs. Older caregivers struggle to maintain an adequate level of energy, enthusiasm, and concentration to meet the needs of their loved one, despite being beset by their own physical and emotional problems. Specific strategies to help caregivers for clients with dementia are detailed in Chapter 6.

In the end, it is critical for clinicians to embody the basic values of kindness, respect, and dignity when working with caregivers and other family members. Caregivers who are educated, supported, and cared for consistently over time will have their burden eased and may even thrive throughout what is undoubtedly a heartbreaking journey. They will also be better caregivers for the ailing client.

Working With Challenging Caregivers

Consider how we might describe "ideal" family members and other caregivers. These individuals would have a good understanding of the client's condition and realistic expectations of care, maintain regular visits and provide for the client's personal needs, and exude a respectful attitude toward the clinician and staff and other residents, if the client lives in a long-term care facility. All too often clinicians and institutions expect such caregivers to fit this description but do not help to adequately cultivate them with sufficient communication, support, and empathy for the burden of their position.

There are some caregivers, however, who play a more challenging role, precipitating conflict through excessive caregiving demands, hostile behaviors, or negligence. Not only can these conflicts disrupt relationships with clients, clinicians, and long-term care staff, but they can poison morale, impede optimal caregiving, and increase both fears of and actual liability on the part of both clinicians and institutions. This section defines the main types of challenging caregivers and reflects upon how to best work with them without compromising standards of care or one's own professional demeanor (Agronin, 2006).

A challenging caregiver may be a single individual or a group of caregivers (usually a family) who precipitate conflict and crises through their attitudes and behaviors toward the care of the designated client and the roles of other involved caregivers. Such conflicts are worsened when clinicians neglect the concerns of the caregiver or react in a defensive or even hostile manner. Some clinicians may react out of anger or fear by actively avoiding contact with the caregiver or with passive-aggressive behaviors such as not following through on caregiver requests or not returning phone calls. It is clear, however, that the resultant impairment in communication becomes a further irritant to the caregiver and serves to exacerbate the situation.

Challenging caregivers can be grouped into four broad categories based on their basic dysfunctional approach—however, keep in mind that some challenging caregivers have features from multiple categories. The degree of how challenging the attitudes and behaviors are varies, ranging from mild as a result of transient stresses or emotional reactions to moderate or severe because of underlying chronic personality problems or psychiatric conditions. These categories, along with their characteristics and possible etiology, are listed in Table 4.2.

The family group that presents with the challenging caregiver may sometimes absorb and buffer noxious behaviors or may serve to amplify them, depending on the underlying family dynamics. Clinicians must keep an eye out for this, because it may be that the "good" sibling and the "bad" sibling are each playing long-standing roles that together serve to perpetuate a dysfunctional situation. Several patterns of challenging family approaches are listed in Table 4.3.

Table 4.2. Types and Characteristics of Challenging Caregivers

Type of Challenging Caregiver	Characteristics	Possible Reasons for Attitudes and Behaviors
Projectors	• Suspicious • Accusatory, blaming • Distrustful • Hostile, angry • Paranoid • Litigious	• Feelings of guilt, inadequacy, or denial • Personality problems: paranoid, antisocial, narcissistic, or borderline features • Psychiatric conditions: bipolar disorder (mania), impulse control disorder, paranoid psychosis
Rejectors	• Indifferent • Absent • Abandoning • Careless • Apathetic • Passive aggressive • Estranged	• Feelings of anger or resentment • History of abuse or neglect by the client • Lack of financial or social resources • Personality problems: antisocial, schizoid, schizotypal, depressive, passive-aggressive, avoidant, or borderline features • Psychiatric conditions: depression, substance abuse, agoraphobia or anxiety disorder that inhibits visitation, dementia
Counters and worriers	• Overinvolved • Overly anxious • Hypervigilant • Hovering • Repetitive • Obsessive compulsive	• Feelings of guilt, dependency, denial, or anxiety • Inability to accept change in client • Personality problems: obsessive-compulsive or dependent features • Psychiatric conditions: obsessive-compulsive disorder, generalized anxiety disorder
Attachers and clingers	• Dependent • Enmeshed, unable to separate • Overly accepting • Constantly present	• History of dependence on client • Lack of independence, incompetence • Lack of adequate social resources • Personality problems: dependent, schizoid, or avoidant features • Psychiatric conditions: developmental problems, mental retardation, dementia, depression, schizophrenia

Table 4.3. Patterns of the Challenging Caregiver Within a Family

Pattern	Description
Single point	Challenging behaviors are limited to a single family member who serves as the sole contact for the client.
Mixed	Challenging behaviors are seen in more than one but not all family members.
United front	Challenging behaviors are seen in all family members.
The assist	Challenging behaviors are seen in only one family member but are supported and sometimes prompted by other family members.
Shifting sands	Challenging behaviors shift among family members.

When one is dealing with challenging caregivers, there are several important questions that can help define the nature and scope of the problem and point toward positive approaches:

- Are you dealing with a single problem, a recurrent situation, or a crisis?
- How is the caregiver making you feel?
- Is there an immediate issue of safety or illegality?
- Are the complaints or issues legitimate? Are *you* part of the problem?
- Is there an underlying issue that is not being addressed (e.g., staffing, environment, psychiatric or medical illness)?

Despite conflicts and crises with challenging caregivers, the chief priority for clinicians and other staff is to maintain proper care of the client in a professional manner. The loss of one's professional demeanor constitutes a serious ethical breach and jeopardizes the clinician's entire role. When frustrated, angry, or fearful, clinicians must seek out other members of the treatment team or colleagues to obtain support and advice and to vent pent-up feelings. Such feelings should never be expressed to the caregiver or client, unless they are central to addressing a clinical or safety issue. All concerns, responses, and inappropriate caregiver behaviors should be carefully and regularly documented to facilitate communication and for risk management purposes. It is also critical to identify and interact with all involved caregivers, and to try to understand the etiology of such behavior (see Table 4.2). More information on family dynamics can be found in Chapter 7.

From the outset, the clinician must communicate with all caregivers on a regular basis to fully listen to, understand, and empathize with them regarding their concerns, and to provide education about the client's condition. Each type of challenging caregiver requires different approaches. For projectors, it is best never to dismiss, ignore, or challenge their concerns without first hearing them out. It is sometimes effective to listen and then redirect the discussion toward more appropriate or practical caregiving issues. For example, the caregiver's anger and inappropriate demands can sometimes be sated by empathic listening coupled with the development of practical steps that approximate the demands.

In clinic or long-term care settings, it is also important to protect less senior and hence more vulnerable staff members from belligerent or bullying caregivers, and to channel all complaints to staff members with sufficient authority to actually effect change. For example, a caregiver who is harassing a secretary should be asked to bring all care concerns to the therapist or the clinic director. Projectors often need appropriate limits to be communicated clearly and by authoritative staff. Sometimes they need to be referred to other practices or agencies, with prior arrangement. In extreme situations when there are threats of harm, the entire clinician-client relationship is jeopardized and the clinician may need to involve local law enforcement to provide protection and then to investigate the risk.

Counters and worriers bring similar caregiving demands but with less noxious and threatening approaches. Communication is again paramount but must involve limit setting. The basic strategy is to structure the roles and concerns of these caregivers into practical tasks and strategies. Sometimes social service or mental health staff can be assigned to work with them. Such caregivers can actually become quite industrious allies of clinicians or staff if they are given appropriate, helpful caregiving roles, and sufficient attention is paid to their anxieties. Attachers and clingers often need more intensive evaluation from social service and mental health staff to support their own deficiencies and losses that have arisen as a result of the client's disability. They may need their own services to help maintain some degree of independence from the client.

Rejectors are known more by their absence than their presence but end up indirectly creating problems and sometimes crises when clients try to get their help or attention. A comprehensive family history is most helpful for understanding why they are neglecting the client; for example, they may have been abused by the client in the past and do not want much contact now that the client is disabled. There may be ways in which the clinician or clinic/long-term care staff can empathize with them regarding their experiences and discuss ways in which they can provide a good enough degree of involvement to satisfy client or staff needs without overstepping their own limits. When the rejector's behaviors are more problematic, such as neglect or abuse of a cognitively impaired outpatient, protective service agencies need to be consulted quickly. The rejector may need interventions for psychiatric illness such as cognitive impairment, psychosis, or substance abuse that is impeding their caregiving abilities.

Regardless of the type of challenging caregiver, clinicians should view the situation as an opportunity to enhance communication with the caregiver and among staff members, and to achieve a better understanding of the world from which the client emerges.

5

THE AGE EQUATION: HOW DOES AGING AFFECT MENTAL ILLNESS?

Many clinicians are daunted by the thought of working with older clients because there seem to be too many moving parts. Cases demand simultaneous reviews of medical history and medication use, decades of psychiatric history, complicated and entrenched family dynamics, immense physical and social needs, and an ever-shrinking horizon of time. A 95-year-old client threw down the gauntlet to me during one meeting in a way that encapsulated this challenge: "I'm 95, depressed, unable to walk, tired, in pain, and have nothing to look forward to. I'm going to die soon anyway. What can you possibly do to help me?" It is easy to sit dumbfounded with such a client, uncertain about what to do. In reaction, we may look for a quick fix, such as a new antidepressant or a referral to someone else. We may even agree with the client's sentiment and give up hope that we can actually help. As with any client young or old, however, we must remind ourselves that therapy is a process, not an event. As such, any intervention must carry with it the promise of a relationship between clinician and client, not just a single encounter. Frustration and fatalism must be replaced by a patient and systematic approach to understanding the client and plotting a meaningful therapeutic course.

But how can this be achieved? In Chapter 1, I presented the following heuristic equation:

$$\frac{\text{Physiological aging process (intellect + personality)}}{\times \text{ Life history (adaptation + maturation)}}$$
$$= \text{ Products of aging}$$

This "age equation" illustrates how a client's presentation (i.e., the "products" of his or her aging process) is shaped over time by the interaction of two primary processes: the impact of physiological aging on intellect and personality, and the manner in which an individual with a specific history and culture has adapted to life challenges. For example, consider the following hypothetical equation of an 85-year-old World War II veteran:

$$\frac{\begin{array}{l}\text{Cerebrovascular disease (average intelligence}\\ +\ \text{aggressive personality)}\\ \times\ \text{World War II combat veteran, laborer}\\ \quad\text{(violent temper + alcoholism)}\end{array}}{}$$
$$= \text{ Divorced, estranged from children, PTSD, depressed,}$$
$$\text{just moved into nursing home}$$

In this case, the client's cerebrovascular disease produced a mild vascular dementia in a man without an extensive cognitive reserve. His poor insight into his condition and aggressive personality led to increased depression and some episodic agitation. His combat experiences during World War II had resulted in a long-standing diagnosis of PTSD, for which he never received formal treatment but instead self-medicated with alcohol. In turn, alcohol exacerbated his violent temper and led to estrangement from most family members. Put together, these factors produced a man who entered late life depressed and with few social or financial supports to help him after a stroke rendered him incapable of living independently. The clinician now is seeing a slice of him as a depressed, irritable, and agitated man. It is not this presentation itself that is unique (in fact, most clinicians see a lot of depressed and agitated older clients), but all the antecedents that have led to it. As a result, the most comprehensive and humane approach to diagnosis and treatment must involve an understanding of the way in which aging and life history have brought the client to his or her current stage.

Of course, this age equation is incomplete, and it is not meant to be used literally in clinical work. The prevailing message is to think broadly about each client's presentation and its antecedents and devise a formulation to account for the journey. A formulation goes above and beyond a mere diagnostic label but provides the *hows* and *whys* of each life history (Horowitz, 1997). Many of the life cycle templates discussed in Chapter 1, such as Erikson's eight stages and Vaillant's developmental tasks, will prove useful.

Although each individual client has his or her own age equation, there are commonalities among many presentations of late-life psychiatric illness that warrant discussion. For example, physical frailty, disability, and chronic pain are often intertwined with psychiatric symptoms. Determining cause and effect can be difficult: Is the client depressed because he has Parkinson's disease, or did Parkinson's disease (or one of the medications used to treat it) cause his depression? The same can be said for cognitive impairment: Does the client have memory trouble because she is depressed, or is the depression an early sign of a memory disorder such as Alzheimer's disease? The answers are rarely clear at first, and such cases require repeated observations over weeks to months. In addition, they might not be mutually exclusive, so one can be depressed or anxious as a result of both psychological and organic causes at the same time.

Another commonality is that aging might confer some advantages in late-life illness: more time to engage in therapeutic activities, greater social support services, fewer individual needs and demands (e.g., one typically doesn't have to care for young children or work to support a family), greater emotional maturity (Carstensen, Pasupathi, Mayr, & Nesselroade, 2000; Gross et al., 1997), and wisdom (see Chapter 1 for a more detailed discussion). All these age-related forces, both positive and negative, influence the following discussion of mental disorders seen frequently in older clients.

Mind, Body, and Brain

A central task with any older client is determining the relative contributions of physical illness and pain versus psychological suffering. For example, to what extent is a depressed client's mood due to a recent stress or loss versus a potential imbalance in a physical attribute such as thyroid hormone levels? Knowing the answer is critical, because psychotherapy can help someone deal with grief, but it certainly won't directly affect a physical organ and its hormonal output. Some researchers would argue, however, that a wide variety of experiences, such as counseling, deep breathing, yoga, and prayer, can affect physiological processes in the body. Consider the power of the placebo effect, in which the belief that one will get better sometimes becomes a self-fulfilling prophecy (Evans, 2004). Modern-day psychiatry hopes to eventually reduce these arguments to a biological formula in which all psychological events are translatable into neuronal impulses and chemical fluxes in the brain. Regardless of one's perspective, it is clear that this debate regarding the roles of mind, body, and brain achieves its greatest relevance and complexity in work with older clients.

Historically speaking, modern philosophical approaches have always struggled to reconcile the role of our physical bodies and brains with that of our minds, the latter being a construct consisting of all our subjective experiences. The French philosopher René Descartes was one of the first modern philosophers to posit that certainty stems from our own subjective experiences: "I think, therefore I am." Existence is known through thought, he proposed, and the role of the brain is ultimately subjugated to this knowledge, which cannot be captured or reduced to a specific physical substrate. As clinicians, we are trained to deal with subjective experiences in this way, as if they were nonmaterial entities that can be recognized, understood within certain dynamics, and manipulated. But working with a thought or emotion is not like working with a piece of clay, which one can easily mold in the desired direction. The way in which we even recognize mental illness is based on observing experiential and behavioral phenomena and then grouping them into categories (e.g., depression, panic, psychosis). But grouping does not make reality.

An alternative view to this Cartesian duality between mind and body/brain is a reductionism that holds that every mental state, whether thought or emotion, is equivalent to a physical state, such as the firing of a particular nerve cell or fiber (Boyd, 1980). Theoretically, then, therapists might someday be able to actually *see* a thought or emotion in the brain and then "zap" it to a more desirable state. Medications do this to some extent, although with minimal precision and modest predictability. The philosopher John Searle has tried to strike a harmonious balance between these two entities: "Mental phenomena," he asserted, "whether conscious or unconscious, visual or auditory, pains, tickles, itches, thoughts, indeed all our mental thoughts, are caused by processes going on in the brain" (1984, p. 18). According to Searle, one can use language—that of psychology or physiology—to speak of them, but the underlying connection between the two doesn't change.

This philosophical discussion is central to our work with older clients. On the one hand, there is a rich philosophical and psychological tradition that obliges us to listen to a client's subjective thoughts and emotions and work with them in ways that are fundamentally different from working with moving particles. We aren't surgeons of the soul. On the other hand, we cannot ignore the physical state of the body or brain, which forms the basic material from which these thoughts and emotions arise. With older clients, in particular, clinicians must have a basic understanding of how both subjective and objective aspects of minds, bodies, and brains change with age and illness.

Medical Disorders

For older clients seen in a clinical setting, the role of physical illness and pain must be identified early on, as the majority of them either have a chronic disease or take medications that can have problematic side effects. How does one recognize such a problem in the first place, especially without medical training? There are several clues that increase the probability that there is a physical factor causing or exacerbating the mental health problem:

- The client's complaints focus on a physical illness or symptom.
- The client appears to be in acute distress (e.g., pained facial expression).
- There has been a recent physical trauma (e.g., bone fracture, head injury).
- The client has experienced recent or ongoing physical illness (e.g., infection, stroke, heart attack, cancer).
- The client currently has physical symptoms (e.g., pain, fatigue, weight loss, tremor).
- The client has experienced mental status changes (e.g., confusion, word-finding difficulty, personality change).
- The client has sensory impairment (e.g., visual or hearing loss) or physical disability (e.g., paralysis) that poses severe functional limitations.

Although these factors may seem obvious when seen in a doctor's office, they might not be picked up on right away in a mental health setting. Whenever a medical or medication factor is suspected, the clinician must refer the client to his or her primary care physician (PCP) for evaluation. In doing so, the clinician can still play a role in helping the client cope with the effects of the physical illness as well as identifying and treating comorbid psychiatric illness. Therapeutic strategies are reviewed in Chapters 7 and 8.

The most common medical conditions in older clients include arthritis, hypertension, diabetes mellitus, hypothyroidism, hearing and visual impairment, anemia, heart disease, and cancer; the most common medical symptoms include constipation, incontinence, weight loss, pain, immobility, and pressure sores (Alessi & Cassel, 2004). Although each one of these conditions deserves its own discussion, a summary of relevant points can be found in Table 5.1.

Medication side effects (reviewed in Table 7.9) in older clients are particularly common causes of sedation, fatigue, and even mental confusion. When one is asking clients about symptoms, it is important to establish a time line; for example, did the symptoms start soon after the client started a medication or changed the dose, or did they predate the medication? Such information must be conveyed to the prescriber when a side effect is suspected and is disrupting the client's health.

Medical illnesses may have primary effects on mental illness, such as when hypothyroidism causes a depressive state or pneumonia causes confusion. Therapy may have to be truncated or even suspended while medical treatment is undertaken. Medical illness may also have secondary effects, such as when the pain or embarrassment of symptoms causes someone to feel anxious or depressed or fearful of recurrent symptoms. Two of the most common fears are a fear of falling and a fear of having bowel incontinence in public. It is not unusual to see complete avoidance of social situations resulting from such fears, and often clients are embarrassed to talk about

Table 5.1. The Impact of Common Medical Conditions and Symptoms in the Older Client

Condition	Impact on Mental Illness
Arthritis	Joint pain and immobility can cause social isolation, insomnia, and increased anxiety over falling. Steroids used to treat rheumatoid arthritis can cause confusion, anxiety, and depression.
Hypertension (high blood) pressure)	The risk of cognitive impairment due to stroke is greatly increased with uncontrolled high blood pressure. Some antihypertensive medications (beta-blockers and others) can cause depression.

Table 5.1. Continued

Condition	Impact on Mental Illness
Diabetes mellitus	Fluctuations in blood glucose levels can impair attentiveness, cognition, and mood. Diabetes is a risk factor for stroke and Alzheimer's disease.
Thyroid disease	Hypothyroidism is more common than hyperthyroidism in late life and is associated with cognitive impairment, sleep disturbances, and depression.
Sensory impairment	Hearing and visual loss can lead to social isolation, loneliness, depression, and unusual sensory experiences that include hallucinations.
Anemia	Low levels of red blood cells are associated with cognitive impairment and depression.
Heart disease	Angina (chest pain) and cardiac arrhythmias can lead to significant symptoms of anxiety and even panic.
Cancer	Certain cancers—including those of the lung, pancreas, and brain, and leukemia—have been associated with an increased risk of depression. Certain chemotherapy agents can also cause depression and cognitive impairment.
Endocrine and metabolic disease	Abnormal levels of calcium, sodium, potassium, cortisol, magnesium, folate, and vitamin B_{12} can cause confusion, cognitive impairment, anxiety, depression, and psychosis.
Parkinson's disease	Parkinson's is associated with high rates of depression and cognitive impairment. Anti-Parkinson's medications can cause delusions and hallucinations.
Incontinence	Bowel and bladder incontinence may lead to social isolation and even social phobias due to fear of losing control in public.
Constipation	Constipation may be caused by antidepressant or antipsychotic medications and may cause social isolation due to discomfort and fear of accidents.

them. In these instances it is important for the PCP to identify and treat the underlying symptoms.

Chronic pain is one of the most common and vexing problems in older clients, affecting between 25% and 50% of them at any given time (Karp & Weiner, 2006). Clients experiencing pain often present to therapy with at least one pain-associated comorbidity, including increased depression, anxiety, prescription drug abuse (e.g., opioid analgesics, benzodiazepines), sleep disturbances, excessive fears, and decreased function (Fishbain, Cutler, Rosomoff, & Rosomoff, 1997). Worrying and preoccupation due to pain can derail substantive, insight-oriented psychotherapeutic work and impair problem solving (Aldrich, Eccleston, & Crombez, 2000). The result may be a clinical picture in which an individual's coping skills and other psychosocial strengths are blotted out by a singular concern with his or her pain. Consider the following case vignette.

Jan was a 75-year-old woman who began suffering from constant, severe lower back pain after being in a car accident. This occurred in the year after her husband passed away. She went from doctor to doctor, seeking relief, and ended up on six different painkillers and muscle relaxants during the day. She also underwent dozens of examinations and scans and had several spinal injections and multiple other procedures. She withdrew from most of her social activities and friends, spending her time either in doctors' offices or lying in bed, knocked out from the effects of sedatives. She met with a therapist but was tired and had a difficult time concentrating during sessions. Her main focus was on how to juggle all her pills and doctor's visits, along with a litany of complaints about the various offices. She admitted to feeling severely depressed and anxious but attributed this to her pain and refused to talk about the loss of her husband or her growing estrangement from friends and family. After several sessions she dropped out of therapy, complaining that it wasn't helping alleviate her pain.

Jan probably had actual pathology from the car accident, such as a slipped disk in her spine and a pinched nerve, but her preoccupation with pain went far beyond what would be expected. Increasing doses of medications did not help her pain much but did impair her cognition and depress her mood. Age-related factors that worsened Jan's situation included persistent grief over her recent widowhood, a less resilient body, and an older brain that was more sensitive to the adverse effects of narcotic medications.

An assessment of the role of pain and its impact on other late-life mental disorders should include a subjective description of the pain and note verbal and behavioral expressions of pain. These may include grimacing, wincing, or frowning, especially with movement; verbalizations of pain or vocalizations indicating discomfort; rigid or restless body movements; mental status changes such as irritability, crying, or increased confusion; and sudden changes in the client's normal activities or interpersonal relationships (American Geriatrics Society Panel on Chronic Pain in Older Persons, 2002). Changes in concentration, alertness, and mood may reflect use of opioid medications (e.g., analgesics derived from opium, including morphine, codeine, hydrocodone, and oxycodone), muscle relaxants, and benzodiazepines. It is critical to ensure that these medications are being monitored closely by a single specialist, as they may have profoundly negative effects on mood and cognition. If they are being taken in large doses without clear relief, an abusive pattern may be present. Such medications are particularly dangerous when mixed with alcohol or other medications, including certain antidepressants and anxiolytics.

When pain is a major barrier to a client's active participation in therapy, it is critical to liaison frequently with the medical specialists who are managing the situation to ensure that they are considering all potential treatment modalities, including medications, physical therapy, massage, and alternative approaches such as acupuncture. Problem-solving therapy can help a client cope better with pain by developing practical strategies of care, whereas cognitive-behavioral therapy can help a client develop realistic perspectives on the pain and find ways to relax tense muscle tissue. Pain is "all in one's head" insofar as multiple brain centers such as the thalamus help mediate pain signals, but trying to force the client to acknowledge the role of mind over body or brain is not useful to treatment. Rather, everyone with pain should be regarded seriously as someone in distress, queried about both physical and psychological causes, and then treated with multiple complementary modalities.

Psychiatric Disorders

The added challenge with older clients is not simply knowing whether they are depressed, anxious, or psychotic but appreciating the ways in which these symptoms and their broader psychiatric disorders differ in later life. Both normal and pathological processes factor into the discussion of how aging affects the most common mood, anxiety, psychotic, personality, somatoform, and substance use disorders in late life. Further discussion of cognitive impairment and dementia follows in Chapter 6.

Mood Disorders

In an interesting and controversial article on the subject of depression in late life that appeared in the *Atlantic Monthly* in 1995, the psychotherapist Stanley Jacobson argued that "oldness itself is reason to be sad if you dwell on it" (p. 46). He went on to assert that "The high rate of depression among nursing-home residents is surely related to the mere fact of their being nursing-home residents, immersed in infirmity and impending death" (p. 50). The larger point of the article is that a lot of what we refer to as depression in older clients is actually a normal response to the travails of aging. Jacobson's arguments resonate with a lot of clinicians who work with older clients in the throes of age-associated losses and ailments. These concerns, however, raise key questions as to how exactly we define and diagnose depression and other mood disorders in late life, and how forthright we need to be with clients who reject such labels and refuse treatment.

Jacobson contrasted his assertions with a 1991 consensus statement on depression in late life that described it as underdiagnosed, undertreated, and not a normal consequence of aging ("Diagnosis and Treatment of Depression in Late Life," 1991), echoing the belief that depression is more common in late life. Interestingly enough, however, research by Dan Blazer published in 1980 found that less than 5% of a community sample of aged individuals were living with major depressive disorder, or MDD (Blazer & Williams, 1980), and these data were corroborated several years later by a larger sample from the Epidemiologic Catchment Area studies, which found MDD in less than 2% of community-dwelling elders (Myers et al., 1984). Surprising many, these rates are significantly lower than those found in young and middle-aged adults.

So how do we reconcile these opposing views of depression: Is it a normal or pathological response to aging? Is it more or less common in late life? The answer depends on what we mean by depression. In "Darkness Visible," the author William Styron provided a rich literary account of his own battle with depression, describing its pain as "quite unimaginable to those who have not suffered it, and [killing] in many instances because its anguish can no longer be borne" (1989, p. 213). He went on to paint a sinister picture of the course of his depression:

> As the disorder gradually took full possession of my system, I began to conceive that my mind itself was like one of those outmoded small-town telephone exchanges, being gradually inundated by floodwaters: one by one, the normal circuits began to drown, causing some of the functions of the body and nearly all of those of instinct and intellect to slowly disconnect. (p. 278)

Styron characterized depression, unlike many other forms of suffering, as complicated by the inability of the mind to see future relief:

> In depression this faith in deliverance, of ultimate restoration, is absent. The pain is unrelenting, and what makes the condition intolerable is the foreknowledge that no remedy will come—not in a day, an hour, a month, or a minute. It is hopelessness even more than pain that crushes the soul. (p. 281)

Styron captured an essential element of depression: that the changes in mood are neither transient nor inconsequential. These changes pervade both mind and body on a daily basis and begin to affect all aspects of being—attention, concentration, sleep, appetite, and motor activity—robbing them of their normal rhythms and vitality. To say, as Jacobson did, that a depressed person is merely sad or a victim of circumstance, for example, as a result of "oldness" or being in a nursing home, defines an emotional reaction, but not MDD. As is quite apparent from Styron's description, MDD is in no way a "normal" consequence of aging, no matter what the circumstances.

A review of the symptoms of MDD as they appear in older individuals can be found in Table 5.2. To meet the criteria of the text revision of the fourth edition of the *Diagnostic and Statistical Manual of Mental Disorders* (*DSM-IV-TR*) for diagnosis, an elderly client would have to be experiencing sadness or depression and a loss of interest in activities nearly every day for at least 2 weeks, along with at least four of the other symptoms cited (American Psychiatric Association, 2000). Diagnosis relies upon the clinician's ability to apprehend the entire context of the client to determine the time course, severity, and source of the symptoms. The main challenge with the older client is to differentiate between medical and psychiatric symptoms that closely resemble each other despite having different causes. This process is particularly complicated by a client with an underlying dementia.

Looking only at MDD and only within community populations provides a limited view of depression in late life. In contrast, broader epidemiological surveys show that MDD affects 6% to 12% of older medically ill individuals in outpatient clinics, 10% to 20% in hospitals, and 12% to 25% in nursing homes. In addition, up to 10% of elderly individuals in the community, 25% in outpatient clinics and hospitals, and 35% in nursing homes meet many but not all diagnostic criteria but still are depressed and functionally impaired, a condition that is captured by the diagnosis of *minor* or *subsyndromal depression*

Table 5.2. Symptoms of Depression and Late-Life Features Based on Diagnostic Criteria from *DSM-IV-TR*

Symptom	Late-Life Features
Sad or depressed mood nearly every day for at least 2 weeks	The clinician may also see irritability, somatization, excessive complaints of pain, or behavioral expressions such as agitation (especially in the setting of dementia).
Anhedonia (loss of interest or pleasure in most activities)	This may be expressed by social isolation and withdrawal from activities and can be easily confused with apathy, a disorder of motivation (not mood) that is common in cognitive disorders.
Significant change in appetite and weight	Usually decreases in both are seen, but the presence of comorbid medical reasons for anorexia and weight loss must be addressed. Failure to thrive is a condition of profound loss of appetite and weight seen in severe depression and late-stage dementia.
Sleep disturbances	The more common sleep disturbance is insomnia. It is important to compare potential sleep disturbances with normal age-related decreases in sleep efficiency and duration.
Psychomotor agitation or retardation	This is variable in late life, but there are strong associations among depression, physical disability, and functional decline.
Fatigue or loss of energy	These symptoms may also be related to several medical disorders commonly associated with depression, including anemia, diabetes, and cardiovascular disease.
Feelings of worthlessness or excessive guilt	These feelings may be referenced to life events that occurred decades in the past, especially those involving child rearing.
Diminished ability to think or concentrate	Symptomatic overlap with cognitive disorders makes it difficult to know the primary source of this symptom. Improvement with treatment is indicative that depression is the likely cause.
Suicidal ideation	Rates of suicide are highest among older white men. Suicidality may be passive ("I wish I would die") or indirect but equally life threatening (e.g., refusing to take life-sustaining medications, tests, or treatments, or refusing to eat or drink).

(Alexopoulos, 1996; Blazer, Steffens, & Koenig, 2009; Parmalee, Katz, & Lawton, 1989).

It is also important to recognize the entire spectrum of mood disorders that occur in late life:

- Major depressive disorder
- Minor or subsyndromal depression
- Psychotic depression
- Pseudodementia
- Depression without sadness
- Bereavement
- Depression secondary to dementia, medical illness, or substance use
- Vascular depression
- Adjustment disorder with depressed mood
- Dysthymic disorder
- Bipolar disorder (manic, depressed, and mixed types)
- Secondary mania due to medical illness or substance use

Psychotic depression and pseudodementia are two particularly serious forms of depression that require intensive pharmacological management and sometimes hospitalization as a result of extreme functional disability. With pseudodementia, depression-induced cognitive impairment gets better with treatment, although these individuals demonstrate a higher risk of later developing an actual dementia compared to older depressed individuals without cognitive impairment (Alexopoulos, Meyers, Young, Mattis, & Kakuma, 1993). Some older clients present with what has been labeled "depression without sadness," or with a "depletion syndrome" characterized by a lack of self-reported or observed sadness or other changes in mood but the presence of many other symptoms of depression (Gallo, Anthony, & Muthen, 1994; Newmann, Klein, Jensen,

& Essex, 1996). Adams (2001) has described a constellation of withdrawal, apathy, and lack of vigor that is commonly seen in older individuals and that represents this gray zone between normal and pathological responses to aging. It is unclear whether these last two phenomena are actual forms of depression or rather a natural part of aging, but they may represent what Jacobson was describing.

Many older clients present for evaluation after experiencing the acute loss of a loved one, typically a spouse. Bereavement (or grief) itself is not considered a depressive disorder unless it is complicated by suicidality, psychosis, or severe and disabling dysphoria that persists beyond the initial few months after the loss. Bereaved clients may be quick to dismiss any talk of depression and attribute all their symptoms to their losses. On this same basis, they may refuse treatment, including counseling and especially medications, out of fear that it would interfere with the natural process of mourning. The therapist must oscillate between a passive role that simply allows the client to talk about his or her concerns and a more active role that probes for more severe symptoms, encourages talk about the loss, and suggests sources of familial, religious, and cultural support.

As noted earlier in this chapter, depression is highly associated with dementia, neurological diseases, and other medial illnesses, including:

- Cardiovascular disease (e.g., myocardial infarction, congestive heart failure)
- Cerebrovascular disease/stroke
- Diabetes mellitus
- Low testosterone
- Hypothyroidism

- Hip fracture
- Parkinson's disease
- Seizure disorders
- Multiple sclerosis
- Alzheimer's disease and other dementias
- Cancer (pancreatic, lung, brain)
- Alcohol withdrawal
- Rheumatoid arthritis
- Vitamin deficiencies (B_{12}, folate)

For example, clinically significant depression (including both MDD and minor depression) is seen in up to 40% of individuals with Parkinson's disease and 50% of those with Alzheimer's disease. The term *vascular depression* has been coined to describe depression associated with multiple cerebral infarcts, either from large cortical strokes or smaller subcortical lacunar infarcts. Damage to neural tracts that connect subcortical regions of the brain such as the striatum with the frontal lobes can produce a corresponding subcortical dementia characterized by depression, apathy, executive dysfunction, and psychomotor retardation (Alexopoulos et al., 1997). Overall, rates of depression are highest with cerebrovascular damage to left frontal and right parietal regions of the brain (Robinson et al., 1983). It should also be noted that certain medications have been associated with depression, including corticosteroids, chemotherapeutic agents, H2 blockers, and beta-blockers.

An adjustment disorder with depressed mood (which may also involve significant anxiety and disturbances in behavior) is a transient depressive reaction to a specific psychological stress that lasts less than 6 months and involves alterations in mood and impairments in social and occupational functioning. Medical illness, sudden changes in roles or finances, and personal losses of loved ones are the most common late-life triggers (Lantz, 2006). Dysthymic disorder, on the other hand, describes chronic, low-grade depressive symptoms that do not rise to the level of MDD but create a tremendous vulnerability to it.

Bipolar disorder is less common than MDD in late life, with rates of less than 0.5% of older individuals in the community but in upward of 10% of nursing home residents and even higher rates in geriatric psychiatry clients (Weissman et al., 1988; Weissman, Bruce, Leaf, Florio, & Holzer, 1991; Young & Klerman, 1992). Bipolar disorder may even present for the first time in up to 10% of individuals after the age of 50 and is often associated with medical or neurological illness or medication side effects (Yassa, Nair, & Iskander, 1988). Mania can be difficult to distinguish from delirium and from agitation and psychosis seen with dementia. Compared with younger individuals, older manic individuals tend to present more commonly with mixed depressive and manic symptoms, and with a greater frequency of irritability, cognitive impairment, and mood-incongruent paranoid delusions (Forester, Antognini, & Stoll, 2006).

It is clear that therapists see older clients with an incredibly wide spectrum of mood disorders, many of which are challenging to differentiate from comorbid medical illness. At the same time, however, therapists should not assume that it is normal to be sad by virtue of age, as this attitude may limit the degree of investigation into the potential causes and permutations of the disorder. It may also engender a sense of fatalism. For if depression is seen as a logical consequence of old age, it might seem equally logical that older clients are entitled to their symptoms and are free to refuse treatment. Unfortunately, therapists encounter profoundly depressed individuals who espouse these views, and who as a result pose a threat to themselves and sometimes to others. The decision to intervene against the wishes, albeit distorted ones, of the client depends upon numerous legal and ethical principles, including personal autonomy and privacy. At those moments a deep understanding of the difference between depression as an illness and mere sadness or dissatisfaction with life's circumstances becomes a critical and even lifesaving skill.

Anxiety Disorders

Complementary roles of body and mind are perhaps best seen within the context of late-life anxiety. From the perspective of the body, anxiety involves various degrees of physiological arousal that prepare the organism for perceived danger. This arousal is readily felt and observed and includes hypervigilance, muscle tremor, diaphoresis, nausea, dilated pupils, and palpitations. When severe, this arousal can be so overwhelming that it becomes the sole focus of concern. Anxiety reactions originate in the amygdala of the brain and are imprinted in the prefrontal cortex. Surrounding neural circuitry in both the medial and the ventromedial prefrontal cortex helps to suppress the amygdala and extinguish fear responses over time—although not successfully in anxiety disorders. Damage to this circuitry can disrupt an individual's ability to modulate the fear response and lead to either poor judgment in dangerous situations or excessive and inappropriate reactions.

From the perspective of the mind, anxiety is much more than physiological arousal. In his seminal work *The Meaning of Anxiety*, the psychologist Rollo May described the existential qualities of anxiety:

It is agreed by students of anxiety . . . that anxiety is a
diffuse apprehension, and that the central difference between fear and anxiety is that fear is a reaction to a specific danger while anxiety is unspecific, "vague," "ob-
jectless." The special characteristics of anxiety are the
feelings of uncertainty and helplessness in the face of the
danger. (1950/1977, p. 205)

May's core definition follows that "anxiety is apprehension
cued off by a threat to some value that the individual holds
central to his existence as a personality" (1950/1977, p. 205).
But what are these values in older clients? They might involve
an individual's role as a spouse or parent or certain attributes
of his or her personal identity such as physical appearance or
function or a skill such as singing or skiing. In long-standing
anxiety disorders, however, there is by necessity a deeper conflict or traumatic experience that can be traced back to childhood or young adulthood. The anxiety may persist well beyond
memories of the original conflicts as mental associations are
substituted or new conflicts reawaken previous ones.

There are six main categories of anxiety disorders: generalized anxiety disorder, panic disorder, specific phobias, social
phobia, post-traumatic stress disorder, and obsessive-compulsive disorder. These are listed in Table 5.3 with basic definitions and late-life features. All these disorders are seen across
the life span, with no specific predilection for late life. However, approximately 8% of older individuals in the community
experience a form of anxiety disorder, and these disorders in
turn are associated with a significant increase in medical visits
and procedures, hospitalizations, disability, and medications.
Anxiety pulls people away from vital activities and socializa-

Table 5.3. Anxiety Disorders and Late-Life Features

Anxiety Disorder	Definition and Late-Life Features
Generalized anxiety disorder	This is characterized by diffuse, constant worry lasting longer than 6 months, with associated physical symptoms (e.g., muscle tension, insomnia, fatigue). New-onset generalized anxiety disorder in late life often occurs in the setting of comorbid depression and has a poor prognosis.
Specific phobias	This describes an irrational fear of and desire to avoid a specific situation, object, or activity. The onset of specific phobias often occurs after trauma. Fear of open spaces (agoraphobia), fear of falling, and fear of incontinence in public are common phobias in late life.
Social phobia	Social phobia is the pervasive fear of and avoidance of potential social embarrassment. Even when social phobia is present, avoidant behaviors in late life are often attributed to other causes.
Panic disorder	Episodic and overwhelming anxiety attacks occur with severe autonomic arousal. Panic disorder is often seen with comorbid medical illness or dementia.
Post-traumatic stress disorder	Individuals reexperience traumatic memories associated with symptoms of hyperarousal and avoidance of triggers. PTSD is common in cohorts of war veterans and Holocaust survivors. Dormant PTSD may be reactivated by news events or anniversaries of traumatic events.
Obsessive-compulsive disorder	Intrusive thoughts or repetitive ritualistic behaviors. Religious sins are a common focus of thoughts, and hygiene is a common focus of behavior.

tion and increases loneliness and depression. In addition, the paralyzing suffering of older individuals with anxiety often prevents them from seeking out appropriate treatment (Lauderdale, Kelly, & Sheikh, 2006).

Despite being the most common psychiatric disorders in late life, anxiety disorders are often obscured by maladaptive behaviors or comorbid medical issues. Consider the following vignettes.

Reuben was an 85-year-old World War II veteran referred to a therapist after making five visits to the VA hospital emergency room in a single month for chest pain, with each workup showing no actual cardiac problems. With a little probing, the therapist learned that Reuben had been in severe combat during the Battle of the Bulge and had been hospitalized for "war neurosis" upon discharge. Recently, Reuben learned that his grandson had been injured while fighting with his marine platoon in Iraq. Watching coverage of the war on TV had triggered traumatic memories, reactivating his PTSD from years ago.

Hortense was a 78-year-old widow who had recently fallen and broken her hip. She was transferred to a rehabilitation unit but refused to participate in physical therapy. Staff noticed that she complained of severe nausea and appeared diaphoretic about a half hour prior to therapy. They initially worried that she was having a heart attack, but the work-up was negative. A therapist was eventually consulted and quickly diagnosed Hortense with a phobia of falling. She was having panic attacks each day as the time for physical therapy approached.

Frances was an 88-year-old woman admitted to a nursing home. Staff requested psychological consultation because Frances was spending hours in the bathroom, refusing any assistance. Her hands were often noted to be beefy red. She would sometimes fly into a rage when staff entered her room and moved any of her clothing or personal items during care. The therapist discovered that Frances had numerous compulsive behaviors, such as excessive hand washing after using the toilet, and she arranged items in her room in specific spots and then rotated them at set times. Any disruption to these compulsions led to severe anxiety, panic attacks, and rage. A discussion with her son revealed longstanding behaviors consistent with obsessive-compulsive disorder.

In each vignette, certain disruptive behaviors presented within medical or long-term care settings and were not recognized immediately as representing an anxiety disorder. In fact, such conditions may persist for months or years in late life and be attributed to inaccurate formulations, such as chronic pain, angina, gastritis, irritable bowels, resistance to care, or malingering. At the same time, older clients may be reluctant to discuss any psychological aspects of their symptoms, insisting that they are due to medical causes, or they may have poor recall of diagnostic events or past symptoms. When there is a failure to recognize the underlying anxiety disorder, resources are wasted on unnecessary medical workups or interpersonal struggles, and definitive treatment is never implemented.

There are several well-established risk factors for anxiety disorders that help explain their origins. These include medical illness; physical trauma; age-related physical frailty; poor self-ratings of health regardless of actual health status; psychological trauma, including the loss of loved ones; lack of social supports; and comorbid psychiatric illness such as depression, dementia, psychosis, and somatoform disorders. For example, 30% to 50% of older individuals with depression have significant anxiety or anxiety disorders. In addition, anxiety disorders are more common in older women (Lauderdale et al., 2006). Finally, it is important to note that research is increasingly identifying biological vulnerabilities to anxiety disorders, one such example being the possibility that smaller hippocampal volumes predispose individuals exposed to trauma to develop post-traumatic reactions (Gilbertson, Shenton, Ciszewski, Kasai, & Lasko, 2002). Medical disorders most associated with symptoms of anxiety are cardiovascular disease/events, pulmonary disease/hypoxemia, anemia, electrolyte disturbances, hyperthyroidism, dementia, stroke, and sensory impairment; medications most commonly associated are stimulants (e.g., caffeine, Ritalin, dopamine), thyroid replacement hormone, corticosteroids, bronchodilators, antihistamines, analgesics (NSAIDS, opioids), antidepressants, and calcium channel blockers.

Clinical assessment of older clients with potential anxiety disorders requires first and foremost a clear inventory of symptoms of physiological arousal during episodes of anxiety, and liaison with the PCP or a medical specialist to ensure that these symptoms are not better accounted for by a medical factor or medication side effect. Consider the following case vignette.

Fredrik was an 82-year-old man with chronic obstructive pulmonary disease, cardiovascular disease, and anemia. He had recently undergone cardiac bypass surgery with a long and complicated recovery in the hospital and then in a rehabilitation center. He was back at home, but his nurse reported that he was having terrible episodes of panic on a daily basis, yelling and screaming for help and cursing at the aide and his wife when they tried to intervene. A visit with a therapist revealed a significant amount of residual anxiety from his hospital stay, along with subjective reports of severe anxiety and panic with objective observations of physiological arousal during these episodes. At the same time, the aide noted that Fredrik's oxygen saturation was significantly low during the day, and a recent blood test found him to be severely anemic.

Fredrik's case illustrates the exact issues that complicate the assessment and treatment of anxiety disorders in late life. On the one hand, Fredrik could certainly be having a post-traumatic stress reaction to the recent hospitalization, as it involved significant discomfort from breathlessness and chest pain, discomfort and confusion during the postoperative period when he was heavily sedated and restrained in the intensive care unit on a ventilator, and then a fear of falling or dying during rehabilitation. These experiences are enough to trigger anxiety and even panic attacks, sometimes manifesting in irritability and anger as well. On the other hand, his chronic obstructive pulmonary disease and anemia are causing low blood oxygen levels that can trigger a fear response in the brain regardless of how Fredrik may feel psychologically. Does he need supplemental oxygen and a blood transfusion or an antianxiety medication? Or both? Ideally, treatment will address all these potential issues and treatment options. But such a process requires the therapist to have a clear recognition of the role of both mind and body, and a willingness to liaise with medical specialists outside office appointments.

Psychotic Disorders

The symptoms of schizophrenia—the quintessential psychotic disorder—are well known to most clinicians: severe and mentally debilitating delusions and hallucinations, disorganized speech and behavior, and an array of disturbances in mood, social function, and volition. Case by case, however, schizophrenia is a coat of many colors, the symptomatic picture of which is as varied as the number of individuals with the disease. The categorizations of schizophrenia—paranoid, disorganized, catatonic, and residual—attempt to capture this variability but succeed only in broad terms. This description of the disease is not meant to obscure its phenotype but is meant to emphasize how important it is to get to know each client as an individual, with his or her unique history and mode of expression. Our expectations flow from this understanding and teach that with optimal care, an older client can be persistently psychotic and yet functional and reasonably content (Agronin, 2007d). In addition, with improvements in both psychiatric and medical care, more individuals with schizophrenia are experiencing longer, healthier life spans.

Interestingly enough, the German psychiatrist Emil Kraepelin, who was one of the first clinicians to classify schizophrenia, or "dementia praecox" as he called it, described this chronic disease as inevitably a *geriatric* illness that metamorphoses from psychosis to dementia over a lifetime (Kraepelin, 1893). To some extent Kraepelin was correct, as aging individuals with schizophrenia do tend to demonstrate less florid psychosis and more social withdrawal, apathy, and cognitive dulling—the so-called negative and residual symptoms of schizophrenia that correlate with increased cerebral atrophy (Heaton et al., 2001; Karim & Burns, 2006). These changes, however, may be less pronounced in individuals with late-onset schizophrenia, in which the disease begins after the age of 40 rather than during early adulthood (Jeste et al., 1997). Such a late onset is more common than most clinicians realize and has been seen in 3% to 10% of psychiatric clients in inpatient settings and in over 20% of older hospitalized individuals with schizophrenia (Harris & Jeste, 1988; Leuchter & Spar, 1985; Yassa, Dastoor, Nastase, Camille, & Belzile, 1993). Although the therapeutic benefits of antipsychotic medications for schizophrenia are well established, their efficacy in late life is less clear and is complicated by multiple drug combinations and drug-drug interactions, age-associated changes in pharmacokinetics and pharmacodynamics, the impact of medical comorbidity, and inadequate social environments (Karim & Burns, 2006).

Other major psychotic disorders seen in late life include schizoaffective disorder, delusional disorder, and psychosis secondary to a variety of medical and psychiatric conditions, including major depression, bipolar disorder, dementia, delirium, and substance intoxication and withdrawal. These conditions and late-life features are listed in Table 5.4. Major medical conditions associated with psychotic symptoms include central nervous system infection, organ failure (renal, hepatic), hypoxia (due to respiratory disease), metabolic and endocrine disorders, seizure disorders (temporal lobe epilepsy), brain lesions (tumor, stroke, trauma), and neurologic disorders (Parkinson's, Huntington's, multiple sclerosis). Medications commonly associated with psychosis include anticholinergics, anti-Parkinson's medications, corticosteroids, antihistamines, stimulants, chemotherapeutic agents, anticonvulsants, antidepressants, and antiarrhythmics.

Psychotic symptoms in late life are similar to those in young-

Table 5.4. Psychotic Disorders and Late-Life Features

Psychotic Disorder	Definition and Late-Life Features
Schizophrenia	Schizophrenia is characterized by chronic psychotic symptoms leading to functional and occupational disability, with multiple subtypes (paranoid, disorganized, catatonic, undifferentiated, residual). Aging brings a decrease in positive symptoms (e.g., delusions and hallucinations) and an increase in negative symptoms (apathy, social withdrawal) correlated with cerebral atrophy. Associated mild neuropsychological deficits may progress with age (Harvey et al., 1999). There is a significant and disproportionate increase in medical comorbidity with age, especially diabetes, cancer, Parkinson's disease, and cardiovascular disease (Jeste, Gladsjo, Lindamer, & Lacro, 1996). Residual subtype representing general attenuation of symptoms is common in later years. Although functioning remains quite impaired, coping skills may improve with age (C. I. Cohen, 1993).
Schizoaffective disorder	Individuals with schizoaffective disorder have chronic psychotic symptoms as in schizophrenia, but also episodes of severe depression, mania, or mixed states. There has been little research in older individuals.
Delusional disorder	An individual demonstrates a prominent, nonbizarre, and specific delusion that doesn't necessarily impair social functioning but can lead to significant social disruptions. An example would be the delusion that one is being poisoned or infested by a parasite. As a rule, older individuals with delusional disorder resist psychiatric treatment but may engage with specialists they believe can help with the delusional concern.
Psychotic disorder due to a general medical condition	In late life, dementia and delirium are the most common comorbid conditions.

Table 5.4. Continued

Psychotic Disorder	Definition and Late-Life Features
Substance-induced psychotic disorder	In older individuals, the most common substances of abuse are alcohol and narcotic analgesics. Anti-Parkinson's medications and steroids are the most common causative agents.
Mood disorders associated with psychotic features	Severe major depression and mania can be associated with psychotic symptoms, including delusions, hallucinations, and disorganized thinking. Somatic and nihilistic delusions are most common in severe depression.

er individuals but when associated with cognitive impairment may involve a greater degree of disorganized thinking and a higher prevalence of delusions of misidentification. As a result of the frequent presence of short-term memory deficits, this type of delusion rarely involves the persistence and organization of delusions of misidentification seen in Capgras syndrome (when someone believes another individual has been replaced by an imposter) or Fregoli syndrome (when someone believes that a stranger is someone familiar). Older clients with severe depression may demonstrate somatic or hypochondriacal delusions or nihilistic delusions, as in Cotard's syndrome, in which the individual believes that certain aspects of his or her body or identity do not exist, or that he or she is dead. Finally, it is not uncommon to see delusions of infestation or parisitosis (also known as Ekbom's syndrome), during which an individual experiences tactile sensations and reports seeing what he or she believes are small insects or parasites infesting the skin or body. Consider the following case vignette.

James was a 78-year-old man who presented to the therapist reluctantly, stating that he was only there because his doctor had insisted. "I don't need a shrink," he said. "I've just got this problem with lice." Clinical history indicated that James had been seen repetitively in both the emergency room and his doctor's office, complaining of itching in his scalp and body, and reporting that he could see small bugs flying in his room and crawling on his skin. He even brought his doctor a small vial of dried skin scrapings and insisted that they were parts of the lice. Despite multiple treatments with anti-lice shampoo and body lotions, he continued to complain of the infestation and to spray his body, hat, and bedclothes with anti-lice products. James refused to take any antipsychotic medications or to continue seeing the therapist, as he firmly believed he had a medical, not a psychiatric, problem. He was eventually seen by a neurologist for complaints of headache, dizziness, blurred vision, and paresthesia, which were attributed to overexposure to toxic anti-lice insecticides.

James's case is particularly frustrating because aside from his delusion, he functioned relatively normally, being able to drive, feed and clothe himself, and run a household, albeit at a reduced pace. He was not cognitively impaired and was not putting himself in such overt danger as to warrant involuntary commitment to force him to take medication. It is even more challenging when an older client has a delusion of being poisoned, because then he or she may more emphatically refuse medication. Even when administered, antipsychotic medications are not always effective or well tolerated by older individuals living with chronic delusions.

Many cases of supposed psychosis warrant investigation to confirm actual psychotic symptoms as well as to identify potentially nonpsychotic components. For example, a somatic delusion may also involve false tactile perceptions that represent either excessive body sensitivity or an actual hallucination. A misidentification may be an actual delusion but may also represent an illusion (i.e., a misperception, as when the nurse actually looks like a visually impaired individual's daughter) or merely confusion on the part of an individual experiencing agnosia due to a stroke or dementia. Sensory impairment can lead to both misperceptions and actual hallucinations, as in the case of Charles Bonnet syndrome, in which an individual with visual impairment reports, often nonchalantly, seeing complex visual hallucinations of, for example, Lilliputian people running around the house (Berrios & Brook, 1982). Organic causes should always be suspected with more uncommon tactile hallucinations (e.g., in alcohol withdrawal state such as delirium tremens) or gustatory and olfactory hallucinations (e.g., in temporal lobe epilepsy or secondary to lithium use; Sims, 1995).

Although it is natural for a therapist to be uncertain about how to effectively build a therapeutic relationship with a chronically psychotic individual, it is critical to never underestimate the importance of such an endeavor. The power of an enduring relationship has been eloquently described by the author Jay Neugeboren (1997) in his writings about the travails of his brother Robert, who lives with schizophrenia and experienced a severe relapse after the departure of his long-standing social worker. Seeing the rapid deterioration transpire before his eyes, Neugeboren wondered why "the medication that worked so well—so miraculously—on Monday stop working on Tuesday? The answer: because Robert was deprived of a relationship that had been a crucial element in his recovery" (2006, p. 17). What Neugeboren (1999) witnessed with his brother was also the single most important component of recovery that he discovered in his interviews with hundreds of psychiatric clients. Establishing such a healing relationship is both a challenge and an opportunity with every older client; it requires persistence, creativity, and courage.

Personality Disorders

Older clients with personality disorders (PDs) pose some of the most challenging and frustrating clinical cases. Depending on the subtype, these individuals present with chronically inappropriate, unusual, belligerent, or overbearing behaviors that create significant interpersonal and environmental conflicts. Many of them come to therapy not by choice but because either their living situation demands evaluation or they are having conflicts that are, according to them, created by others. Such pervasive disturbances in interpersonal relationships lie at the root of these disorders and serve to disrupt and sometimes even destroy an older client's support system. As a result, the therapist must often take on case management responsibilities. PDs are inevitably embedded in other psychiatric disorders such as major depression, generalized anxiety and panic, somatization, and substance abuse (Zweig & Agronin, 2006). PDs complicate both diagnosis and treatment and engender some of the strongest negative countertransference along the way.

PDs are classified under Axis II of the *DSM-IV-TR* as being characterized by an enduring and pervasive pattern of inflexible and maladaptive inner experiences and behaviors that deviate from cultural expectations and lead to significant disruptions in four areas: cognitive interpretation and perception, affective expression, interpersonal relations, and impulse control. PDs are believed to originate in early development, although such history is rarely available with older individuals.

There are 10 categorical personality disorders under the current classification system, grouped into three clusters based on similar phenomenology. Cluster A, the odd cluster, consists of paranoid, schizoid, and schizotypal subtypes; Cluster B, the dramatic cluster, with antisocial, borderline, histrionic, and narcissistic subtypes; and Cluster C, the anxious cluster, with avoidant, dependent, and obsessive-compulsive subtypes. In addition, there are two provisional disorders (depressive and passive aggressive) listed in the appendix of *DSM-IV-TR,* and a not-otherwise-specified diagnosis for PDs with features that do not fit into any existing category, or that represent criteria of several disorders. Each PD is defined by eight to 10 diagnostic criteria, and an individual must meet a specified number of them in any combination in order to qualify for a diagnosis. The major features of these disorders in both adults and elderly individuals are listed in Table 5.5.

Clinical work with late-life PDs involves several key challenges. Diagnosis is limited by the lack of longitudinal data, which leads to difficulty distinguishing between acute symptoms and more long-standing character traits. Even when there is extensive past history, acute symptoms of comorbid Axis I disorders can mimic PD symptoms. Consider the following case vignette.

Ronald was a 76-year-old man with a long-standing history of rage attacks and alcohol abuse. He had become a successful investment banker who was known for being an extremely unpleasant person to be around because of his constant bragging, cruel put-downs of others, and ruthless business practices. After a major medical crisis, he had to stop drinking, and this precipitated a manic psychosis. After successful treatment with both a mood stabilizer and an an-

Table 5.5. PDs and Late-Life Features

PD	Definition and Late-Life Features
Paranoid	The client is suspicious and distrustful of others and may become rageful, agitated, and even transiently psychotic when interacting with others, especially when his or her needs are not met.
Schizoid	The individual with schizoid PD is isolative, aloof, and eccentric, with few if any friendships and little desire for socializing. He or she often avoids contacts with others and can be difficult to engage in activities and treatment. In late life, such individuals have a very difficult time adapting to congregate and long-term care settings.
Schizotypal	The schizotypal personality is characterized by odd, bizarre, and eccentric beliefs, appearance, or speech. The individual is detached from and uncomfortable with social relationships. Others may be uncomfortable with his or her odd appearance and statements, leading to further isolation or even anger at and social ostracism of the individual. Long-term care placement may prompt resistant and belligerent behaviors.
Antisocial	Antisocial PD is characterized by aggression, recklessness, impulsivity, deceitfulness, and a lack of regard for social norms, as well as a lack of conscience for behaviors. Those with antisocial PD frequently have a history of criminal behaviors and substance abuse. Late-life presentation often involves depression and ongoing substance abuse. In long-term care and congregate living settings, individuals may be aggressive, assaultive, reckless, and inappropriate, sometimes prompting expulsion.
Borderline	The individual is impulsive, self-injurious, and rageful, with unstable interpersonal relationships and poor self-image. Emotional lability and impulsive behaviors may prompt crises and conflicts with others. Depression is a common end point.
Histrionic	The client is overly extroverted and provocative, sometimes in a sexually inappropriate manner. He or she is emotionally shallow and attention seeking. Such behaviors may exhaust others and provoke hostility or ostracism. Histrionic PD may resemble frontal lobe disinhibition, hypomania, or even adult attention-deficit/hyperactivity disorder.

Table 5.5. Continued

PD	Definition and Late-Life Features
Narcissistic	The narcissistic personality is arrogant, entitled, and grandiose, with little regard for others. He or she may react with anger, paranoia, and indignation to long-term care placement. Age-associated losses can prompt rage, depression, and paranoia. Those with narcissistic PD are frequently in conflict with others over personal demands and complaints.
Avoidant	Individuals with avoidant PD are timid, socially inhibited, and fearful of rejection. Loss of long-held social contacts can be devastating. Comorbid anxiety and depression are common.
Dependent	The client is clinging, needy, and dependent on others to make decisions for him or her. He or she may tax and even exhaust others with neediness, sometimes reacting with anger and panic when needs are not met. Comorbid anxiety and depression are common.
Obsessive compulsive	Obsessive-compulsive PD is characterized by a preoccupation with orderliness and perfectionism, coupled with a rigid and overly conscientious approach to activities. In late life, such individuals may have medical illnesses or cognitive impairment that impedes the ability to regulate schedules and routines and maintain their environment in desired ways. Relocation to long-term care and other structured settings may increase rigidity and prompt resistance and belligerence when demands are not met. Major depression is common.
Passive aggressive	The individual is resistant to demands and responsibilities, noncompliant, and hostile to authority. He or she may agree to but then resist daily care needs, medications, and other treatments, prompting conflict with others.
Depressive	The depressive personality is gloomy and pessimistic and has poor self-esteem and overly critical attitudes. He or she is often resistant to and pessimistic about care. This condition is often difficult to distinguish from major depression, and the two may occur simultaneously.

Note. Based on "Personality Disorders," by M. E. Agronin, in *Psychiatry in Long-Term Care* (2nd ed., p. 218–219), edited by W. E. Reichman & P. R. Katz, 2009, New York: Oxford University Press. Copyright 2009 by Oxford University Press, Inc. Adapted with permission.

tipsychotic medication, Ronald's narcissism and cruelty faded away, and he became a rather calm person who could actually build relationships with others.

What started off as an initial diagnosis of a PD with narcissistic and antisocial features turned out to be chronic bipolar disorder modulated by alcohol. Once both problems were treated, Ronald had a more pleasant personality. On the flip side, there are individuals diagnosed with chronic depression or bipolar disorder who respond poorly to treatment because their symptoms are driven mostly by personality dysfunction.

Another major challenge is that the criteria for PDs are based on the symptoms shown by young and middle-aged adults and have never been adapted for late life. For example, antisocial PD criteria such as "repeatedly performing acts that are grounds for arrest" and "repeated physical fights or assault" and borderline PD criteria for self-injurious and impulsive behaviors with respect to spending or sex simply do not apply as well to older clients. In fact, one study found that younger and older individuals with similar degrees of personality dysfunction endorsed about 30% of PD criteria quite differently. As a result, younger adults were more likely to be diagnosed with avoidant and dependent PDs, whereas older adults were more likely to have schizoid and obsessive-compulsive PDs (Balsis, Woods, Gleason, & Oltmanns, 2007). In trying to correct this or "age-adjust" criteria, the clinician runs the risk of invalidating the PD in question (Agronin & Maletta, 2000).

These diagnostic challenges may account for the lower prevalence rates of PDs in older adults. Epidemiologic studies in younger individuals in the community have found that prevalence rates range between 10% and 20%, with one large study of over 43,000 individuals in the United States finding a prevalence rate of 14.79% (Grant, Hasin, & Stinson, 2004). In contrast, rates of PDs in individuals 65 years or older range from 5% to 13% (Abrams & Horowitz, 1996). These rates increase two- to threefold in the presence of comorbid Axis I disorders, particularly major depression, seen in both inpatient and outpatient mental health settings (Zweig & Agronin, 2006).

What happens to individuals with PDs as they age? There are three possibilities: They get better, they stay relatively the same, or symptoms change over time so that the PD presents differently. Longitudinal data are sparse but point toward symptomatic improvement and significant rates of remission in middle age for individuals with antisocial PD (Black, Baumgard, & Bell, 1995; Robins et al., 1984) and borderline PD (McGlashan, 1986; Paris, Brown, & Nowlis, 1987). This stability may erode in later life, however, as age-associated losses accumulate and underlying dysfunctional traits reemerge, but in more age-appropriate ways. Narcissistic and histrionic PDs may follow a similar pattern.

It is believed that odd cluster disorders generally stay the same or worsen with age, especially because many individuals with schizoid, schizotypal, and paranoid PDs enter late life without many close family members or friends as supports, and they tend to alienate others who try to help. At the same time, these individuals may be less vulnerable and reactive to age-associated losses in relationships or social attributes. Anxious cluster disorders are at great risk for symptomatic exacerbation, as aging might disrupt long-time social supports and force individuals into long-term care settings that may not adequately address dependency needs, require undesirable social contacts (such as in congregate dining halls or with roommates), and interfere with long-held daily routines and rituals. Consider the following vignettes.

Edna was an 82-year-old woman with an obsessive-compulsive PD. She had been widowed for 10 years but had gotten along reasonably well in her small condominium, where she could control her daily schedule and keep her surroundings extremely clean and spartan. After falling and fracturing her hip, Edna was admitted to a rehabilitation facility. She came into immediate conflict with staff, whom she accused of disrupting her normal routine and not keeping her room as clean and organized as she would like.

Maxwell was a 77-year-old recently widowed man with a dependent PD. Maxwell began losing weight and secluding himself inside his home following the loss of his wife, who had previously managed all his affairs, down to telling him what to wear each day and what to eat at each meal. Maxwell became extremely depressed and anxious and ended up calling 911 one day when he felt unable to function. A county social worker found Maxwell's home in disarray and determined that he was incapable of living independently. She assigned him a care manager to oversee his personal affairs and arranged for him to move into an assisted living facility that offered three meals a day and medication management.

Although anxiety and depression were the initial symptomatic expressions for both Edna and Maxwell, neither an anxiety nor mood disorder was driving the underlying problems. Rather, it was unfortunate life events that destabilized rigid personality styles and led to the reemergence of extremely dysfunctional behaviors consistent with underlying PD diagnoses.

There are several basic principles regarding treatment for late-life PDs. First, the goal of treatment is not to cure the PD itself but to reduce the frequency and intensity of its most problematic symptoms—including those of associated Axis I disorders. For example, the target symptoms for an older client with dependent PD may include panic attacks and anxiety over one particular area of decision making. A therapist who seeks to do too much and transform the client will probably enter into eventual conflict with the dysfunctional dynamics and develop countertransferential frustration, anger, and burnout. Keep in mind that dysfunctional interpersonal relationships lie at the heart of each PD, and these are activated in the therapy. A client with antisocial or narcissistic traits may start off therapy quite pleasant and charming, but this veneer can quickly give way to noxious behaviors that test the boundaries of therapy. Having multiple informants to provide history and progress reports as well as multidisciplinary treatment team members helps defuse conflicts and provides additional avenues of therapy.

Psychotropic medications are aimed at both Axis I disorders and select symptoms of the PD. For example, for an individual with dependent PD, an antidepressant may help reduce symptomatic anxiety during decision making. This selectivity is key because there are no medications that treat an entire PD itself. Medications can be hazardous with clients who engage in unsafe or abusive behaviors, such as taking too many pills or mixing them with other pills or substances without regard to a doctor's instructions. Some clients with obsessive-compulsive, passive-aggressive, and dependent traits may use the medications to perpetuate dysfunctional dynamics. Consider the following vignette.

> Jules was an 82-year-old man with dependent PD. After being started on an antianxiety medication, he would frequently show up unannounced at the doctor's office, seeking advice on the timing and dosing of the medication, and reporting specious side effects. He would also stop taking it or alter the dose on his own and then seek out the doctor when he claimed to be feeling worse. It became clear that the medication was not helping any of the symptoms of Jules's PD but was serving as a convenient vehicle to further a dependent relationship with the doctor.

PDs in late life require tremendous patience and courage on the part of the therapist if he or she is to persevere over the long haul. Treatment guidelines for late-life PDs include the following:

- The goal of treatment is clinical management of target symptoms, not cure of the PD.
- Treat any underlying Axis I disorders first and foremost.
- Rule out underlying cognitive impairment.
- Address underlying medical symptoms such as pain and physical disability and medication side effects that may be negatively influencing mood and behavior.
- Consider the following target symptoms: paranoid ideation, extreme and transient dysphoria or panic, impulsive aggression, rage attacks, self-injurious behaviors, hypochondriacal complaints, medication abuse, nonadherence to medication regimens, or complaints of excessive and unusual side effects.
- A multidisciplinary team approach may help defuse con-

flicts and can be used to approach dynamics from several modalities.

- Cognitive-behavioral and dialectical behavior therapy may be helpful for borderline PD and other dramatic and anxious cluster disorders.
- For older clients with poor social supports, initial placement in congregate living or long-term care settings can exacerbate underlying dynamics and precipitate crises.
- The therapist or a designated case manager can help troubleshoot and provide a buffer for older clients with PDs, especially those with anxious and odd cluster disorders.

Somatoform Disorders

The general category of somatoform disorders represents a group of seven heterogeneous conditions all characterized by physical symptoms or complaints that lack objective organic causes and are strongly associated with psychological factors (American Psychological Association, 2000). Each disorder is listed in Table 5.6 along with salient characteristics.

The term *somatoform* comes from the Greek word *soma*, meaning *body*, and originated in the belief of the Greek physician Hippocrates (460–377 BCE) that emotional disorders were rooted in the body. For example, emotional lability, or hysteria, was thought to result from a wandering *hystera* or womb, whereas emotional disorders associated with digestive problems were believed to be centered in the anatomic region below the ribs termed the *hypochondrium*. It wasn't until the 1600s that the English neuroanatomist Thomas Willis first postulated that emotional disorders were localized to the brain. The birth of the modern-day concept of *somatization*, referring to psychological distress communicated through the body, was popularized by Sigmund Freud's work with women experienc-

Table 5.6. Characteristics of Somatoform Disorders

Somatoform Disorder	Definition and Characteristics
Somatization disorder	The client has multiple physical complaints without organic basis across four or more pain sites or dysfunctions, in addition to gastrointestinal, sexual, and pseudoneurological symptoms. Somatization disorder has an early age of onset, at less than 30 years. Symptoms are often presented in a vague yet exaggerated manner and tend to be worse during times of stress. This disorder has a chronic, fluctuating course, with significant social and occupational impairment.
Undifferentiated somatoform disorder	At least one somatic symptom with over 6 months' duration that cannot be explained by medical workup. This is seen in 14% to 20% of community samples and is commonly seen with chronic pain.
Hypochondriasis	Hypochondriasis involves a preoccupation with the fear of having a deadly disease, coupled with anxious ruminations about misinterpreted bodily symptoms. Medical reassurance does not calm fears. This disorder typically has a chronic course with waxing and waning symptoms.
Conversion disorder	The client experiences at least one motor or sensory deficit without organic basis. Symptoms may be causally related to psychological factors (especially abusive or traumatic experiences). Examples include paresthesia, paralysis, double vision, aphonia, blindness, deafness, ataxia, aphonia, and pseudoseizures. Twelve percent or more of clients with conversion disorder have concurrent neurological illness. Most episodes resolve rapidly but can be recurrent. Chronic symptoms are less common.

Table 5.6. Continued

Somatoform Disorder	Definition and Characteristics
Body dysmorphic disorder (BDD)	BDD involves preoccupation with an imagined or small defect in appearance. Individuals with BDD often seek repetitive, unnecessary plastic surgery. Examples of preoccupations include facial asymmetry, size of nose, breast size or shape, and hips. Individuals with BDD often spend excessive amounts of time repetitively viewing the body part in the mirror, touching or picking at it, and seeking reassurance from others. Fifty percent of individuals with BDD may be delusional. BDD tends to be chronic.
Pain disorder	Pain occurs in at least one anatomical site and is the main focus of attention. Psychological factors play a role in the onset, severity, exacerbation, and maintenance of pain. Diagnosis is challenging in elderly individuals, among whom chronic pain is common.
Somatoform disorder, not otherwise specified	This is a residual diagnosis for individuals with somatic symptoms that do not meet criteria for any other somatoform disorder (e.g., nonpsychotic hypochondriasis for less than 6 months, unexplained physical complaints for less than 6 months).

Note. Adapted from "39 Doctors," by M. E. Agronin, 2007, *CNS News, 9,* pp. 12–13. Copyright 2007 by McMahon Publications. Adapted with permission.

ing hysteria. Using hypnosis and later talk therapy, Freud and his colleague Josef Breuer discovered a link between memory and physical symptoms: "For we found . . . that each individual hysterical symptom immediately and permanently disappeared when we had succeeded in bringing clearly to light the memory of the event by which it was provoked" (Breuer & Freud, 1895/1955, p. 6). As Freud elaborated throughout the corpus of his psychoanalytic theory, these provoking memories and their associated affects are hidden in the unconscious mind but find indirect means of expression through psychiatric symptoms. In somatoform disorders, these symptoms take the form of physical ailments. Consider the following case vignette.

Prior to her first appointment with Etta, Dr. P. received strict instructions from the client's son: "Don't tell her she's better—then she'll feel worse!" Indeed, after each session, Etta complained of feeling worse. She begged for help from Dr. P. but rejected all suggestions. Etta was 75 years old and had lived in the United States for over 40 years after her family left Cuba. As a child, she was the youngest of six siblings and was doted on by her parents, who ran a successful fabric business. When Etta was 12, however, her mother died suddenly from a brain infection that resulted from a dental abscess. Although her siblings described Etta as appropriately traumatized by this event, she never spoke of it. Even with several therapists over the years, Etta would only refer to her mother's death incidentally and without emotion. Etta's early adulthood was marked by a series of mysterious ailments involving joint and muscle pains and transient paralyses, eventually leading her father to move the family to Miami to seek better medical care. This move coincided with the loss of both his business and his fortune as a result of the Castro dictatorship, and the once wealthy family was forced to live quite modestly.

Fortunately, Etta's health improved following the move to Miami, and by age 35, she was married, with one son and another on the way. After her second son was born, Etta experienced severe postpartum depression and ended up being hospitalized and treated with electroconvulsive therapy. She left the hospital only moderately improved and again began experiencing transient, unexplained aches and pains, including incapacitating jaw pain, spasms in her calf muscles, and dyspareunia that caused her to refuse sexual relations with her husband. In 1970, her husband sought a divorce after Etta discovered he was having an affair with her best friend. She again descended into a severe depression.

Another trial of electroconvulsive therapy and subsequent treatment with an antidepressant were helpful, but Etta emerged from the hospitalization a near invalid, claiming that the electroconvulsive therapy had ruined her body. She developed multiple tic-like movements that she claimed disrupted both her walking and her vision. These various unexplained pains, muscle spasms, and tics continued throughout her adulthood, and Etta went from doctor to specialist to therapist, accumulating a 4-inch thick dossier of tests and scans and consultations—all without any definitive findings or therapy. She had multiple surgeries for various dental and orthopedic complaints and ended up being prescribed numerous painkillers, muscle relaxants, anxiolytics, antipsychotics, and antidepressants over the years. With her current therapist, Etta voiced a litany of complaints about her previous doctors, none of whom, according to Etta, had ever provided definitive diagnosis or treatment (Agronin, 2007e).

Etta's case reveals clear dynamics to her symptoms, as they started shortly after the traumatic loss of her mother and always involved the highly symbolic symptom of jaw pain— reminiscent of the dental abscess that led to her mother's death. From a psychodynamic perspective, Etta's permanent recapitulation of this pain may represent an attempt to restore the profound loss of a parent; she yearns for healing, and yet the possibility of healing means loss of the memory, even on an unconscious level. Thus, as she begins to feel better—she feels worse! At the root of Etta's pathology is a 12-year-old child frozen in time, unable to comprehend what has transpired.

Her resultant symptoms thus represent a conversion of anguished and overwhelming emotion, such as anger toward her mother for dying, into more psychologically tolerable physical symptoms that she can feel, manipulate, and move throughout her body—with the doctor as a perpetual interlocutor in her search for meaning. Such conversion symptoms are actually relatively common, seen in up to 3% of medical clients in outpatient settings, and tend to come and go regardless of treatment (Rabinowitz, Hirdes, & Desjardins, 2006). The diagnostic key with conversion disorder and all other somatoform disorders is to identify that their primary gain is to relieve an unconscious impulse, unlike the intentional nature of malingering, in which individuals have the conscious goal of avoiding some responsibility (e.g., work) or the semiunconscious goal of those with factitious disorders to assume the sick role.

There are other dimensions to somatoform disorders beyond unconscious dynamics, and many of these are seen in Etta's life history: her inability to identify and describe emotions, known as alexithymia; her hypersensitivity to bodily sensations and subsequent amplification of minor symptoms (Barsky, 2001); her depressive personality; and the later onset of major depression (Agronin, 2009c). In the end, Etta's mind-body structure was a perfect storm of somatization. Even when conversion symptoms subsided, she remained a hypochondriac, convinced that she had a deadly disease but unwilling to trust any doctor's reassurance. She would misinterpret minor bodily sensations as harbingers of dysfunction, and her vigorous attempts to self-diagnose, examine, and then correct these symptoms produced even more physical discomfort and functional impairment. Thus, a pain in her jaw implied a bone disease, and her constant examination of her mouth and tensing of her cheek and jaw muscles to counteract the oral sensation resulted in facial muscle spasm, inflammation, and an odd winking movement. The individual with body dysmorphic disorder shares a similar preoccupation with a bodily defect, such as a misshapen nose or uneven breasts, but takes it a step further by seeking repetitive surgical correction. Etta followed this path on several occasions, her preoccupation assuming the appearance of a somatic delusion.

As her illness gained steam, Etta's clinical picture was most consistent with somatization disorder, one of the most challenging to address because of its multiple defining symptoms that lack organic etiology and include four or more sites of pain or dysfunction, two gastrointestinal symptoms, one sexual symptom, and one pseudoneurological symptom.

With older somatoform clients who present initially to medical specialists, there are clear expectations of finding underlying medical causes, such as an occult malignancy or a neurodegenerative condition. These expectations are actually important for two reasons. First, it is necessary for a doctor to take every client's complaints seriously and to look for organic causes, especially as a means to establish a trusting relationship with the client with somatoform disorder. Second, many cases of somatoform disorder do have underlying medical problems that may be triggering or exacerbating his or her psychopathology (Rabinowitz et al., 2006). For example, in one study of conversion disorder, approximately 12% of individuals had an actual neurological disorder (Moene et al., 2000). Individuals with pain disorder truly suffer from pain, but they amplify the pain experience and resultant disability to an unreasonable level because of psychological factors. As clients age and accumulate medical conditions with actual organic pathology, it becomes more and more difficult to determine what constitutes unreasonable symptomatic expression. And consider this statistic: Up to 80% of nursing home clients live with chronic pain (Won et al., 2004). Sometimes it is just too complex and time consuming to sort out the reasonable from the exaggerated.

The diagnosis of somatoform disorder in late life faces other challenges as well. There are few clinical descriptions or studies in the literature that can guide our clinical work. Even when we suspect a somatoform disorder, we often lack sufficient longitudinal history to trace symptoms back to young adulthood, when most disorders begin. We do know that about 5% of older individuals demonstrate a somatoform disorder, and that somatization, a component of every individual somatoform disorder, does increase in frequency with age, especially in the context of depression (Sheehan, Bass, Briggs, & Jacoby, 2003; Waxman, McCreary, Weinrit, & Carner, 1995). The pitfalls of missing somatoform symptoms in older individuals are potentially catastrophic; in one study, for example, 2.4% of patients receiving a tissue plasminogen activator for acute stroke turned out instead to have somatoform symptoms (Mouradian et al., 2004).

On the flip side, some clinicians are too quick to label certain symptoms in older clients purely psychological, perhaps causing them to curtail appropriate clinical studies or treatments. This may happen as a matter of course when doctors become angry with somaticizing patients who fail to follow their instructions or fail to get better.

The treatment for Etta was quite rocky but involved many important principles:

- Foster doctor-client trust and rapport by listening to the client's complaints with a patient and nonjudgmental demeanor.
- Never challenge the client's veracity in reporting symptoms.
- Involve a treatment team that includes medical, psychiatric, and social components.
- Practice conservatism in terms of number of doctor's visits, referrals, lab tests, and procedures in order to avoid iatrogenesis. Workups should take the client's concerns into consideration but be driven by objective findings.
- Identify and treat comorbid medical and psychiatric conditions.
- Focus on symptom/pain reduction and rehabilitation rather than on cure.
- Provide education on stress reduction.
- Provide regular, scheduled follow-ups.
- Slowly introduce the idea of psychiatric treatment.
- Multiple psychotherapeutic modalities can be used to increase emotional expression, identify relevant losses, reduce depression and anxiety, and focus on coping with somatic symptoms.
- Pharmacotherapy is typically based on target symptoms of anxiety, depression, and in some cases transient somatic delusions.
- Several somatoform disorders—pain disorder, hypochon-

driasis, and body dysmorphic disorder—have been shown to respond well to antidepressants. (Agronin, 2009c)

Unfortunately for Etta, her intelligence, determination, and wholly unconscious motivation enabled her to craft her doctor appointments in such a way as to guarantee failure. First, she would precede each meeting with a detailed letter to the clinician explaining her various concerns, conjectures, and previous treatments. During the appointment, she would describe a litany of symptoms in excessive detail and often argue with the doctor about his or her thoughts. After listening to the doctor's recommendations, she would haggle over which tests or treatments she would agree to and then ask repetitive questions about her symptoms that the doctor had just attempted to explain. Several doctors lost their temper with her, whereas others maintained their composure but urged her to see a psychiatrist. She did see many psychiatrists, and by the time she reached Dr. P., she had, by her own account, tried every viable treatment, all without success.

The treatment approach with a client with a somatoform disorder is similar in some respects to that with personality disorders: Check your ego at the door and realize that the goal is to manage, not cure, what is certainly a chronic disorder. The treatment has to be less about the identity of the therapist whose mission is to heal a sick individual, and more about the client's need for acknowledgement. The challenge is to conduct the therapeutic relationship between two opposing forces: the client's persistent expression of symptoms and the near-simultaneous rejection of medical advice and symptomatic relief. Etta was trying to communicate something through her symptoms, but it was a language difficult for others to understand because she herself did not have access to its basic rules. In some clients, psychotherapy can tap into the unconscious dynamics that drive the symptoms; in others, it can merely support the client's attempt to manage them. Regardless, the steady and persistent hand of the therapist is key.

In the end, Etta's symptoms did not improve. Over time, her accumulating ailments associated with aging merged with her waxing and waning somatoform symptoms, making them even more difficult to tease apart. Her social supports withered away, leaving only her two sons and a long-standing aide, and she was eventually admitted to a nursing home. She is still seen on a regular basis by her physician, who provides exams and advice when appropriate, but with low expectations for gratitude or compliance.

Healing with Etta was quite elusive, but less complex older clients with somatoform disorders can show substantial bene-fit over time. Patience and hope must be two key virtues for any therapist who wades into these waters.

Substance Use Disorders

Imagine the following encounter with a client.

Alice was a 78-year-old married woman who was referred for an evaluation of potential cognitive impairment and de-pression. At the evaluation, Alice presented as a thin and nicely dressed and groomed woman with a refined air and a very friendly demeanor. Her husband was a portly, rumpled man who sat quietly during the meeting. Alice had some mild word-finding difficulty, partial disorientation to place, and mild short-term memory impairment. However, she was so verbal and outgoing during the appointment that the therapist did not see significant evidence of depression. The daughter expressed concern about her parents' alcohol use, but they dismissed it as their "daily cocktail" that they had enjoyed for decades. Several weeks after the evaluation, Alice was hospitalized after falling and bruising a hip and was found to have pneumonia during her workup in the emergency room. Within 24 hours of being in the hospital, she became tremulous, agitated, and confused. Doctors discovered that she was in full-blown alcohol withdrawal.

The fact that Alice was an elderly individual with a substance use disorder is not as salient here as the fact that the diagnosis was missed. Unlike younger substance abusers, older clients often present without the pronounced social, legal, and work-related problems that tip the clinician off to the diagnosis. It is more likely that medical and psychiatric problems, which both result from substance abuse and mask its underlying existence, will present. This fact, combined with the dearth of treatment programs for elderly people and the stereotype that older individuals—especially woman—do not abuse substances, results in alcoholism among older individuals being described as an "invisible epidemic" (Widlitz & Marin, 2002). It is clear, however, that although the prevalence rates of various substance use disorders decrease in later life, these rates are certain to climb with upcoming cohorts of aging individuals who grew up in an era of more widespread abuse of illicit drugs (Oslin & Mavandadi, 2009). In fact, rates of illegal drug use have doubled and the prevalence of alcohol abuse or dependence has tripled in the last decade in select populations of adults older than 50 years (Grant, Dawson, et al., 2004; Office of Applied Studies, 2007).

The most common substance use disorder in late life involves alcohol, followed by prescription drugs and then illegal substances. Tobacco is also a common substance of abuse that can result in equally dire health consequences. Specific features of each substance of abuse can be found in Table 5.7.

The term *abuse* applies when an individual is demonstrating at least one social, interpersonal, or legal problem as a result of his or her substance use. Substance *dependence* applies when there are three or more recurrent problems that typically include increased tolerance to larger quantities of the substance, withdrawal symptoms, and increased time spent obtaining the substance or recovering from its effects. Older individuals develop a greater sensitivity to substances, particularly alcohol, and so the risks and rates of health consequences increase dramatically.

For example, heavy or chronic alcohol use causes peripheral neuropathy and impairs cerebellar function, which governs coordination and balance, leading to increased falls, fractures, and subdural hematomas (Biglan, 2008). Alcohol use worsens the symptoms of diabetes and increases the risk of hemorrhagic stroke, cardiomyopathy, muscle weakness and pain, and liver disease. Over half of individuals with chronic alcoholism also develop various forms of dementia. Of greatest relevance to therapy, however, is the risk of both depression and suicide associated with alcohol abuse and dependence. Not surprisingly, the rates of depression and suicide drop dramatically when the alcohol problem is resolved (Llorente, Oslin, & Malphurs, 2006). In addition, treatment outcome for depression improves when alcohol intake is reduced (Oslin, Katz, & Edel, 2000).

Abuse of and dependence on prescription drugs such as benzodiazepines, opioid or narcotic analgesics, antihistamines, and muscle relaxants often begins innocuously during hospi-

Table 5.7. Late-Life Features of Substance Use Disorders

Substance of Abuse	Late-Life Features
Alcohol	• Alcohol abuse is seen in 3.1% of adults above 65 years in the community (Grant, Dawson, et al., 2004) but prevalence may be as high as 10% to 23% across mental health, inpatient, and nursing home settings (Llorente et al., 2006). • Problem drinking (enough to cause at least one problem related to use) is seen in 10% to 15% of older individuals in primary care settings. • Older individuals are advised by the National Institute on Alcohol Abuse and Alcoholism and the Center for Substance Abuse treatment to drink no more than 1 *standard drink* daily, defined as 6 oz wine, 1 can of beer, 4 oz liqueur, or 1.5 oz (or a small shot) of hard liquor (Blow, 1998). • Symptoms of alcohol use include a history of falls and other injuries, sleep problems, memory impairment, anxiety, depression, psychosis, incontinence, peripheral neuropathy, worsening of diabetes and other medical conditions (e.g., liver disease, cardiomyopathy), poor nutrition, dizziness, and social isolation (Oslin & Mavandadi, 2009). • Medical workup may find abnormalities in the physical examination (enlarged liver, peripheral neuropathy, ataxia) and blood serum analysis (increased liver enzymes, decreased albumin, alteration in blood count and red blood cell volume).
Benzodiazepines	• Benzodiazepines are often prescribed initially during operative procedures, hospitalization, or treatment for anxiety or sleep disturbances. Diazepam (Valium) and temazepam (Restoril) are the most popular benzodiazepine prescriptions, followed by alprazolam (Xanax), lorazepam (Ativan), and clonazepam (Klonopin).

Table 5.7. Continued

Substance of Abuse	Late-Life Features
	• Over one third of older individuals continue to refill their benzodiazepine prescriptions after hospital discharge (Grad et al., 1999). • Around 10% of geriatric psychiatry clients in outpatient settings demonstrate benzodiazepine dependence; this is much more common among women than among men (Holroyd & Duryee, 1997). • Benzodiazepine use significantly increases risk of falls with subsequent injury such as hip fractures.
Narcotics and opioid analgesics	• Narcotics and opioid analgesics are often prescribed initially for pain, with rapid development of tolerance and dependence. • Common side effects include sedation, confusion, incoordination, visual impairment, constipation and impaction, and increased risk of falls and hip fractures (Llorente et al., 2006).
Tobacco (nicotine)	• Rates decrease with age, but over 15% of individuals age 65 to 75 and over 8% of those 75 and older smoke (Llorente et al., 2006). • Rates of smoking are higher in individuals with mental illness or substance use disorders. • There is a clear association with multiple medical problems, particularly heart and lung disease, multiple cancer types, and osteoporosis. • Older individuals have higher rates of success with smoking cessation treatment.
Illegal substances (marijuana, cocaine, heroin, methamphetamine, hallucinogens)	• Prevalence across the board is less than 1% of older individuals, but this is higher in veteran populations (Office of Applied Studies, 2007). • There are little data on the use of these substances after age 65 because of the rarity of use; however, this is projected to increase in the coming decades.

talizations, operative procedures, or ongoing treatment for anxiety, sleep disturbances, or pain. Many older individuals are given medications while hospitalized and then simply continue taking them after discharge without adequate monitoring or education on their risks. When relief is not obtained from pain or discomfort, a pattern of increased use and tolerance may develop over time, leading to problems such as drug-seeking behaviors, cognitive impairment, and increased risk of falls and other injuries.

Every older client who presents for an evaluation for therapy should be screened for substance abuse, and the clinician should keep in mind that one or more of the client's prescription medications may be the culprit. Several tips on the evaluation are presented in Table 3.2. There are several short instruments used to screen for alcohol abuse, including the CAGE interview (see Table 3.2); the Short Michigan Alcohol Screening Test–Geriatric Version, or SMAST-G; and the Alcohol Use Disorders Identification Test–C, or AUDIT-C. The SMAST-G has been validated for use with older adults and focuses on a variety of behaviors associated with alcohol abuse (Barry & Blow, 1999), whereas the AUDIT-C is more explicit about the frequency of alcohol consumption (Bush, Kivlahan, McDonell, Fihn, & Bradley, 1998). The Severity of Dependence Scale can be used to screen for benzodiazepine dependence (de las Cuevas, Sanz, de la Fuente, Padilla, & Berenguer, 2000).

When a substance use disorder is present, the therapist must sort out several issues. First, is detoxification needed? If so, this will take precedence over any other form of therapy. Second, when there is a dual diagnosis, such as bipolar disorder and alcohol abuse, can general psychotherapy proceed while the substance use is being treated? Finally, are there medical, social, or legal issues being perpetuated by the substance use that are interrupting therapy? Consider the following case vignette.

Edmund was a 72-year-old Korean War veteran who presented with complaints of depression, anxiety, and difficulty adjusting to a recent nursing home placement. Edmund did not report any substance use during the evaluation but complained about how his stepdaughter moved his wife out of town and would not let him have any contact with her. He hated the nursing home and was angry at the county social worker who arranged for his placement after he was hospitalized for pneumonia. When contacted, the social worker reported that Edmund had long-standing alcohol dependence and was well known to the police for domestic violence while intoxicated. That is why his stepdaughter forbade contact with his wife. She also reported that the nursing home suspected he was becoming intoxicated and belligerent from drinking cologne, mouthwash, and even the hand sanitizer in the facility.

Despite his desire for counseling, Edmund's problems all related to ongoing alcohol use and were not going to improve until that was addressed. Disease-specific evaluation and treatment were needed instead, including a formal detoxification, restricted access to alcohol-containing substances, an evaluation for potential cognitive impairment, and referral to both a 12-step program and individual and group alcohol programs. If anxiety and depression persisted beyond abstinence, dual-diagnosis treatment would be necessary. But as it stands with Edmund and many individuals abusing alcohol and other substances, much of the psychiatric comorbidity resolves once abstinence has been attained (Llorente et al., 2006; Oslin & Mavandadi, 2009).

A Final Word on Strengths

On the basis of the discussion in this chapter, it would be easy to see the impact of aging on mental illness as primarily negative. Age-associated physical symptoms and disorders confound diagnosis and complicate treatment for most late-life psychiatric disorders. It is important to ask, however, whether aging can also bring benefits that help mitigate long-standing mental illness or prevent new onset. In other words, are there age-associated factors that are both protective and adaptive for the older client?

First, there are numerous psychosocial strengths that accumulate with aging that can play positive roles, including emotional maturity, wisdom, and spirituality. Late life may also bring added time for reflection, leisure, and socialization. Levels of impulsivity and depression tend to decrease. Both socioemotional selectivity theory (Carstensen et al., 2000) and selection, optimization, and compensation theory (Baltes & Baltes, 1990) describe how older clients can bring these strengths to bear on daily living. According to socioemotional selectivity theory, aging individuals recognize the shrinking horizon ahead and begin to place more emphasis on seeking more positive and meaningful emotional experiences. This theory is supported by research showing that older individuals feel less negative emotion and are able to maintain a generally positive emotional state, even in the face of criticism (Charles & Carstensen, 2008; Nielsen, Knuton, & Carstensen, 2008). Selection, optimization, and compensation theory describes three processes through which older individuals can successfully manage new challenges by selecting among finite personal resources and refining these to achieve specific goals, while simultaneously maintaining normative functioning. For example, dependency in late life can be seen not as a weakness or potential manifestation of depression but as a way for the older individual to balance gains and losses in order to maintain control over certain aspects of life (Ong & Bergeman, 2007).

Although we understand how these processes of positive or successful aging may improve the life of an aged client, we do not know exactly how they affect mental illness. Moreover, the presence of cognitive impairment can derail them, as is discussed in Chapter 6. Both socioemotional selectivity theory and selection, optimization, and compensation theory were developed for normative, not pathological, aging. But it will become clear in a review of psychotherapies in Chapters 7 and 8 that psychosocial strengths are the foundation of most therapeutic change. We ignore them at the peril of our clients.

6

WORKING WITH COGNITIVELY IMPAIRED CLIENTS

Here is a tale of two clients. The first client, named Jan, was an 88-year-old woman who was referred for an evaluation for depression and cognitive impairment. At the appointment Jan sat quietly and calmly, smiling at the therapist but not responding to any questions. The therapist assumed that Jan was not speaking because of aphasia associated with an underlying severe dementia and called her daughter to get more history. Over the phone the daughter instructed the therapist to put the phone up to her mother's left ear. "Oh yes, I'm fine," Jan suddenly exclaimed into the phone, seeming to spring to life in front of the therapist. "I'm just sitting and waiting to talk to this nice doctor." Contrary to the therapist's thinking, Jan was not demented but had severe hearing loss and had forgotten to wear her hearing aids to the appointment.

The second client was a 76-year-old widower named Edward who showed up for his appointment wearing a Green Bay Packers sweatshirt. The therapist—being a huge football fan—spent the first 15 minutes listening to Edward's description of being at the famed Ice Bowl when the Packers won the

1967 NFL championship. By the time the therapist began to probe Edward's current complaints of moodiness, he was so enamored of his spirit and background that he could not imagine him being very cognitively impaired. After the appointment Edward was found by security staff wandering around the parking lot, looking for his car. The therapist had never probed his short-term memory enough to diagnose obvious cognitive impairment.

This tale illustrates some fundamental lessons of working with cognitively impaired clients. First, not every client who seems cognitively impaired has an actual cognitive disorder. There are several conditions that either mimic cognitive impairment (e.g., severe sensory impairment, dysphasic speech) or involve transient impairment in attention or concentration (e.g., depression, dissociation) and falsely give the impression of an enduring cognitive disorder or dementia. Second, certain cognitive strengths (e.g., sociability, verbal fluency, motor skills) may outpace memory impairment to such an extent that they give the false impression that the individual in question is cognitively intact. Third, brief interviews and cognitive screens (such as the Mini–Mental State Examination) do not capture well key aspects of cognitive disorders related to frontal, temporal, and parietal lobe impairment such as personality changes, compulsive behaviors, and neglect syndromes. And fourth, many individuals with cognitive disorders are poor historians because they have limited insight into their impairment.

As outlined in Chapter 3, the clinical interview must obtain sufficient history from both clients and informants in order to establish a baseline of cognitive abilities and the course of any recent change. The MSE must probe not only memory function but also language, recognition, motor abilities, and executive function. Even with an in-depth interview, however, formal neuropsychological testing remains the gold standard for establishing the spectrum and degree of actual cognitive impairment. In addition, such testing can identify extant strengths critical to shaping therapy and therapeutic activities. For example, stimulating activities for individuals with memory impairment can draw upon cognitive, motor, and perceptual skills such as creativity, imagination, humor, compassion, sensory enjoyment, and movement.

Cognitive impairment may also be associated with severe psychiatric conditions including schizophrenia, depression, and substance use. The impairment seen with schizophrenia tends to be chronic and worsens with age. Depression impairs attention and concentration and may affect memory, especially in more severe states such as pseudodementia. This "false" dementia, by definition, involves reversible cognitive impairment that improves with antidepressant therapy but carries with it an increased risk of later development of actual dementia (Alexopoulos et al., 1993). Alcohol is the most common substance of abuse in late life that may be associated with reversible cognitive impairment as well as permanent dementia. Specific neuropsychological impairments associated with each condition are listed in Table 6.1.

Differential Impact on Therapy

The different forms of cognitive disorders, ranging from mild cognitive impairment to various dementia types such as Alzheimer's disease were described in Table 1.1. Across the board, the most common impact on therapy, regardless of the type, is the failure of clients to retain insights or skills acquired in a session because of short-term memory impairment. At the same

Table 6.1. Cognitive Impairment and Mental Illness

Condition	Neuropsychological Impairment
Schizophrenia	Cognitive impairment is an intrinsic part of the diagnosis and worsens with age. Areas of impairment include attention, memory, processing speed, reasoning, problem solving, and verbal fluency. Some of this impairment may be due to the effects of antipsychotic medications. The functional impairment of schizophrenia is linked to underlying deficits. Cognitive rehabilitation has been shown to improve deficits (Green, Kern, & Heaton, 2004; Keefe & Eesley, 2009; McGurk, Twamley, Sitzer, McHugo, & Mueser, 2007).
Depression	Mild to moderate depression may cause distractibility and poor concentration. Severe depression and pseudodementia involve impairment in attention, short-term memory recall, motor speed, and syntactic complexity (Alexopoulos et al., 1993). Impairments improve with antidepressant treatment.
Alcohol abuse	Severe alcohol abuse has been associated with two forms of dementia seen in 4% to 20% of abusers: (1) Wernicke's encephalopathy, which involves transient confusion and neurological impairment and is reversible with thiamine supplementation but can otherwise progress to Korsakoff's syndrome, which involves more permanent, severe impairments in short-term memory, and (2) alcohol dementia, which involves global cognitive impairment and brain atrophy. With abstinence, a significant percentage of these individuals can improve over time (Agronin, 2008; Schuckit, 2009).

time, the lack of insight into these deficits may rob a client of motivation and emotional investment in therapy. Disinhibited behaviors, mood lability, and psychotic symptoms can interfere with attention and cooperation in therapy. Ultimately, therapeutic modalities that are more insight oriented may be impractical with increasing cognitive impairment. The specific impacts of various dementia types are described in Table 6.2.

Table 6.2. Major Dementia Types and How They Affect Therapy

Dementia Type	Impact on Therapy
Mild cognitive impairment	Mild impairment in short-term memory for therapeutic issues can be compensated for by written summaries of sessions and frequent reviews of insights, tasks, and the like.
Alzheimer's disease	Depending on the stage of illness, it is likely that material from previous sessions may not be remembered well, but a consistent relationship can still be established. The focus of therapy should be on resolving anxiety and other conflicts in the moment or on recognizing and enhancing personal strengths.
Vascular dementia	The type of impairment (memory, language, motor, or a combination) limits certain skills but not others. A neuropsychological profile is key to plotting a therapeutic plan. Subcortical vascular dementia may be associated with bradyphrenia (i.e., slowed thinking), apathy, and response latency, which require patience on the part of the therapist.
Dementia with Lewy bodies	Parkinsonism may be associated with reduced facial expression of emotion. Psychosis may interfere with attention and cooperation with therapy. Fluctuations in cognition are common, and poor performance at one session may be improved at the next.
Frontotemporal dementia	Language dysfunction is prominent and may limit therapeutic approaches that require strong verbal skills. Personality changes, bizarre behaviors, and compulsions may interfere with attendance and attention during therapy.
Dementia due to medical illness or injury	A strong emphasis on cognitive rehabilitation is key because many medically caused forms of dementia can be either static or improve with time.

Shirley was a 75-year-old woman with a previous diagnosis of major depression but no formal diagnosis of cognitive impairment. Her daughter brought her for a psychological evaluation because she had been increasingly tearful and socially withdrawn. She loved knitting but had stopped doing it for the last month. Her sleep and appetite were poor. The therapist found Shirley to be an articulate, forceful woman who spent most of the session complaining about feeling lonely and overwhelmed because no one came to visit her. She also expressed concern that when her children visited they always seemed to take things with them. The therapist engaged Shirley in what appeared to be a cathartic discussion about coping with loneliness and disappointment. Shirley was smiling at the end of the session and exclaimed, "Finally I've met someone who understands me!" She thanked the therapist profusely and expressed interest in meeting again. The therapist felt that she had allowed Shirley to vent much of the frustration underlying her depression. On the basis of the session, the therapist began to construct a basic case formulation. Two weeks later Shirley returned with her daughter for the appointment. The therapist was surprised when Shirley introduced herself as if they had never met. She had no recall of the therapist or the last session and began talking about how lonely she felt and how upset she was over losing her purse. "Maybe my son took it!" she wondered.

It may seem most natural to jump into sessions with older, talkative, and sociable clients and allow them to take the lead in sharing their thoughts. Listening, reflecting, and problem solving with the client can easily take priority over due diligence in terms of a screen for cognitive impairment. But in this case the therapist had no clue that Shirley was experiencing marked short-term memory impairment, which was driving most of her complaints. Although such a mistake may strike the reader as contrived, it is a common occurrence across many clinical settings in which therapists are not attuned to the older client. The early stages of Alzheimer's disease and other dementias can look a lot like depression and can involve impairments in attention, concentration, sleep, appetite, and social withdrawal. Shirley stopped knitting not because she was depressed and lost interest, but because she could no longer mentally process what to do. She was crying and upset less because of depression and more because she could not remember when family members visited. Her anger fueled a growing paranoia as she blamed others for taking items that she had misplaced and could not find because she could not remember where she put them. Without a basic memory screening, Shirley's emotions were accurately gauged but the underlying causes and the case formulation itself were way off the mark.

Adaptations to Therapy

As the therapist reflects on the impact of cognitive impairment on the therapeutic process, the first question is whether therapy is even viable. The answer is an unequivocal yes! In fact, it would be a grave mistake to think that cognitive impairment, even in moderate degrees, should preclude some form of therapy. Instead, therapy needs to be adapted in order to accommodate cognitive deficits while simultaneously leveraging residual cognitive strengths.

Step 1, as previously emphasized, is to conduct a thorough enough evaluation that includes a cognitive screen and perhaps even formal neuropsychological testing in order to get clear knowledge of the diagnosis and the degree and areas of impairment. Informants here are key. The overall case formulation must take into account the role of associated psychiatric symptoms, including changes in mood, personality, thinking, behavior, and perception. Paranoid ideation is common but often subtle in early stages of both Alzheimer's disease and dementia with Lewy bodies. It is relatively common in individuals with Parkinson's disease and associated dementia. Executive disturbance is seen in all forms of dementia as a result of damage to the frontal and temporal lobes or to subcortical neural connections to these lobes. Such damage disrupts an individual's ability to organize and prioritize issues from therapy, as well as the motivation to seek change. Equally important, cognitive impairment can limit the therapist-client relationship, which is central to therapy, especially psychodynamic approaches that rely upon an analysis of the transference.

During the period of evaluation, keep in mind that verbal reports of affect may be inconsistent in later stages of dementia. For example, some individuals share that they feel nervous at one moment, but an hour later, they do not report feeling that way. Some individuals become panicked on and off because of a temporary annoyance, but they then return to their baseline after minutes or hours. Look for enduring patterns of symptoms that continue to manifest with a clearly negative impact on daily function and care.

Step 2 is to develop a case formulation and the goals of therapy. The formulation includes the working diagnoses as well as an account of the previous baseline and the current landscape. For example, in the case of Shirley, the diagnosis was Alzheimer's disease with moderate impairment in short-term memory and associated paranoid ideation. Prior to onset, Shirley had been a very active and outgoing individual. She did not have any major medical problems that were causing pain or disability. In addition to paranoid ideation, she had insomnia and had been taking, it was discovered, a sleeping pill that was worsening her memory. The current landscape included a highly unstructured living situation with a supportive daughter but no one at home to provide monitoring and assistance. The daughter expected the therapist to do much of the heavy lifting: cure Shirley's mood and behavioral problems, help with home health care, counsel the family, speak with her PCP, and provide insight into Shirley's ability to manage her own affairs. These expectations were symptomatic of a daughter and larger family that neither understood Shirley's condition nor appreciated its risks, along with a therapist who did not conduct a thorough enough examination. Under these circumstances, therapy was untenable.

At the same time, many of Shirley's personal and social strengths were clear: She was premorbidly a very bright and active woman with an extraverted personality; her language function was intact and she could clearly verbalize her thoughts, feelings, and needs; she was a creative individual who still retained some ability to knit; she was physically fit and enjoyed exercise; and she had adequate financial resources and a loving extended family that was motivated to help.

On the basis of this case formulation, it is clear that any form of therapy that requires short-term memory, such as insight-oriented and cognitive-behavioral modalities, would not be practical. Second, additional structure was needed in Shirley's home situation in order to reduce the sense of isolation and paranoia that came with living alone. Such structure would likely reduce the intensity of many of the issues brought to therapy. What would be helpful would be providing emotional support as well as sensory, social, and cognitive stimulation, either one on one or in a group. One groundbreaking study demonstrated that such social interaction and support in the form of brief psychosocial therapy could even reduce agitation in individuals with Alzheimer's disease (Ballard et al., 2009). In addition, the therapist could provide the family with education and referral to relevant support systems (e.g., the Alzheimer's Association) and other professionals in the community (e.g., a geriatric psychiatrist or neurologist to work up the dementia and consider cognitive-enhancing and other appropriate psychotropic medications).

It is true that this process might severely limit or even negate the role of the therapist in some circumstances, such as when the cognitive impairment or behavioral problems are severe. At the same time, many of the modalities appropriate for Shirley and similar individuals might be considered not psychotherapy as most therapists would conceive, but forms of occupational therapy or therapeutic programming. That is the reality of working with such clients. It is imperative to have either a formally established team in place or a loose network of colleagues, programs, and institutions in order to provide for all of these clients' needs.

Individuals with milder degrees of cognitive impairment are, on the other hand, appropriate for most forms of psychotherapy, but again with adaptations in order to accommodate their limitations. For example, clients with mild short-term memory impairment should always be provided with clear information and frequent reminders about therapy, including the name of the therapist, the practice location, and topics covered from session to session. The use of preprinted handouts or notes during therapy might be useful. Sessions might include formal introductions and recaps of the previous session at the beginning of the hour. The therapist may need to take a more active role in terms of initiating conversation and directing the client through the session. Such techniques are particularly useful for individuals with executive impairment, who get distracted easily or have difficulty organizing their thoughts.

Regardless of the degree of impairment, the therapist often has to assume a more active management role than is common or even appropriate with younger clients, such as contacting and involving informants, helping with transportation, and even assisting with mobility into the room. At the same time, the therapist must be mindful of how these roles will necessarily affect the transference relationship and carry the risk of breaching the autonomy and privacy of the client. The rule is not to assume a paternalistic role but to be open to the unique needs of the client and work these out during the course of therapy.

Many clients with cognitive impairment end up surprising the therapist with strengths that fluctuate during the course of therapy, sometimes disappearing for awhile, then returning, or emerging from out of nowhere to seemingly transcend the established cognitive limitations. It may be that transient medical conditions suppressed these skills during the evaluation phase. But even in progressive forms of dementia, particularly dementia with Lewy bodies, there are fluctuations in attentiveness, concentration, and memory that must be expected. With many of these individuals, however, short-term memory impairment will limit how much information is remembered from session to session. Although this limits the client's sense of continuity and coherence in therapy, it does allow the therapist to continually refine the therapeutic approach.

Beverly was an 84-year-old widowed woman who was an artist and previously ran a successful art gallery. Over 18 months she had developed mild to moderate cognitive impairment due to several small strokes. She had a long-standing history of depression but had done reasonably well in the past with weekly psychotherapy and antidepressant medication. After a lengthy hospitalization and then rehabilitation following a hip fracture, Beverly returned to therapy, although with more pronounced short-term memory impairment. She remembered the therapist well and appreciated their history together, but she could not recall details of previous sessions and had lost her entire sense of their progress. At the same time, she did not dwell on many of the stressors that had bothered her before, mainly because she had forgotten about them. During some sessions Beverly was quite sharp and almost seemed like her old self, whereas during others she was distant and fatigued.

Despite Beverly's increased cognitive impairment, the therapist knew her well enough from their time together to adapt the therapy to her strengths. On days when she was sharp, they picked up on many themes from before, such as Beverly's struggle with loneliness and feelings of abandonment. On days when Beverly was fatigued or distant, she encouraged her to talk about her art, sometimes prompting conversation by putting a piece before Beverly and asking about the creative process. During times of stress, Beverly retrieved the therapist's phone number from the large-print notepad she kept next to the phone and called the therapist—something she never would have done in the past. The momentary contact was usually successful in calming her worries and redirecting her to more pleasant thoughts. Despite the absence of the more intellectual and emotionally laden issues that they once discussed, Beverly was buoyed by the connection she always felt with the therapist and was able to maintain a sense of continuity in the process of therapy more than in the content. In addition, she was acquiring coping skills in a more indirect, nuanced manner that helped her even though she could not always articulate them.

Therapists should recognize that the presence of cognitive impairment may offer some advantages in therapy. A decline in neurotic concerns resulting from the loss of memories of previously upsetting issues may give the client greater openness to talking about feelings. By necessity, a greater spectrum of therapeutic approaches, such as sensory stimulation, life review, and creative arts therapy, might awaken dormant skills and provide a sense of well-being that would not have been achieved in the past. And finally, there may be greater support systems in place to bring clients to therapy and follow through with recommendations.

Brain Training

Concerns about memory impairment arise often in therapy with older clients, even in the absence of actual cognitive impairment. Memory lapses might be reported as a source of great concern, as it is common knowledge that Alzheimer's disease and other dementias are primarily diseases of the aged. The therapist must be able to distinguish between benign memory lapses (such as the ubiquitous "tip-of-the tongue" experiences) and more serious problems that warrant investigation. In addition, therapists must have some knowledge about the potential for cognitive training or rehabilitation, for they will inevitably be asked about whether anything can be done to boost memory and other skills.

The analogy of the use of mental exercises to improve brain function—in a manner similar to how physical exercise improves muscle tone and strength—has gained much currency lately in light of the plethora of so-called brain games on the market. Ranging from relatively inexpensive Internet sites and handheld video games to more sophisticated and costly computerized systems, these widely touted interactive products claim to bring significant improvements in mental functioning and subtly, if not subliminally, promise to slow cognitive decline associated with aging. The obvious question is whether these claims are true. More important questions are whether any mental exercise–induced improvements in discrete cognitive functions, such as memory and processing speed, offer practical benefits in daily life, and whether they stave off not simply age-associated cognitive decline but more devastating forms of dementia (Doraiswamy & Agronin, 2009).

A published study by Smith and colleagues (2009) is one of the largest randomly controlled trials to actually attempt to answer at least one of these critical questions. The Improvement in Memory With Plasticity-Based Adaptive Cognitive Training (or IMPACT) study utilized the computer-based Brain Fitness Program by Posit Science to test whether its stimulatory exercises on auditory system functioning would provide significantly greater generalized cognitive improvement than a more conventional cognitive learning program. The IMPACT study enrolled 487 cognitively intact individuals 65 years or older (with a mean age of around 75 years) and randomized them to the treatment group, which involved hour-long computerized training sessions 5 days a week with the Brain Fitness Program, or an active control group, in which participants observed DVD-based educational programs, which were followed by quizzes testing attention and learning. Outcome measures included scores on a standard neuropsychological test battery, with a focus on auditory memory and attention, as well as pre-post ratings of participants' perceptions of their cognitive abilities in day-to-day life.

Researchers found that after 8 weeks of engaging in these brain games, participants in the Brain Fitness Program group demonstrated modest but significantly greater improvements on tests of auditory memory and attention, processing speed, delayed verbal recall, and digit span than the active control. The former group also reported a significantly greater degree of positive perceptions of their cognition, although the differences in raw scores were minimal. These results confirmed earlier findings from a smaller version of IMPACT conducted by Mahncke, Connor, Appelman, and Merzenich (2006), as well as findings from the much larger Advanced Cognitive Training for Independent and Vital Elderly (ACTIVE) trial by Ball and colleagues (2002), which looked at the effects of non-computerized cognitive training modules in a sample of over 2,800 cognitively intact elders.

But is research simply stating the obvious? The fact that cognitive performance improves after some form of training should not come as a surprise; after all, the ability to learn does not end in old age. So why all the fuss? Several studies have already demonstrated that exercise and socialization in later life have positive effects on cognition, and both of these are free and immediately accessible. What, then, is the rationale for using brain games that cost money, require computers or trained instructors, and are more difficult to access? The immediate answer is that we do not yet know. The underlying thrust of IMPACT, ACTIVE, and similar studies was that structured forms of learning hold the promise of more focused improvements in cognitive skills such as memory and processing speed that are most affected by aging of the brain.

Future studies will need to determine how long these benefits last, and whether longer-term training is needed for more pronounced gains. We also need to know whether these brain games may actually overstress the brain and, paradoxically, lead to frustration or even boredom, which is counterproductive to the mission. In terms of practical benefits, we only know that participants in the IMPACT study rated themselves as having improved cognitive abilities, but we do not yet have quantitative evidence of noticeable benefits in terms of daily function. To underscore this concern, the ACTIVE trial showed similar improvements in cognition, but a measure of functioning for activities of daily living did not change after 2 years of training.

For the subgroup of aging individuals who are cognitively intact but concerned about potential decline—whom we call the *worried well*—their high baseline of performance in terms of memory and other cognitive functions may limit the measured benefits of brain games. And despite their promise, a recent review of cognitive interventions in healthy elderly individuals by Pap, Walsh, and Snyder (2009) found no evidence that these programs prevent the onset of dementia.

But what about for therapy clients who already experience varying degrees of cognitive impairment? For example, the pioneering work of Loewenstein, Acevedo, Czaja, and Duara (2004) has demonstrated that cognitive rehabilitation helped individuals with early stage Alzheimer's disease improve on several discrete tests of cognitive ability, at least initially and for 3 months after the targeted intervention was completed. These benefits, though likely to degrade quickly in the face of a progressive dementing process, certainly compare favorably to what can be achieved with cognitive-enhancing medications such as memantine and the cholinesterase inhibitors.

What has not been factored well into any of these studies is the role of a therapist. The intensive, focused social interactions with a therapist might be just as effective as a cognitive-enhancing computer game or other module. Or perhaps a combination of a human guide and a structured program might yield the best results. Many day programs and forms of therapeutic programming rely on this combination because they are designed for older, cognitively impaired individuals who cannot otherwise participate effectively in individual therapy. These activities involve a variety of modalities including group exercise, music, art, trivia, and pet therapy and are aimed at providing stimulation, orientation, socialization, and soothing in a comfortable and meaningful way.

Therapeutic Help for Caregivers

With many older clients, the therapist may need to assume two different roles for caregivers: that of an educator who provides advice, education, and support for the caregiver and that of a formal individual or family therapy provider. I have already discussed in detail the great burden that a caregiving

Table 6.3. Caring for the Caregiver

Strategy	Examples
Provide education about the cognitive disorder.	• Provide basic information on the diagnosis and its course, including associated disturbances in mood and behavior. • Make referrals to relevant organizations that can provide literature and more in-depth education (see Table 6.4 for specific listings).
Empower the caregiver by providing basic caregiving skills.	• Teach optimal ways to communicate with the client based on his or her level of impairment, including using nonverbal methods and compensating for hearing and visual loss.

Table 6.3. Continued

Strategy	Examples
	• Suggest ways to enhance memory in the home situation, such as using large-print calendars, labels on items, and written reminders.
	• Develop a structured daily routine that accommodates the client's preferences when possible and allows for attention to privacy and dignity during hands-on care.
	• Know when a caregiver has reached certain limits and needs outside help, such as a certified aide.
Engage the caregiver and client in meaningful, stimulating activities.	Have the caregiver take stock of the client's interests and strengths in order to find appropriate pursuits. The following questions will help.
	• What is the client still able to do at his or her current stage?
	• What did the client love to do earlier in life?
	• Are there people or cultural or religious items, rituals, foods, music, or languages that held great meaning for him or her?
	• What form of sensory stimulation can he or she still enjoy?
	Encourage the caregiver to look for community programs that can help clients engage in some of these interests by contacting the local Area Agency on Aging through the Eldercare Locator, a nationwide toll-free directory that can be reached at (800) 677-1116.
Energize the caregiver by suggesting respite time from caregiving responsibilities.	• Encourage the caregiver to set aside time to continue to pursue previous interests and relationships.
	• Other caregivers such as home health aides need to be involved in order to give the main caregiver time off.
	• Many nursing homes offer respite programs for clients to stay at for several days if the caregiver needs to travel out of town.
	• Civic, religious, and community organizations often offer support programs specifically for caregivers.

Table 6.4. Support Organizations for Caregivers

Alzheimer's Association
The Alzheimer's Association is the largest organization of its kind dedicated to education, research, support, and advocacy.
Web site: www.alz.org
Phone: (800) 272-3900

National Family Caregivers Association
The NFCA provides support, information, and advocacy for individuals who care for chronically ill, older, or disabled family members. Their goal is to strengthen the self-care and self-advocacy of caregivers so that they can control their own situations.
Web site: www.nfcacares.org
Phone: (800) 896-3650

Well Spouse Foundation
The WSF is a nonprofit association of spousal caregivers that provides support and sponsors respite programs for the spouses and partners of chronically ill or disabled individuals.
Web site: www.wellspouse.org
Phone: (800) 838-0879

---

role can incur. Table 6.3 summarizes ways in which the therapist can help the caregiver. Several key caregiver resources are listed in Table 6.4. It is clear from the two tables that therapists need to educate themselves about local resources and integrate some degree of care management into their approaches. It is unrealistic to expect to conduct successful therapy for either older clients or their caregivers without this.

7

FORMS OF PSYCHOTHERAPY

An older client has entered the threshold of the therapeutic setting, and therapy is about to begin. Hopefully the therapist has laid much of the groundwork for a successful encounter, including obtaining basic demographic information and ensuring that the client has been brought to the setting and oriented to its purpose. Formal introductions are then made by the therapist and the client and perhaps at least one caregiver or informant as well. As a general rule, the therapist should then meet with the client alone. There may be circumstances where severe cognitive or behavioral disturbances warrant the presence of a caregiver or aide, and the therapist will need to decide whether this should occur at the start of the session or after some time.

Many clients of the existing older cohort have not had previous experience with psychotherapy and thus do not know what to expect in terms of what happens in therapy, the role of the therapist, how often they will come for appointments, and for how long. It can be helpful to provide some orientation to such a client about the therapeutic process itself, and to probe for expectations. A client who expects to be cured in one session is unrealistic; a therapist who expects an older client to be able to come weekly for months or years may be equally unrealistic. A discussion about therapy not only provides education and reassurance to clients but also helps to reduce the stigma of being treated for mental illness and allow the very beneficial opportunity for them to have choices in terms of the type and course of therapy (Gallagher-Thompson & Thompson, 1996; Wyman, Gum, & Areán, 2006).

The most common issues that older clients bring to therapy usually involve one or more of the following stressors:

- Grief over recent or past personal losses
- Physical frailty, illness, pain, or disability
- Dependency on others
- Intergenerational conflicts
- Inability to cope with or manage the current living situation
- Impending death

The psychiatric symptoms and disorders underlying these problems are legion and the most common include anxiety, depression, cognitive impairment, agitation, psychosis, substance abuse, somatization, noncompliance with medical or psychiatric care, self-neglect or self-harm, and failure to thrive. At the end of one or two sessions the therapist should have a case formulation that includes not only a list of these issues but a formal diagnosis and an understanding of why and how the client has arrived at these circumstances.

Several key barriers with older clients need to be addressed at the outset, including client factors such as physical and cognitive limitations and therapy factors such as transportation and finances. Many of these factors and ways to manage them are listed in Table 7.1. The central theme behind these factors is that the therapeutic frame used with younger clients is often

Table 7.1. Management of Age-Specific Challenges to Therapy

Challenge	Management
Cognitive impairment • Disorientation • Short-term memory deficits • Language disturbances (aphasia) • Impaired recognition (agnosia) • Impaired motor sequencing (apraxia) • Executive disturbances	• Provide extra verbal cues for orientation. • Provide written reminders and materials for sessions. • Select a type of therapy that emphasizes support and stimulation in the current session rather than recall of previous sessions. • Build upon cognitive strengths less affected by short-term memory, such as long-term memory, sociability, creativity, humor, motor memory (i.e., ability to engage in overlearned motoric tasks), and altruism. • Provide structured, consistent therapy sessions in a consistent location. • Consider shorter sessions to account for changes in attention span and concentration. • Simplify therapeutic tasks and use a notebook (e.g., to log homework assignments). • Slow down the pace of therapy to ensure adequate comprehension. • Consider recording sessions for future review.
Sensory impairment	• Encourage clients to wear sensory aids, including hearing aids and glasses. • Have hearing amplifiers available. • Use large-print materials.
Speech impairment (e.g., dysarthria, stuttering)	• Demonstrate patience in the face of slow verbalization and latent responses to questions. • Make certain that receptive aphasia is not interfering with the client's understanding of what is being said.
Physical symptoms (e.g., pain, shortness of breath)	• If possible, have the client treat symptoms ahead of time with analgesics, inhalers, and the like.

(continued)

Table 7.1. Continued

Challenge	Management
Mobility in therapy	• Consider flexible length and timing of sessions in case physical symptoms cause interruptions. • The office should be handicapped accessible. • Be prepared to help a client in a wheelchair or using a walker, and have extra space in the office for maneuvering.
Stigma of being in psychotherapy	• Provide education and reassurance about psychiatric diagnosis and the benefits of therapy.
Difficulty making and managing appointments and payments	• Provide explicit orientation to the method of making appointments and payments, and provide the therapist's and staff's contact information. • Office staff should have their own orientation to working with older clients and their caregivers and be schooled in being patient when dealing with sensory and physical impairments.
Transportation to therapy	• Have information handy to send or hand out to clients regarding subsidized (e.g., STS) and public transportation. • Consider home visits or sessions in alternate locations other than an office, such as in long-term care facilities or senior centers.
Financial limitations	• Devise sliding-scale fees.

inadequate or too rigid for older clients and must be adapted (Wyman et al., 2006). As a result, decisions regarding the timing and length of sessions, location of sessions, and form of therapy must be made in an open-minded way and must sometimes stray from traditional approaches.

At the same time, the therapist is aided by the client's age-associated strengths, including increased knowledge and life experience, greater openness to change, decreased impulsivity, more positive emotions coupled with less focus on negative thoughts and feelings, deepened spirituality, and an expanded approach to problem solving that falls under the rubric of *wisdom* (Ardelt & Oh, 2010; Charles & Horwitz, 2010).

The Clients: Sarah and Abe

As of way of illustrating the adaptations to therapy as well as the different forms of therapy with older clients, I have selected two representative clients named Sarah and Abe, who are based on actual individuals but with sufficient changes made so as to render them fully anonymous. Although the case formulations and treatment approaches for Sarah and Abe that are described for each form of therapy are based on actual circumstances, they are contrived from a composite of the experiences of clients in order to show how the process works. Allow me to introduce each client.

Sarah

Sarah was a 77-year-old woman who presented for therapy, complaining of depression, physical pain and disability, and conflict with her two daughters. Three months before the appointment, she had been admitted to an assisted living facility after a lengthy hospitalization and subsequent rehabilitation stay at a nearby nursing home. Previously she had been living with her youngest daughter, Rebecca, who now emphatically insisted that she could no longer care for her mother in her home. Sarah sought therapy herself because she was having a difficult time adjusting to her new surroundings.

Her medical history was complicated and included atherosclerotic heart disease, breast cancer, hypothyroidism, diabetes mellitus, anemia, osteoporosis, and severe back pain. She was moderately obese and had both visual loss and nerve pain in her legs and feet due to her diabetes. She had recently developed extreme shortness of breath and weakness while living with her daughter Rebecca and was found to be in congestive heart failure. She subsequently underwent surgery for replacement of a heart valve and contracted postoperative pneumonia. During her rehabilitation she tried valiantly to regain her strength, but after nearly 8 weeks of physical therapy, she was still not able to walk safely. As a result, Sarah spent most of her time in a wheelchair. She was taking many medications for her various medical problems but continued to report persistent pain in her back, knees, and feet.

In terms of psychiatric history, Sarah reported several bouts of depression but never sought or received any treatment. She was started on both an antidepressant and a sleeping pill in the rehabilitation facility but did not feel that either pill made much of a difference.

The oldest of two girls, Sarah was born in a small town in Pennsylvania. Her father was a coal miner and her mother a homemaker. When she was 6 years old, her mother abandoned the family and had no contact with them for nearly 5 years. Her father was a hardworking and caring man but relied upon several of his sisters to help raise his two girls. When Sarah was 11, her mother inexplicably returned to live with the family. Sarah graduated from high school and was married at the age of 18. However, her husband was in the service and was immediately sent to fight in the Korean War. Upon his return, they had a baby girl but divorced within 2 years. During this time Sarah worked as a waitress and later a bank teller. She remarried at the age of 36 and had another daughter. She and her husband started a relatively successful bakery, which they ran for the next 20 years. Sarah then discovered that her husband was cheating on her, and they got divorced. A year later she was diagnosed with breast cancer and underwent a radical mastectomy followed by radiation and chemotherapy. As a result of both the divorce and her illness, the business faltered and Sarah and her ex-husband ended up selling it at a loss. Alone, ill, and now impoverished at the age of 58, Sarah experienced her first bout of depression. She resisted getting any help, however, and was able to pull herself out of it by going back to work. At the age of 70, Sarah began experiencing increasing health problems, including diabetes and associated painful neuropathy in her feet. She also had recurrent breast cancer and had to undergo a lumpectomy and radiation. She temporarily moved in with a grandson and then moved to Florida to live with her youngest daughter. Her oldest daughter lived nearby but was going through a divorce and had little time for Sarah. The daughter was also wrestling with an addiction to narcotic painkillers and had been in and out of drug rehabilitation at the time.

As her health deteriorated, Sarah began feeling more and more depressed and isolated and was having frequent fights with her daughter Rebecca, who was pregnant with her second child. Sarah described this time as the worst of her life, given the physical pain and tension with the one person whom she still trusted to care for her. After Sarah's hospitalization, Rebecca refused to allow her to return to her home, stating that she was overwhelmed by her care needs at a time when she was also caring for two small children. Sarah felt betrayed and angry and grew increasingly depressed. However, she still held out hope of moving back with Rebecca and continued to pay a high monthly fee to keep all her furniture in storage until that day arrived.

At their first meeting, the therapist found Sarah to be a nicely dressed and groomed, moderately obese woman in a wheelchair. She was friendly and initially presented with a bright affect, but this quickly gave way to sobbing when she spoke about her recent losses. Sarah denied suicidal ideation but stated that she didn't care if she never woke up: "I would be free of all of this pain," she suggested. She was fully oriented and articulate and had intact short-term and long-term memory. There was no evidence of psychosis. She complained that her daughter did not call enough and did not always return her phone calls. She also complained about her roommate, stating that she tried to help her but felt taken advantage of. She continued to express hope that she would move back with her daughter and felt overwhelmed at the thought of living long term in the assisted living facility. Aside from this unrealistic thinking, her insight and judgment were intact.

Abe

Abe was a 72-year-old man with a history of cognitive impairment and anxiety associated with a stroke. He was referred to a therapist by his wife because of severe anxiety and panic attacks. Although Abe was described as a chronically anxious individual, the panic attacks began approximately one year ago after the death of his son and had increased in frequency and intensity ever since. During his attacks he experienced hyperventilation and palpitations and quickly became restless, angry, and distraught. He often screamed at his wife and would sometimes throw whatever he could grab from the confines of his wheelchair. On several occasions he threw his body onto the ground. He consistently refused to take any medications for his symptoms, as he blamed his son's death on a medication overdose.

Abe's medical history was notable for uncontrolled hypertension, insulin-dependent diabetes mellitus, and end-stage renal disease requiring hemodialysis. He had a major stroke in the left thalamus of his brain 2 years prior to being seen for therapy and was in a coma and on a ventilator for several months before being transferred for a lengthy stay in a rehabilitation facility. He continued to have slurred speech, right-sided paralysis, and some mild memory impairment. Abe was on multiple medications to prevent further strokes but refused all medications for anxiety and panic except an occasional dose of alprazolam when his wife insisted.

Abe was born into a wealthy family in Cuba that owned a large textile factory. The family's business was confiscated by the Castro regime after it took power in the early 1960s, and Abe and his family were forced to flee the country. They settled in Miami, where Abe helped run a new family business. He later got a business degree and then left the family business to work for a large manufacturer in south Florida. This move infuriated much of his family, especially because his success rivaled that of several respected uncles.

Abe and his wife had been married for nearly 50 years and had a relatively stable marriage. They had a son and a daughter and raised both in Miami. Their daughter was married and lived with her husband and three children down the street from Abe and his wife. His son had been married and divorced and had problems with depression, alcohol dependence, and prescription drug abuse. The son's death a year prior to Abe's first therapy session was sudden and probably the the result of a mixture of alcohol and pills, but Abe denied that his son was an alcoholic and blamed everything on the doctors who gave his son multiple pain medications.

Abe's wife described him as having a self-centered, obsessive, and driven personality that allowed him to be successful but deprived him of any close relationships. Up until his stroke, his entire focus was on earning money, and he was emotionally devastated by major losses in his investments in the past year. Aside from his strong personality with clear narcissistic and obsessive-compulsive features, Abe did not have any reported past psychiatric history.

During their first meeting, Abe sat in his wheelchair in a restless manner, describing himself as having a choking sensation whenever he tried to speak. His speech was slurred and he tried to convince the therapist to speak only in Spanish. His affect was anxious and irritable, and he repeatedly asked the therapist for reassurance that she was not a psychiatrist who would force him to take pills. He denied feeling suicidal but stated that during panic attacks he wished he would die so the pain would go away. Although he was suspicious of his wife's motives for bringing him to the therapist ("Is she trying to put me away?"), there was no evidence of overt paranoid ideation or other psychotic symptoms. He was alert and oriented to person and knew the day of the week, month, and year but could not remember the date. He knew that he was at a clinic in Miami, Florida. He could only remember one of three objects after several minutes. His visuospatial skills, attention level, and concentration were generally intact. He knew that he needed help and agreed to see the therapist for several sessions.

Forms of Therapy

There is an exhaustive list of therapy types that can be used with older clients, and the goal here is neither to enumerate them all nor to explain the detailed workings of select therapies. Rather, the goal is to orient readers to how each is applied and adapted to age-relevant issues and tasks. The cases of Sarah and Abe will be put into motion for each therapy.

Psychodynamic Therapy

In his classic work on psychotherapy for older individuals, George Pollack wrote that

> It has become evident that a very crucial element for successful aging is the ability to mourn for prior states of the self. When one can accept aging and its changes and mourn for the past the result can be a liberation, a freeing of energy for current living, including "planning for the future." (1987, pp. 12–13)

Contained within this description is the essential process of psychodynamic psychotherapy with older clients, involving an active exploration of the past and its impact on the present, and the pursuit of change that occurs when psychic energy that was previously bound by intrapsychic conflict is freed up. More detailed assumptions that underlie this approach are enumerated by Fonagy and Target (2009):

- Both unconscious and conscious psychic forces produce the conflicting thoughts and feelings that comprise symptoms.
- Identification and exploration of developmental history, unconscious expectations, psychic defenses, internal representations of interpersonal relationships, and the therapist-client relationship are key therapeutic activities.

In late life, these dynamic forces continue to evolve and play active roles in shaping experience and behavior and are perpetually open to exploration. At the same time, there are accumulating losses of personal attributes and relationships, as well as the approaching horizon of death, that challenge these forces in new ways (Cath, 1984; Nemiroff & Colarusso, 1990; Pollack, 1987).

One form of psychodynamic therapy that has been developed and used with older clients is brief psychodynamic psychotherapy, or BPP (Gallagher-Thompson & Steffen, 1994; Lazarus et al., 1987). Compared with standard psychodynamic and psychoanalytic therapy, BPP involves fewer sessions (fewer than 24), a shorter timeframe (less than 6 months), a more active therapist, a faster development of therapeutic alliance, and a narrower problem focus. In addition, it is more selective in terms of candidates, generally favoring individuals with less severe pathology and good object relationships (Dewan, Weerasekera, & Stormon, 2009). In terms of the older client, these criteria translate into a more cognitively intact nonpsychotic individual who has generally stable interpersonal relationships.

Sarah represented an excellent candidate for BPP because she was cognitively intact, articulate, sociable, and motivated to change. The initial evaluation immediately focused on Sarah's chronic feelings of insecurity in relationships, dating back to her mother leaving her as a child and then reappearing several years later without an explanation. Sarah smothered her first husband upon his return from Korea, angrily demanding to know his whereabouts at all times out of fear that he was either cheating or making plans to abandon her. Her second husband was a relatively passive man whom she could keep her eye on because they worked together every day, but as the marriage progressed he began to feel burdened by his wife's intrusiveness and demands. Sarah caught him having an affair with a much younger employee at the bakery, whom she described as her opposite: passive and adoring of her husband, never putting demands on him, and acceding to his every whim. More recently, Sarah had been imposing demands on her daughter to spend time with her, even when Rebecca was pregnant and trying to please a husband and care for a young child.

The psychodynamic case formulation postulated that Sarah's chronic depression was ultimately tied to her ambivalence toward her mother. On the one hand, she had always yearned for a more secure attachment to a loving mother. On the other hand, she felt deep anger toward her mother for abandoning her, but had never been able to express it to her mother when she was alive. Instead, Sarah directed it inward, creating chronic dysphoria. To a certain extent, Sarah's approach to relationships with her husbands and daughters provided unconscious gratification as she re-created an internalized mother figure. However, this approach led her to end up infantilizing, bullying, and alienating the individuals with whom she sought a connection.

Armed with this formulation, Sarah and her therapist began meeting weekly over the course of 4 months. Each step along the way, based on the framework of Dewan et al. (2009), is described in Table 7.2.

Interpersonal Therapy

Interpersonal therapy (IPT) is rooted in the interpersonal theory of psychiatry, which postulates that depression and other mental disorders arise in a social context consisting of interactions, relationships, and roles. Although it was developed for individual therapy with depressed adults, it has been adapted for a variety of other age groups, therapy formats (individual, couples, group), and psychiatric disorders, including anxiety

Table 7.2. Brief Psychodynamic Psychotherapy With Sarah

Therapeutic Element	Session Material
Narrowed problem focus	On the basis of the case formulation, the therapist communicated to Sarah that "You have always been a very loving wife and mother in spite of having lost your own mother for several years in your childhood. But you find yourself easily depressed when you try so hard to care for others but do not feel that they care for you in return." The focus of therapy, to which Sarah agreed, would be on this discrepancy between what she expected from relationships and what she felt she actually got in return.
Increased therapist activity: Use of transference	The relatively short duration of the therapy demands that the therapist leap in and begin analyzing aspects of the relationship. With respect to their relationship, the therapist noticed that Sarah expressed great concern when the therapist sneezed several times during a session. Sarah began quizzing the therapist about any other symptoms that might reflect an underlying illness and then got visibly angry:

Sarah: God bless you! Have you been sneezing all day? Does your throat hurt? I know that there is a flu going around— maybe you should see a doctor.
Therapist: It sounds like you are worried about me.
Sarah: Of course! Why wouldn't I be? You're an important person to me! Why would you even ask me such a thing?
Therapist: Are you upset with me?
Sarah: Not at all! I'm just saying that I care about you!
Therapist: I wonder whether the way you are feeling now is how you sometimes feel when you are with your daugh-

Table 7.2. Continued

Therapeutic Element	Session Material
	ter Rebecca. You try to care for her but she seems to resist.
	Sarah: That's true. All I want is to be a good mother for her, to be there for her, and for her to appreciate that.
	Therapist: Is that what you wanted from your own mother?
	The transference toward the therapist was a recapitulation of Sarah's relationship with her daughter, which was in turn a reaction formation to Sarah's own experience of an uncaring and abandoning mother.
Increased therapist activity: Use of countertransference and clarification	At the next session, Sarah again asked the therapist how she was feeling, and whether she ever got sick. She then pointed to a photograph of the therapist's children in the office and asked whether they had been sick in the last week. The therapist felt intruded upon by this line of questioning, and her immediate impulse was to tell Sarah that they were there to talk about her, not the therapist. Instead, the therapist took the opportunity to communicate to Sarah an important point about her interpersonal style, but in a less intrusive way by restating her own words.
	Therapist: I know that it's important for you to express such concern about me and my family. Maybe it's difficult for me to know how to respond. Does the same thing happen with your daughter?
	Sarah: My daughter—you better believe it! Although you're a lot nicer about it. She just yells at me and tells me to stop prying.

(continued)

Table 7.2. Continued

Therapeutic Element	Session Material
	Therapist: Prying? **Sarah:** Yes—I guess that she thinks I am overreacting to little things and then trying to tell her what to do, as if she's a baby. **Therapist:** So your daughter thinks that you treat her like a baby? **Sarah:** She does. And yet she is a grown woman with two babies of her own! I guess I do baby her. Maybe I'm trying to do the same with you.
Here-and-now focus	Although Sarah's past relationships were important to her current pathology, her symptoms were best approached with a focus on current struggles. This is particularly relevant to older clients who have faced many recent losses. For several sessions Sarah kept on reciting a litany of hurt feelings she experienced from her first marriage. The therapist tried to redirect her to a current conflict in order to begin moving toward practical changes.
	Sarah: That no-good louse promised to care for us when he returned from Korea, but it was more important for him to booze it up with his buddies. I was home alone with our daughter and he couldn't understand why I yelled at him when he came home at all hours of the night. **Therapist:** Are you feeling angry at him today? **Sarah:** Today? No—I haven't thought about him for years until now. **Therapist:** But you're feeling angry now? **Sarah:** At this moment, yes. I feel angry and depressed about living here. I mean, it's not a terrible place, but I want to live with my daughter again.

Table 7.2. Continued

Therapeutic Element	Session Material
Increased therapist activity: Interpretation	As a means of facilitating more rapid progress in therapy, the therapist may throw out hypotheses to the client to explain what may be happening in the therapy on an unconscious level. Several sessions into the therapy, Sarah was complaining about how her daughter Rebecca was not calling her back. **Sarah**: I call and leave messages, but it takes her days to get back to me. She's a spoiled, inconsiderate bitch. I'm so angry I could kill myself! **Therapist:** You would kill yourself? **Sarah:** Well no, I mean I'm angry at Rebecca, but I wouldn't kill her—perish the thought! I am just so furious with her and I don't know how to contain it. I can't stand it when she rejects me! **Therapist:** Maybe this anger has a different source and is related to your mother leaving you when you were a little girl. I wonder whether it's easier to feel anger toward Rebecca than to feel hurt and rejected by your own mother.
Termination	After 4 months of treatment, Sarah had a better understanding of how her early feelings of abandonment led her to become an overbearing mother to her daughter Rebecca. She felt able to let go of much of the anger that was masking hurt feelings. She felt close to the therapist without having to mother her and as a result was also less intrusive with her own daughter. In the last session Sarah discussed her current situation.

(*continued*)

Table 7.2. Continued

Therapeutic Element	Session Material
	Sarah: I finally signed a yearly contract with the assisted living facility—it's my home now.
	Therapist: How are you feeling about that?
	Sarah: I'm sad to let go of my dream of returning to live with Rebecca, but she needs to focus on her family without having to worry about me every day. I know that was too much for her.
	Therapist: You don't sound angry.
	Sarah: I'm just happy for the time I do spend with her and the girls. The little ones are so precious. [Sarah pulls out recent photos to show the therapist.] By the way, did you hear the news?
	Therapist: No—tell me.
	Sarah: I've just been elected president of the residents' council! I've got a lot of things I want to change around here.
	Overall, Sarah was feeling significantly less depressed. She had established many new relationships at the assisted living facility and was getting along well with her daughter. Her underlying desire to mother others was channeled into more adaptive and creative pursuits in the residents' council, representing the healthier defense mechanism of sublimation.

disorders and eating disorders, and for marital discord (Hinrichsen, 2009). IPT is most associated with the work and theory of the psychiatrist Harry Stack Sullivan, but influences from Sullivan's mentor, Adolf Meyer, and several noted figures in the social sciences and psychoanalysis including George

Herbert Mead, Karen Horney, and Frieda Fromm-Reichmann can also be traced (Lipsitz, 2009; Sullivan, 1953). Since the publication of the first influential text on IPT in 1984 (Klerman, Weismann, Rounsaville, & Chevron, 1984), this psychotherapeutic technique has been used widely and has been found to be efficacious with elderly individuals living with depression (Hinrichsen, 1997; Reynolds et al., 1999). There is a standard IPT treatment manual for therapists (Weissman, Markowitz, & Klerman, 2000), a companion guide for clients (Weissman, 1995), and even a treatment manual for IPT with depressed older individuals (Hinrichsen & Clougherty, 2006).

In practice, IPT takes as its focus one or two salient interpersonal problems with the goal of defining losses and stressors, helping the client develop better interpersonal coping skills, and ultimately decreasing the depressive (or other) emotions associated with the problems. In IPT, depression is regarded as a diagnosable syndrome that is distinct from one's personality. As in a medical model, the depression is seen as the culprit that is causing problems for the client, and he or she is allowed to play the "sick role," described by Talcott Parsons (1951) as involving two key responsibilities: first, a desire to get well, and second, the responsibility of the client to seek out medical (or psychiatric) assistance. In a larger sense, the encouragement of a sick role emphasizes the goal of extirpating the illness versus learning to live with it.

Although IPT and psychoanalytic therapy share a concern with exploring the meaning and impact of key relationships, IPT differs in its greater focus on current relationships, limits in terms of both the scope of therapy and the number of sessions, a more pragmatic focus on specific goals, the cultivation of a collaborative therapist-client relationship and avoidance of interpretation of transference, and the emphasis on explaining the diagnosis (e.g., depression) and seeking its resolution (Lipsitz, 2009).

In terms of interpersonal problems, IPT prompts the client to inventory relationships and look for the following problem areas: role transitions (e.g., assuming a caregiving role for an ill spouse, retirement, moving into an assisted living facility, becoming medically ill), grief (e.g., loss of loved one or of a beloved home), role disputes (e.g., marital discord following a stressful life event or transition), and interpersonal deficits (e.g., social isolation). For the older client, there are a multitude of age-associated stressors (such as those just listed) that prompt interpersonal problems across these four domains. It is the job of the therapist and client together to select the one or two areas that seem most relevant to the current depression or other diagnosis.

IPT is broadly divided into three phases. During the initial sessions, the diagnosis is defined and psychoeducation is provided. The therapist assumes a warm, supportive, and active role as both a partner and a guide. Clients are allowed to assume the sick role insofar as this encourages them to view their symptoms as a disorder that can be treated successfully—providing a key message of hope. Working as a team, the therapist elicits an inventory of relationships from the client to begin to explore the interpersonal problem areas, making connections between depressed moods and upsetting or negative interpersonal experiences. The eventual goal of the first phase of treatment is to select an interpersonal problem that seems most relevant (and antecedent) to the genesis of the depression or other disorder being treated (Wyman et al., 2006).

During the intermediate phases of treatment, the therapist and client explore current interpersonal interactions in order to understand their impact on mood. As noted, the therapist-client relationship is seen as a mutual journey to understanding interpersonal problems outside the therapy and is not itself a focus of therapy (Lipsitz, 2009). The disorder is used to explain symptoms and serve as a target for recovery. Through communication analysis, the therapist might actively clarify (but not interpret) in detail interpersonal interactions in order to understand associated emotional responses, see what works and what doesn't in terms of facilitating problem resolution, and suggest more adaptive ways to communicate. Additional psychoeducation is provided as needed. The client is encouraged to increase socialization and pleasurable activities to counter the depression or other symptoms in question.

The final or termination phase of IPT consists of two to three sessions during which the therapy is reviewed and areas of improvement are highlighted, persistent areas of vulnerability are identified, and whatever follow-up is needed is planned for. It is important to manage feelings of loss that may present in the older client who came into therapy with grief as a central theme, so as not to reverse any improvements in mood. It is appropriate for the therapist to praise the work of the client and even to express his or her own satisfaction with the therapy and even feelings of loss in order to normalize those that may be felt by the client. Future work together is always a possibility.

For an older client who is relatively cognitively intact and verbal, IPT can work well at capturing many interpersonal struggles that accrue with age, including multiple losses of loved ones and associated grief, changes in long-held roles, and struggles with dependency on others due to physical illness.

During the initial phase of therapy, Abe took an immediate liking to the therapist both because she reminded him of his favorite niece and because their families came from the same region of Cuba. Seeing that Abe was trying to assume a paternalistic role in the therapy, the therapist deliberately decided against pointing that out to him and instead reframed the therapy as the two of them working together as a team. The chairs were positioned in the room nearly side by side instead of facing each other on opposite sides of a desk, and the therapist often leaned forward in Abe's direction to project a friendly and eager attitude. She explained to Abe that he was having panic attacks and that these were proving debilitating to him in many ways. She provided some education on what causes panic and how the body responds physiologically. Abe was happy to blame the panic attacks for many of his problems instead of feeling like they represented character flaws.

Once the therapy was underway, the therapist worked with Abe to inventory the key relationships in his life, both past and present. The most painful loss he experienced was when his son died, especially because he had always had a very conflicted relationship with him. He blamed everyone and everything for his son's problems, except for the role he himself played as a harsh and demanding father who had little patience for his underachieving son. Given his intense feelings of grief and the fact that the son was no longer alive, the therapist refocused Abe on the relationship with his wife, which seemed more relevant to his current problems. They discussed how Abe's role as the unquestioned patriarch of the family changed after his stroke, making him dependent on his wife. His panic attacks began occurring after this major and unexpected role transition, and the two seemed directly related. The therapy that followed is outlined in Table 7.3.

Table 7.3. Interpersonal Psychotherapy With Abe

Initial Phase	*Sessions 1–2*
Diagnosis	Based on a systematic review of Abe's symptoms, a diagnosis of panic disorder was made.
Psychoeducation	The therapist reviewed with Abe the physiological symptoms of panic based on the fight-versus-flight response and talked about how they prompted his temper tantrums.
Sick role	A medical model of illness was presented with panic disorder as the target. Abe was allowed to adopt the sick role as a patient with an illness that precluded certain responsibilities, such as being the central leader of his family and business, but that encouraged him to tend to his illness, seek out a doctor, and express an interest in getting better.
	Abe: I blame myself for my weakness here. I just can't handle things anymore. **Therapist:** It's hard to run a business when you're ill. This panic disorder has taken over your life at times. **Abe:** You're right—if I could just get rid of these panic attacks, I could do a lot more! **Therapist:** That's exactly what we'll work together on—getting you better so that you can play a more active role in your affairs.
Interpersonal problem	The therapist led Abe through an inventory of his social relationships, looking for the source of his anxiety and panic.
	Therapist: With whom do you spend most of your time? **Abe:** I still have many cousins in Miami, and of course my daughter I see every week. But my wife is here every day. **Therapist:** How do you get along with her? **Abe:** Not good. A lot of fighting. It started after my stroke. She gets me angry with her demands, and the stress makes me panic.

(continued)

Table 7.3. Continued

Initial Phase	Sessions 1–2
	The impaired relationship between Abe and his wife was selected as the focus of treatment because his symptoms of panic seemed to occur mostly when they were together.
Case formulation	The case formulation held that a role dispute between Abe and his wife was at the root of his problems. This problem area also involved a significant role transition for Abe from his role as the family patriarch to a dependent, isolated figure. The therapist presented the formulation to Abe.
	Therapist: Your stroke was quite devastating and left you unable to care for yourself for many months. Even as you have recovered, the residual physical and cognitive impairment robbed you of the ability to run your business and other affairs as you did before, forcing you to rely on your wife. This change in your role has produced tremendous anxiety. As you have recovered even more, you still have not been able to take back these roles from your wife, and this has led to a lot of fighting between the two of you. You get so nervous and angry when you and your wife argue over your limitations that you literally feel panicked and out of control.
Treatment contract	The therapist and Abe agreed on the diagnosis and formulation and the need to work together. The therapist then outlined the treatment plan and provided words of encouragement and hope.
	Therapist: We've agreed that we need to improve your relationship with your wife, since it seems clearly connected to your panic attacks. If you can improve the way the two of you interact, your anxiety should lessen and the panic attacks should melt away. Let's plan

Table 7.3. Continued

Initial Phase	Sessions 1–2
	to meet every week for 10 sessions total to work on this. **Abe**: Doc, you think it will work? I'm a tough person. **Therapist**: This is a tried and true method, Abe, and I am really confident that you will be feeling a lot better after just a few sessions. **Abe**: OK, I'm ready.

Middle Phase	Sessions 3–12
Focus on mood and recent life events	**Therapist**: How have you been since our last session? **Abe**: OK, I guess. I'm still having panic attacks. **Therapist**: At the last session you reported having five panic attacks the week before. How many did you have this past week? **Abe**: I think three. **Therapist**: What prompted these attacks? **Abe**: On Tuesday my wife showed up and reported a leak in our roof. I told her to call Manny, but she said she already called a different roofer. I screamed at her for doing this because only Manny is reliable. Then I started feeling like my heart was beating out of my chest, and the panic began. **Therapist**: What was it about your wife's answer that made you so anxious and upset? The therapist was skillfully trying to make a direct connection between the role dispute between Abe and his wife and his anxiety and panic.
Communication analysis and role play	The therapist worked with Abe to understand what transpired in his conversations with his wife, asking him at some points to demonstrate his tone of voice with his wife. Using

(*continued*)

Table 7.3. Continued

Initial Phase	Sessions 1–2
	leading questions, the therapist helped Abe to recognize his problematic way of communicating with his wife and to understand how his anxiety made it worse. They then came up with more adaptive approaches.

Therapist: What did you tell your wife when you heard she called another roofer?
Abe: I told her that she was wrong and didn't know what she was doing.
Therapist: What exactly did you say?
Abe: Something like "Why are you so stupid here? You know better! I always call Manny first!"
Therapist: How did your wife react?
Abe: She stood above me and screamed that I wasn't there to help and she had to do something before the roof fell in.
Therapist: How did that make you feel?
Abe: Seeing her standing above me reminded me that I can't walk, and I can't even get to the house to look at the leak without her driving me there and pushing me into the house. I felt so low and no good, and then this pressure started building in my chest.
Therapist: So you get panicked when you see your wife taking over for you?
Abe: Yes—exactly.
Therapist: I wonder whether the word *stupid* made her mad.
Abe: Oh, no doubt. That really set her off and made her stand up in front of me. Maybe it wasn't the best word to use.
Therapist: What else could you have said? Try it out here.
Abe: I could have said, "Honey, it was good to call a roofer, but why not Manny?"
Therapist: You told me you felt upset not being able to help out. Would you ever be

Table 7.3. Continued

Initial Phase	Sessions 1–2
	able to tell your wife, "Hey, I feel so nervous when there's something at home that I can't help out with."
	Abe: But that won't change anything.
	Therapist: Sometimes just saying how you feel can help.
	The therapist used the detailed content of the conversation to illustrate what Abe was doing to worsen communication, how that in turn led to increased anxiety and panic, and how he could speak to his wife in a less noxious and more productive way that conveyed his feelings without making his wife feel like everything she did was wrong.
Explore options	Because Abe did have some short-term memory issues, the therapist wanted to help him write down and think about what he wanted to achieve in the relationship with his wife. They began to keep a written log of panic attacks and their triggers for Abe to review each week, and it became clear that Abe wanted to be more involved in decision making. The therapist prompted Abe to write down the questions he had for his wife in order to get him more involved in aspects of their home, family, and business.
Psychoeducation	As the therapy progressed, the therapist taught Abe how to recognize the early physiological changes in his body that presaged a panic attack, and they talked about ways in which these symptoms could be stopped. One option was the use of anxiolytic medications, and a psychiatrist was involved to review options with Abe.
Interpersonal problem: Further work	For role disputes, there are three stages of dispute in IPT: (1) renegotiation, in which the individuals are actively but unsuccessfully

(continued)

Table 7.3. Continued

Initial Phase	*Sessions 1–2*

trying to work out a dispute; (2) impasse, in which there is no active negotiation and a stalemate exists; and (3) dissolution, in which no resolution is expected and the relationship is ending. Abe and his wife were clearly in Stage 1, and the therapist sought to intervene to decrease the emotional intensity of the arguments and improve the overall communication. The therapist worked with Abe to help him express his feelings to his wife without blaming her, and to find ways to communicate and be involved without feeling useless and panicked that he was being shunted aside:

Therapist: So let's role-play what happened with your wife. She came in and told you there was a leak and she had called the roofer. What could you have said to her?
Abe: Something like this: "That's terrible! Let's call Manny right away."
Therapist: Tell your wife how you are feeling.
Abe: I wish I could be there to help.
Therapist: Were you feeling nervous?
Abe: Yes, very. But my wife didn't care.
Therapist: Maybe she didn't know. How about something like this: "I am nervous that there is a leak, but I am glad that you called someone. Do you think we should get a second estimate from Manny?"

It was clear that Abe's stroke had caused some increased mood lability and memory impairment, which limited his ability to learn quickly how to communicate better. Still, after much role play Abe was improving and reporting fewer arguments and fewer panic attacks.

Table 7.3. Continued

Initial Phase	Sessions 1–2
Protecting the therapeutic relationship	On several occasions Abe blamed the therapist for jumping ahead of him and making decisions for him. Instead of pointing out to Abe the obvious transference, in which he viewed the therapist as he did his wife, the therapist listened to Abe and acknowledged his feelings. She emphasized their collaboration. **Abe**: Why are you telling me what to do here? **Therapist**: Are you angry with me? **Abe**: I am angry. You have to give me time to decide! **Therapist**: I am glad you are telling me how you feel. Thank you for telling me to slow down here. **Abe**: I don't mean to tell you how to do your job. **Therapist**: We're a team here and I can't do my job alone. I need your input.
Enhance activity	Because Abe spent so much time feeling anxious and on the verge of panic, the therapist encouraged activities that would be relaxing. Abe loved walking along the beach when he was well, so the therapist suggested that he ask his daughter and his niece to take him there on the weekends. This provided several hours of relaxation that Abe looked forward to every week. It also got him to spend more enjoyable time with his family without feeling that he wasn't meeting family obligations.

Termination Phase	Sessions 13–14
Assess remaining needs	The therapist recognized that Abe was having significantly fewer panic attacks but was still quite anxious and irritable. The use of an

(*continued*)

Table 7.3. Continued

Initial Phase	Sessions 1–2
	antidepressant medication helped to further reduce these symptoms.
Reinforce gains	In reviewing Abe's notebook, the therapist noted a significant reduction in both arguments with his wife and panic attacks, and she congratulated Abe on his progress.
	Therapist: How have you done this? **Abe**: My wife knows how I feel and she doesn't press me as much. And I let her run the things that I really can't anymore. **Therapist**: That's a huge accomplishment. I think you are ready to graduate!
Manage feelings of termination	Abe started crying during one of the last sessions, saying that he didn't know how he could have done it without the help of the therapist.
	Therapist: It's normal to feel sad at the end of therapy—but I can see that you are not panicking. You know what to do.
Avoid blaming the client	Like Abe, many older clients may not meet all treatment goals perfectly by the end of the therapy. It is important to blame the therapy rather than the client, and to keep the door open for future work together.
Future work	In the last session the therapist scheduled with Abe a series of phone calls so that she could hear how he was doing. She reviewed with him how he could reach her if he needed to, and they read over the list of strategies to reduce anxiety and panic. The therapist indicated that she would be happy to work with Abe again in the future.

Note. Based on Swartz and Markowitz (2009).

Cognitive-Behavioral Therapy

Cognitive-behavioral therapy (CBT) is one of the most widely used and best-supported forms of therapy for older clients across a wide variety of diagnoses and is particularly useful for depression and anxiety (Gallagher-Thompson & Thompson, 1996; Moss & Scogin, 2008). It is rooted in the belief that the psychological symptoms that present in therapy ultimately stem from distorted and negative thoughts and beliefs. These thoughts and beliefs tap into the basic ways in which an individual thinks about him- or herself and the surrounding environment and tend to occur automatically. An example is our client Sarah's core belief that she is an unlovable person, which she uses to explain why she has been abandoned by multiple individuals throughout her life. Although this belief does not explain reality and can be easily disproved by an outside observer, it is an unshakable aspect of reality to Sarah and it shapes not only the way she thinks about relationships but the negative emotions and dysfunctional behaviors that often erupt within them. A primary goal of CBT is to identify and change these underlying negative beliefs in order to effect change in the symptoms they produce.

There are two primary methods used to identify and challenge distorted beliefs. The first method involves taking an inventory of underlying distorted beliefs and then challenging their veracity. For example, Sarah's belief that her daughter does not love her is an example of dichotomous thinking, in which she takes an extreme position related to a deeper core belief that she is unlovable, and ignores more moderate views to the contrary. The second method is teaching mindfulness, in which clients allow themselves to become aware of certain thoughts as they arise, but in a nonjudgmental and relaxed manner. Once certain cognitive distortions are identified, mindfulness can help an individual signal to him- or herself that the thought is present and begin to adopt different compensatory responses that are more realistic and positive.

Cognitive change must be coupled with behavioral change in CBT, and there are a variety of techniques that are applicable to older clients. Relaxation techniques such as deep breathing and progressive muscle relaxation can reduce symptoms of anxiety. Behavioral tasks and homework assignments help structure the therapy by helping the client plan out specific activities that can put changed feelings and thoughts into action. One example is exposing the individual to phobic situations in a gradual manner in order to slowly reduce the fear response. Another example is scheduling pleasant activities and having the individual rate his or her mood before and after and take note of the effect (Wyman et al., 2006).

Dialectical behavior therapy, or DBT, is a form of CBT that was developed initially for individuals with borderline personality disorder but has been adapted for elderly individuals with depression (Lynch, Morse, Mendelson, & Robins, 2003). DBT focuses on making clients mindful of both the triggers and consequences of maladaptive behaviors and then teaching them strategies to avoid them (Livesly, 2002).

Sarah presented with changes in mood and behavior that suggest a diagnosis of a recurrent MDD. Although she had true pain and physical disability, these symptoms were exaggerated by her underlying mood disorder, and they impeded optimal rehabilitation. Her difficulty adjusting to the assisted living facility stemmed in part from her unrealistic hope that she could return to live with her younger daughter, Rebecca, coupled with the belief that Rebecca did not love her, just as her husband and mother did not love her. She felt that her roommate disliked her and only sought to take advantage of her. An increasingly depressed mood led Sarah to withdraw from most activities.

After an initial evaluation, the therapist met with Sarah and oriented her to therapy by explaining the basic process of CBT, the use of homework, and the goal of bringing about change in 10 to 20 sessions. They began by talking about Sarah's frustrations with her daughter, and then the therapist worked with Sarah to challenge her underlying cognitive distortions, as outlined in Table 7.4. Once these negative beliefs were identified, Sarah's weekly homework was to keep a tally of how often she had each thought, thus promoting mindfulness.

The second phase of CBT with Sarah involved promoting some more positive and pleasant activities to lift her mood and make her feel more loved. The therapist arranged for Sarah to work with a pet therapist and receive unconditional love from a large and friendly dog that visited every week. Sarah rated her mood before and after each visit and was surprised to see the dramatic improvement, even if short lived. Because one of Sarah's strengths was her ability to speak in public, one homework assignment was to attend the residents' council meeting at the facility. Sarah spoke so beautifully at the meeting that she was later elected council president. This was an incredibly gratifying experience that challenged her core belief that she was unlovable. Finally, the therapist worked with Sarah to help her realize that her roommate's isolative behaviors had nothing to do with her. Once she stopped taking her roommate's behaviors so personally, she was able to feel compassion for her rommate and stop feeling so unloved.

Table 7.4. Sarah's List of Cognitive Distortions

Cognitive Distortion	Challenge
"My daughter hates me." *Dichotomous thinking: viewing one's experience in an extreme way while ignoring more moderate possibilities* Underlying core belief: "Nobody has ever loved me."	• Rebecca told Sarah on many occasions that she loved her. • Sarah was asked to bring into the session the many beautiful cards sent by her daughter and read them aloud. • Sarah was asked to imagine her daughter having an alternate, more moderate thought: "I am frustrated caring for a mother and young children at the same time."
"My roommate doesn't care about me." *Personalization: assuming that certain unrelated events have personal meaning* Sarah based her statement on her observations that her roommate sometimes didn't want to talk to her.	• More detailed questioning about the roommate revealed that she was often in pain and did not feel like talking to anyone at those times. • The therapist strategized about ways that Sarah could express her concern without expecting any significant conversation in return.
"My back pain is crippling." *Magnification: exaggerating the importance or extent of an event*	• Sarah was given homework to keep a rating of her pain and activity level twice daily. After a few days she was able to see that she actually experienced less pain on the days she was physically active

Note. Based on Clark, Hollifield, Leahy, and Beck (2009).

Abe's main presenting symptoms were anxiety and panic attacks. Given their severity, the therapist's first goal was to educate Abe about how the body changes during a panic attack, to help him become more mindful of the automatic physiological reaction. Abe was then taught relaxation techniques involving slow, deep breathing and progressive muscle relaxation. These techniques were key, because he initially refused medication. Because Abe had some memory impairment, he was provided with relaxation tapes using verbal instructions and guided imagery to cue him on what to do. As Abe learned to use these techniques, the therapist explored with him two key cognitive distortions and ways to counter them, outlined in Table 7.5.

Problem-Solving Therapy

Problem-solving therapy, or PST (and its variant for primary care settings, labeled PST-PC), is a well-established form of therapy with some similarities to CBT that has been used to treat older individuals with depression (Areán, 2009; Areán et al., 1993). It is based on the premise that depression is related in part to faulty decision-making and coping skills in the face of stress (Nezu, Nezu, & Perri, 1989). For older clients, these difficulties may be acquired or lifelong, but either way, they feed into a loss of self-confidence and hope. They are exacerbated by cognitive impairment, especially when it affects executive functions such as the ability to prioritize, organize, and motivate oneself to act. Each step of the therapy outlined in Table 7.6 is designed to counteract these deficits, regardless of the cause, although their ultimate success requires at least moderate cognitive integrity.

PST involves training and problem solving and is held in weekly 50-minute sessions over at least 12 weeks, although in PST-PC the training is held in one session and then the therapy involves six to eight biweekly 30-minute sessions (Wyman et al., 2006). Adaptations to PST for some clients may involve shorter sessions and a more truncated course, depending on the extent of the depression and specific problems identified. Individuals with cognitive impairment require more active intervention by the therapist and more written materials. One approach for these cognitively impaired clients may be to fast-

Table 7.5. Abe's List of Cognitive Distortions

Cognitive Distortion	Challenge
"A prescription pill may kill me." *Arbitrary inference: making a conclusion without evidence or in the face of contradictory information* Underlying core belief: "Pills are evil (since they killed my son)."	• Without directly challenging Abe's theory and grief about the loss of his son, the therapist reviewed the risks versus benefits of various medications, providing reassurance about the use of low doses. • The therapist and Abe made a list of "no go" medications and then a list of medications that he might consider taking for anxiety. • Abe took a single dose of an anti-anxiety pill in the presence of the therapist, and they scored his anxiety level before and after, along with his pulse and blood pressure, to show him how safe the pill was. • Abe was allowed to find a "friendly" pill based on new evidence that he had not considered in the past.
"Financially, I'm ruined." *Selective abstraction: highlighting one detail to the exclusion of other more pertinent ones* Abe only considered the overall stock market index without keeping in mind his complete list of assets.	• The therapist asked Abe to provide an inventory of how the stock market drop affected his major asset categories. By doing this, he realized that most of them were secure. • The therapist and Abe together wrote up a brief "safe" portfolio that he could look at to remind himself that he was still financially secure. • Relaxation techniques were used before and during these reviews to build up an association between a state of relaxation and thinking about his financial affairs.

Note. Based on Clark et al. (2009).

Table 7.6. Six Steps of Problem-Solving Therapy

Step	Description
Problem orientation	Provide education about depression and orientation to how PST works. Help clients to see problems as discrete, solvable issues.
Problem definition	Select a specific realistic problem to be addressed, break down a larger problem into discrete units, or identify an achievable goal amid a seemingly insurmountable problem.
Brainstorming	Think broadly, creatively, and nonjudgmentally about five to 10 possible solutions to the problem, in order to begin overcoming resistance and hopelessness.
Decision making	Review each decision to consider how practical it is, review pros and cons, and estimate its impact on others. Then select a solution to try.
Planning	Review and list what needs to be done for the selected solution.
Implementation	Put the plan into action.
Solution verification	After attempting the solution, the client reviews with the therapist the relative success or failure of the plan.

References: Areán (2009) and Wyman et al. (2006).

track planning and implementation so as to improve motivation and provide rapid gratification for their abilities (Areán, 2009).

Older clients typically have many more practical constraints that may interfere with their ability to engage in PST, including limited finances, transportation and mobility issues, limited caregiver assistance, and physical disability. The therapist must be prepared to play a case management role in many of these situations to improve the chances for success. Having ancillary services available (e.g., transportation service, home health aide agency, nurse-practitioner) may facilitate the process. Therapists should also remember that regardless of the outcome of a solution for a specific problem, the process of working with a therapist can have enormous benefits in terms of the therapist-client relationship.

> During the initial meeting with Sarah, it was clear that she felt overwhelmed and hopeless about changing her situation. She identified her main problems as not being able to walk, not being able to live with her daughter, and not being able to stop her older daughter's substance abuse. Clearly there were no feasible solutions to any of these problems, as one of them involved a permanent physical problem and two of them involved changing the lives of two people other than Sarah. The therapist asked Sarah to focus at first on something less daunting. Sarah decided that if she couldn't actually live with Rebecca, she at least wanted to have more contact with her. The six steps of PST that followed are outlined in Table 7.7.

Reminiscence Therapy

There are many antidotes to the dehumanizing aspects of aging, and one of the most powerful involves asking clients not only about their symptoms but about their lives as well (Agronin, 2007b). Simple questions concerning where they grew up, what sort of work they did, what their interests are, and the state of their relationships, among many other types of questions, can lead to a deeper understanding of and appreciation for their strengths and weaknesses. This exploration, whether done in a few minutes or over the course of an hour, signals to clients that someone is truly listening to them, and that their symptoms, like their lives, have some meaning to the therapist. These questions also prompt the client to engage the key memory function of reminiscence, defined as "the act

Table 7.7. Six Steps of Problem-Solving Therapy for Sarah

Step	Therapy
Problem orientation	Sarah's initial problems could not be solved and the therapist talked about her grief over losses of physical abilities and independence. However, the therapist redirected Sarah to the fact that there might be aspects of her insurmountable problems that could be improved upon.
Problem definition	Sarah decided to identify the main problem as not having enough contact with her daughter—as opposed to the problem of not living with her daughter.
Brainstorming	Sarah and the therapist talked about the following potential solutions:

1. Establish an agreed-upon time to talk with her daughter every week.
2. Write letters to her daughter.
3. Learn to write e-mails to her daughter.
4. Get a cell phone and learn to send text messages.
5. Sell her furniture and use the money to hire a driver to take her to visit her daughter.
6. Learn to use the handicapped bus service to visit her daughter.

Decision making	Sarah reviewed each potential solution with the therapist and came to the following conclusions:

1. Sarah didn't think her daughter could be relied on to always be available, as she had two small children to care for, and missed calls would increase her frustration.
2. Letters were too impersonal.
3. Sarah had never used a computer before and worried about getting regular access to the computer room, because she was in a wheelchair. She also thought e-mails were no better than written letters.

(continued)

Table 7.7. Continued

Step	Therapy
	4. Sarah didn't want to spend money on a cell phone for texting that she wouldn't otherwise use.
	5. Sarah thought this made the most sense because it allowed for face-to-face contact and would permit her to be flexible to accommodate her daughter's schedule.
	6. Sarah thought that the handicapped bus service would not take her as far as her daughter's house.
	In the end Sarah selected #5 as the most practical and satisfactory solution.
Planning	Sarah and the therapist devised the following list of tasks for Sarah:
	1. Speak to her daughter about the plan to see if she was agreeable to such visits.
	2. Ask her daughter to remove the furniture from storage that she wanted before selling the rest.
	3. Offer to pay her son-in-law part of the proceeds from the furniture sale if he would help her.
	3. Select a publication in which to advertise her furniture for sale.
	4. Contact the publication and its Web site to learn about how she might sell the furniture.
	5. Place ads for the sale.
	6. Work out an arrangement with her son-in-law to negotiate a price if a buyer was interested.
	7. Set up a checking account for the money.
	8. Hire a driver.
Implementation	Sarah placed ads on Craig's List and within days had several interested buyers. Her son-in-law screened the calls and ended up showing and then selling her furniture to several buyers, including a college student, a young family mov-

Table 7.7. Continued

Step	Therapy
	ing into a new house, and an antique dealer. She earned a total of $3,600, of which she paid her son-in-law $600 for his help. Sarah then hired as her driver a retired man who agreed to take her to and from her daughter's house twice a month for $100/trip. Sarah had enough money to pay for 30 trips, which she realized would cover nearly 2 years' worth of visits.
Solution verification	After her first visit to her daughter's house, Sarah met with the therapist and expressed elation at how smoothly it went. Sarah got to spend some relaxing and enjoyable time with her daughter, who was much calmer because she didn't have to worry about the transportation issue taking time away from her responsibilities at home. Sarah stated that the regular visits had lifted her spirits and made her feel less depressed. It also gave her confidence that she could solve other problems.

or process of recollecting past experiences or events" ("Reminiscence," 2009).

On another level, reminiscence lays the basis for what Robert Butler described as "the universal occurrence in older people of an inner experience or mental process of reviewing one's life" (1963, p. 12). Butler felt strongly that this life review process is both natural and healthy and can help aging individuals revisit and come to terms with unresolved conflicts. Tapping into remote memories and long-held beliefs as well as current thoughts and self-observations can provide an individual with a sense of continuity and strength, especially during times of rapid change or loss. Under ideal conditions, life review holds the promise of bringing increased "candor, serenity, and wisdom among certain of the aged" (Butler, 1963, p. 12).

The process of life review is facilitated by several factors in late life. First, individuals may have more time for self-reflection and greater motivation to think about past experiences. Second, there is the development of postformal thinking, through which aging adults acquire the ability to examine and balance the needs of competing relationships, systems, or perspectives (see Chapter 1 for a full discussion). Reminiscence therapy (RT) thrives on this expanded view of reality that allows for greater patience, acceptance, and pragmatism with complex situations, whether present or past.

Although RT is not used as commonly as other modalities, its use in a group format does have some evidence-based support (Areán et al., 1993; Hsieh & Wang, 2003). The process of reminiscence itself is also often used as part of other therapeutic modalities such as psychodynamic psychotherapy and CBT (Watt & Cappeliez, 1995). Typically based on Erikson's eight stages of development, RT involves asking the client to recall experiences and conflicts from previous stages of life (sometimes prompted by audiovisual materials, props, or personal items such as clothing or photographs) in order to revisit how he or she faced and resolved them. In turn, reminiscence therapy can help some individuals in achieving Erikson's eighth-stage strength of integrity or Vaillant's fifth development task of becoming a Keeper of the Meaning.

When using RT, whether alone or as part of any other therapeutic modality, therapists should keep in mind that reminiscence can reactivate traumatic memories and even trigger depression in some older clients. A review of one's life may only highlight mistakes or losses. It may be rendered useless by denial of one's past, by distorted or even grandiose recollections, or by memory loss. Other individuals may be able to acknowledge past transgressions but feel hopeless about the possibility for forgiveness. In *The Life Cycle Completed*, Erik and Joan Erikson described how still other individuals are too paralyzed by daily life to even engage in the process:

> In one's eighties and nineties one may no longer have the luxury of such retrospective despair. Loss of capacities and disintegration may demand almost all of one's attention. One's focus may become thoroughly circumscribed by concerns of daily functioning so that it is enough just to get through a day intact, however satisfied or dissatisfied one feels about one's previous life history. Of course despair in response to these more immediate and acute events is compounded by earlier self and life evaluations. (1997, p. 113)

What the Eriksons offered in response is exactly what the therapist has: a sense of trust that can be enlivened within the therapeutic encounter. As Rhonda Parker (1995) emphasized, life review is not intended to be a solo trek but is meant to be shared, guided, and even shaped within the context of a relationship.

The therapist who met with Abe suggested that he participate in a reminiscence group but he refused, stating that he did not like to share his problems with others and was afraid of having a panic attack in front of them. He agreed to meet individually, and the therapist decided to use RT to help Abe tap into life events that might help him understand the origin of his symptoms and dormant strengths that might prove therapeutic. Using Erikson's developmental stages, Abe and the therapist reviewed the memories described in Table 7.8.

Table 7.8. Reminiscence Therapy With Abe

Erikson Stage	*Reminiscence*
Trust versus mistrust (infancy)	Abe recalled accounts of his mother being depressed and having a very difficult time breast-feeding him. He reflected on how he never felt any warmth from his mother and viewed her as a dysfunctional person.
Autonomy versus shame, doubt (early childhood)	Abe had only one memory from this time, which was an image of himself throwing a gift from his aunt and uncle at them because it was a stuffed animal that frightened him. Many years later this same aunt and uncle, furious at him for leaving the family business, labeled him an ungrateful nephew and accused him of throwing temper tantrums with the family just as he did as a child. He saw himself as very anxious and speculated that his depressed mother provided little direction while his father was working all the time. He saw himself as an abandoned and overwhelmed little boy who had to learn to do things on his own.
Initiative versus guilt (play age)	Abe extended his need to do things for himself into his play stage, recalling that he always played alone and would get very nervous whenever other kids came over. He recalled getting a beating from his father after he hid all his toys from his cousins when they came to visit. He recalled feeling even worse when his grandfather scolded him for being selfish. But at the same time he recalled feeling vindicated after being forced to bring out his toys and finding several of them broken by his cousins. He later brought a broken toy to his father and threw it at his feet and re-

Table 7.8. Continued

Erikson Stage	Reminiscence
	membered his father looking astonished at his son's audacity.
Industry versus inferiority (school age)	Abe recalled being a very serious and nervous overachiever in school who made his parents very proud with his schoolwork but refused to ever let them help him. He became a leader at school but recalled getting terrible stomachaches every morning before class. However, he kept his pain hidden from his parents.
Identity versus role diffusion (adolescence)	Abe always assumed that he would take over his father's business and began working there in high school while continuing to be a star pupil. Although he saw his father as ineffective at home, he began to model his own behavior after his father's ferocious demeanor at work, even bullying relatives who worked with him. Abe had very few close friends and assumed the role of a forceful leader more than that of a peer.
Intimacy versus isolation (young adulthood)	Abe was in his mid-20s when the family business was confiscated and they had to flee Cuba. He remembered with great bitterness and disappointment that he was abruptly separated from several women whom he was courting and felt that he was never able to recreate the status he had in Cuba, which attracted so many women. The stress of the move on Abe and his family took a toll on his father, and Abe felt that he had to prematurely assume a leadership role in the new business venture. He recalled with pride his ability to guide the family through the

(continued)

Table 7.8. Continued

Erikson Stage	Reminiscence
	ordeal but also remembered having panic attacks when he first came to Miami without the wealth they had previously enjoyed. He felt alone and did not pursue any friendships or romantic involvements for several years after the move.
Generativity versus stagnation (adulthood)	Abe was a successful businessman in part because of his take-no-prisoners attitude and workaholic style. He made a lot of money but also ended up angering and alienating much of his family, including his son, whom he drove incessantly to do better. As long as Abe was busy with work, he felt productive and in control. The death of his son was a crushing blow to his dream of passing along his business acumen, but he had for years ignored or denied his son's substance abuse. He dealt with his grief by blaming others for failing his son and by throwing himself even more ferociously into his work.
Integrity versus despair (old age)	Abe's life came to a crashing halt, in his view, when he had a stroke that left him cognitively impaired and physically disabled. He could no longer work or run things at home and had to move into a nursing home because his wife did not feel able to meet his needs at home. Abe now had a difficult time in the moment because of his anger and frustration with day-to-day tasks, especially when his wife was present. It was extremely difficult for him to feel a sense of wholeness or pride in his accomplishments because he felt so inadequate.

Couples and Family Therapy

Caregivers and informants frequently play a necessary role in work with older clients. These roles expand as older clients face increasing dependence resulting from frailty, physical disability, and cognitive impairment. At the same time, many of these caregivers face their own age-related challenges and mental health issues, sometimes as a direct result of the demands of caregiving. As a result, therapists may need to offer assistance to clients' spouses, partners, or other family members. Although the scope of this book does not allow for a detailed description of the wide range of therapeutic modalities for both couples and families, there are a number of critical points to be emphasized.

There are two frameworks that are particularly relevant to clinical work with couples and families. The first is a family systems orientation, which posits that the clinical problems of an individual have a larger context within a family. Emotions and behaviors in one individual influence and are influenced by family members in unique and telling ways, and this entire system must be seen as well within the context of the shared beliefs, cultural norms, and historical moment of a particular society. The second framework involves features of intergenerational relationships that create conflict, including conflicts over family loyalties and assumed obligations; feelings of entitlement to care, attention, or assets; demands for balance and fairness among family members; and the resultant legacy of unresolved issues or reactions to them carried into successive generations (Nagy & Spark, 1973). Couples and family members compete along these lines within and between generations, with the increased needs of the oldest family members imposing particular stresses (McEwan, 1987).

Consider Abe's family dynamics. His father ran a successful business in Cuba that was shared by his siblings. The Cuban revolution created a schism in society that stripped Abe's family of their assets and forced them to flee the country. The scarce financial resources that the family initially had in the United States, coupled with the tremendous loss of lifestyle and status, was a blow to each and every family member, and this led to tensions as they tried to resurrect their previous success. Abe's split from his uncles and cousins created extreme enmity in the family and deprived him of support from both relatives and the larger Cuban émigré community. The belief among many of his cousins that he had betrayed the family and unfairly amassed wealth led to jealousy and conflict, which prompted some of Abe's underlying anxiety and distrust.

The legacy of these conflicts played out in Abe's relationship with his son, whom he drove mercilessly to be successful in order to reclaim his place in the family. Abe's poor relationships with several grandchildren and the resultant lack of support in his later years can be traced to these same conflicts. Of course, not every family or individual would react the same way to such historical trauma. In addition, family dynamics must be coupled with individual personalities and behaviors in order to enable a full understanding of the course of any given family member.

For many older individuals, the transition between roles can be the trigger for larger family strife. When a parent has a debilitating physical, cognitive, or mental illness, the family must compensate by providing care (versus engaging in neglect) and assigning members to fill the fully or partially vacant role. In Abe's family, his stroke imposed an extreme stress on his wife and daughter and led to the main conflicts that presaged Abe's symptoms. Sometimes a genogram can be useful for visualizing the relationships between family members, whereas a time line can plot the progression of events and suggest causality (Rolland & Walsh, 2009). An analysis of this information may reveal certain family narratives that are driving much of the conflict—such as rigid and burdensome demands for loyalty and obligation that are driven by generations of familial, cultural, and even societal forces. Family members who can come to recognize these forces, express their feelings about them, and receive some acknowledgement from other family members and the therapist might then be able to adapt and even rewrite the narratives in a more harmonious way. A sample genogram for Abe's family can be found in Figure 7.1.

Techniques With Challenging Clients

All the therapeutic techniques discussed in this chapter have been demonstrated to be both practical and efficacious for older clients, particularly for cognitively intact individuals with depression. In practice, though, many therapists end up combining elements from two or more modalities. They also have to adapt the therapies to account for cognitive impairment, nondepressive diagnoses, gaps in treatment due to illness or other interruptions, and the involvement of caregivers and other informants.

Two major challenges with older clients that pose significant resistance to therapy are clients' lack of insight into the underlying problem or disorder and the pervasive stigma of mental illness. Lack of insight might be related to poor education about mental illness, denial, or brain trauma–induced anosognosia. Stigma is a more insidious problem. The existing cohort of older clients did not grow up in an era when psycho-

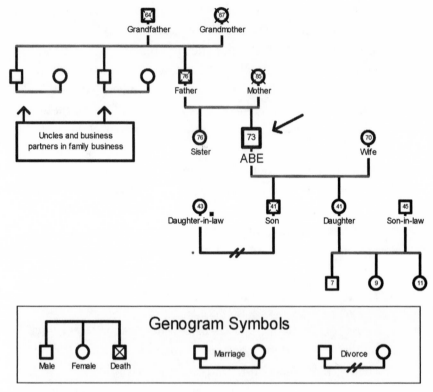

Figure 7.1. Abe's genogram.

therapy was widely used. Psychiatric treatment was associated with insanity, the need to be "locked away," or frightening treatments such as shock therapy while the client was awake, insulin coma therapy, and frontal lobotomies. As a result, the therapist must spend extra time educating both clients and caregivers about to the nature of psychotherapy, the roles of each participant, and the rules of confidentiality.

In addition, there are several types of very challenging clients who may defy the typical confines of therapy:

- Clients brought to therapy under duress by a caregiver or in a long-term care institution.
- Clients with severe or debilitating psychiatric symptoms.
- Clients with organic impairment such as impulsivity, mood lability, or personality changes.
- Clients with cognitive impairment.
- Clients with severe PDs, chronic mood or psychotic disorders, or treatment-resistant symptoms.
- Clients with severe substance use disorders.

For all the aforementioned client types, an effective and comfortable approach may be supportive psychotherapy, which is aimed at providing a consistent and structured setting through the use of a variety of techniques. The therapist adopts a conversational style and engages in interested and empathic listening without excessive probing or attention to issues of transference or unconscious motivation. Provision of ample praise, reassurance, and encouragement can bolster the client's self-esteem, and this is coupled with efforts to reduce anxiety and teach more adaptive skills in order to enhance ego function (Rosenthal, 2009). Supportive therapy is particularly useful for skeptical or resistant older clients who expect to be probed and judged; they are often surprised and gratified by a therapist who simply wants to listen in a friendly manner and expresses a desire to help. Once the client has been acclimated to therapy and a therapeutic alliance is established, the therapist may be able to utilize more active interventions.

For individuals with severe or disruptive symptoms, sessions may need to be shorter, more focused, and flexible, with appropriate limit setting. Consider how the therapist responds to Abe when, during a panic attack, Abe cries out: "Why the hell am I here? I can't stand it now—oh, oh—I need help! What are you doing to help me? Take me out of here!" and pounds his hands on the desk, knocking off some papers.

At this point the therapist could choose to end the session and give Abe some time to relax, perhaps with the help of an antianxiety medication. Or he or she could try to set limits and work through the attack.

> **Therapist:** Abe, I'm here to help. Tell me what's wrong.
>
> **Abe:** Oh, I feel so terrible! The panic is on me, help!
>
> **Therapist:** Abe, I'm here to help you. Try taking a slow deep breath now. I know you can do it.
>
> **Abe:** I can't, I can't!
>
> **Therapist:** What would be helpful now?
>
> **Abe:** I need some space!

The therapist then allows Abe to sit outside for a few minutes, all the while teaching him to use relaxation techniques. A similar approach may be needed with clients who are in pain or are severely fatigued and cannot keep awake. Recurrent problems with physical discomfort may require some liaison with the client's caregiver or health care professional to provide symptomatic relief prior to the appointment (e.g., using an analgesic or an inhaler).

For most clients, but particularly those with persistent or severe psychiatric symptoms, psychotherapy is routinely combined with psychopharmacologic treatment administered by the therapist if he or she is a psychiatrist or a psychiatric nurse-practitioner. The advantage of combining these two approaches is that they can work synergistically to reduce symptoms and accelerate the process of recovery. With Abe, for example, the use of an antidepressant to eliminate his panic attacks allowed him to work in a calmer and more organized fashion on coping with his physical disability and improving his relationship with his wife. Some individuals such as those with vegetative depressive symptoms, psychosis, or agitation may not even be able to effectively participate in therapy until medications have provided sufficient improvement. Every therapist should have an understanding of the major classes of medications, several of the major players within each class, their uses, and major side effects. A practical summary can be found in Table 7.9.

Older clients with chronic severe or debilitating symptoms or even treatment-resistant symptoms such as those found with organic or dementia-related impulsivity or mood lability, severe PDs, and chronic psychotic disorders such as schizophrenia are sometimes poor candidates for therapy. The combination of any of these disorders with dementia and medical illness can seem overwhelming and hopeless to the therapist. Still, therapy can play a vital role in terms of the formation of therapeutic alliances, provision of outlets for venting and basic psychoeducation, increased socialization, mental stimulation and soothing, and enhancement of coping skills through modeling by the therapist and shaping of the environment.

More important than the content of therapy for many of these individuals is the presence of the therapist. In his capacity as a caregiver for his brother, the author Jay Neugeboren found that sometimes the most important factor in symptomatic reduction can be "a relationship with a human being . . . who say[s], in effect, 'I believe in your ability to recover, and I am going to stay with you until you do'" (2006, p. 17). Such an approach can often transcend the role of medications and structured settings because it provides a basis for trust and hope that is accessible by even the most severely impaired individuals.

Table 7.9. Common Psychopharmacologic Agents for Older Clients and Their Uses and Side Effects

Class of Medication	Specific Agents	Uses	Most Common Side Effects
Antianxiety medications	Benzodiazepines • Alprazolam (Xanax) • Diazepam (Valium) • Lorazepam (Ativan) • Clonazepam (Klonopin)	• Acute and chronic anxiety and panic • Agitation • Insomnia	• Sedation • Dizziness • Unsteadiness/falls • Confusion
Antidepressants	Selective serotonin reuptake inhibitors ➤ Fluoxetine (Prozac) ➤ Sertraline (Zoloft) ➤ Paroxetine (Paxil, Pexeva) ➤ Citalopram (Celexa) ➤ Escitalopram (Lexapro) • Serotonin-norepinephrine reuptake inhibitors ➤ Venlafaxine (Effexor) ➤ Desvenlafaxine (Pristiq) ➤ Mirtazapine (Remeron) • Duloxetine (Cymbalta) • Bupropion (Wellbutrin) • Tricyclic antidepressants	• Depressive disorders • Anxiety disorders • Impulse control disorders • Eating disorders • PTSD • Obsessive-compulsive disorder	• Nervousness • Agitation • GI disturbances (nausea, stomach-ache, diarrhea) • Headache • Weight gain • Sexual side effects • Sedation • Insomnia

Category	Drugs	Uses	Side effects
Mood stabilizers	Valproic acid (Depakote) Carbamazepine (Tegretol) Lamotrigine (Lamictal) Also see *Antipsychotics*	• Bipolar disorder • Agitation • Impulse control disorders	• Sedation • Dizziness • Unsteadiness • Confusion • Liver dysfunction • Skin rashes
Antipsychotics	• Conventional/typical antipsychotics ➤ Haloperidol (Haldol) ➤ Fluphenazine (Prolixin) ➤ Perphenazine (Trilafon) ➤ Trifluoperazine (Stelazine) ➤ Thiothixene (Navane) ➤ Chlorpromazine (Thorazine) ➤ Thioridazine (Mellaril) • Atypical antipsychotics ➤ Clozapine (Clozaril) ➤ Risperidone (Risperdal) ➤ Olanzapine (Zyprexa) ➤ Quetiapine (Seroquel) ➤ Aripiprazole (Abilify) ➤ Ziprasidone (Geodon)	• Psychosis • Schizophrenia • Delusional disorder • Delirium • Agitation	• Sedation • Muscle stiffness • Tremor • Abnormal movements or spasms • Drooling • Restlessness (akathisia) • Sexual dysfunction • Weight gain • Increases in glucose and lipid levels • Blood pressure drops

(continued)

Table 7.9. Continued

Class of Medication	Specific Agents	Uses	Most Common Side Effects
Sedative hypnotics/ sleeping pills	• Temazepam (Restoril) • Zolpidem (Ambien) • Eszopiclone (Lunesta) • Zaleplon (Sonata) • Ramelteon (Rozerem) • Trazodone (Desyrel)	• Insomnia	• Sedation • Dizziness • Unsteadiness/falls • Confusion

Cognitive enhancers	• Acetylcholinesterase inhibitors
	  ➤ Donepezil (Aricept)
	  ➤ Rivastigmine (Exelon)
	  ➤ Galantamine (Razadyne)
	• Glutamate (NMDA) receptor antagonists
	  ➤ Memantine (Namenda)
		• Alzheimer's disease
		• Dementia due to Parkinson's disease
			• GI disturbances (nausea, vomiting, diarrhea)
			• Weight loss
			• Slowed heart rate
			• Increased pulmonary secretions
			• Nightmares
			• Confusion

Note. This list is *not* meant to provide treatment guidelines for any particular client or disease and is *not* a complete list of all agents, uses, and potential side effects. It is solely intended to show some of the most widely used agents and their properties for older clients. The common uses listed for the various agents are not restricted to indications approved by the Food and Drug Administration. Several of the agents listed are generally contraindicated for use in older individuals, especially in long-term care settings. There are additional side effects not listed above, including several serious ones for which the FDA has issued specific warnings.

Older clients with severe substance use disorders are best directed initially to detox programs, substance abuse counseling, and 12-step programs before any form of psychotherapy can be useful. Otherwise the effects of the substance will distort the underlying psychopathology (e.g., causing de novo anxiety or depression or making preexisting symptoms significantly worse), obscure the case formulation, and significantly disrupt and reverse any potential gains of therapy.

Final Points of Wisdom

In the introduction I suggested that there are three key virtues that serve the therapist well—curiosity, caring, and courage. Translated into therapy, these virtues drive a sincere interest in and concern for the older client and a willingness to persevere through many challenges. Although these are broad suggestions, they can be supplemented by several more detailed and specific points of wisdom for the therapist, regardless of the client profile or the form of therapy. These points include the following:

- There are as many strengths as there are weaknesses in the cognitive, emotional, and psychosocial realms of the older client, and we are too programmed to seek out the weaknesses and pathology without recognizing, encouraging, and celebrating those elements that, in the end, carry the day with successful therapy.
- Despite the best of intentions, the devil is always in the details when one is conducting therapy with older clients, as small issues—ranging from not being able to get a ride to the session to feeling achy or constipated to not liking the receptionist—can completely disrupt and derail ther-

apy. These "devils" occur as forms of resistance across the life span, but in older clients they are less often unconsciously motivated and more often actual facts. They require a proactive style on the part of the therapist.

- For many older clients, although not all, the pace of therapy is slower than with younger clients, and the therapist needs to be more active and less reflective.
- Time is short and what isn't resolved soon may never be. To borrow a cliché from pharmacologic management of the older client, "Go slow, but *go*."
- Hope does spring eternal. Death is rarely the central concern of most older clients; instead, these clients are yearning for resolution of some very mundane issues, which will bring tremendous improvement in well-being.
- It is neither the content nor the process that ultimately proves healing for many older clients, but the sustained presence of a caring and concerned therapist.
- Be open to surprises. When all possibilities seem exhausted and little hope is left, do not give up.

These points of wisdom are ways to appreciate the gifts of age, to truly honor one's elders, and to advance the ethic of care as an antidote to the indifference and disdain for the aged that is so commonplace.

8

STRENGTH IN NUMBERS: GROUP PSYCHOTHERAPY

Several years ago I received a book in the mail titled *An Exaltation of Larks* written by James Lipton (1977). This wonderful volume is a compendium of names for groups of animals and professions, including well-known terms such as a *gaggle* of geese and lesser-known ones such as a *leap* of leopards or the eponymous *exaltation* of larks. Lipton's book was sent to me by the daughter of a client to express both gratitude and, I am certain, an endorsement of a certain therapeutic approach. In that situation I had worked with not only an elderly man living with severe anxiety and depression but his entire family unit. The collective efforts yielded much success, more than I alone could have accomplished. And that was the point: A group (or a gaggle or a leap!) has unique and often unexpected properties. I have also seen this phenomenon quite clearly in a group program for older women with early-stage memory disorders. When seen individually in the clinic, each woman is timid, anxious, and completely exposed in her cognitive deficits. After all, the goals of clinic visits are to probe the progression of the disorder. In a group, however, these same women are able to transcend their memory loss by supporting one another and engaging in activities that empower them, such as laughter, creativity, and socialization. A visit to this group and its dynamic, stimulating, and *fun* atmosphere truly reveals that there is strength in numbers.

This principle applies well to many older clients, suggesting that group therapy may be able to provide benefits not available from individual work alone. Consider the following case vignette.

Frieda was an 84-year-old woman who was seen repeatedly in an outpatient medical clinic for complaints of headache and fatigue. After several years of failed attempts to improve her symptoms, she was referred for psychological evaluation and therapy. During her first session, she was quite clear with the therapist. "My problems all start here," she said, pointing to a spot in the back of her head where her pain centered, and then insisting, "But it's not depression!" For several sessions Frieda engaged the therapist in lengthy discussions about what depression was, each time arguing that she did not have it. It was clear from her symptoms, however, that Frieda was living with considerable depression and anxiety, stemming in part from her personal history. Frieda had grown up in Poland before World War II and had had, by her own description, a rather idyllic childhood. At the outbreak of the war in 1939, however, Frieda fled with her brothers into Russia to escape the advancing German army, knowing that their Jewishness would put them at grave risk. The small band of teenagers was arrested by the Russian authorities and sent to Siberian labor camps for several years, and their entire remaining family in Poland was murdered by the Germans. Within the blink of an eye, it seemed, her entire world disappeared. After her release from the labor camp, Frieda walked several thousand miles across Russia, eventually reuniting with a brother. Later they were able to come to the United States. She had one brief failed marriage but never married again or had children. Although Frieda would discuss these traumatic events, she often used them to denigrate being older and living in an assisted living facility, arguing, quite incredibly, that her current situation was actually *worse* than the gulag!

Her first therapist felt that Frieda was not getting better and referred her to a psychiatrist for antidepressant therapy. Although she reluctantly agreed to try medication, Frieda continued to insist that she was not actually depressed and would persistently engage the doctor in endless arguments about whether she actually had depression. She failed multiple medication trials, each time complaining of major side effects after only a few doses and then refusing to continue taking the medication. Over the years Frieda engaged in a similar pattern with successive therapists, begging for help with headaches but then resisting therapy, all the while feeling victimized by the way in which she was labeled depressed (Agronin, 2007c).

In Frieda's case, there were clear elements of depression, anxiety, and post-traumatic stress all stemming from unresolved grief from World War II but accompanied by the accumulation of many other intrapsychic conflicts in the ensuing years. Eventually, one frustrated therapist decided that individual therapy was not working because Frieda continually resisted the singular authority and clinical labeling that came along with it. The therapist took note of Frieda's strengths: she loved singing in a choir at her assisted living facility and was quite sociable with certain other residents. Perhaps a group could provide a more active form of therapy that would bring positive attention to Frieda's strengths along with the chance to give something to others.

The Goals and Types of Group Therapy

Although the main activities of group therapy with older clients vary, depending on the type of group and its makeup, the central goal is always to provide some degree of peer-to-peer interaction. Such interactions allow group members to share their own problems and perspectives, hear from others, and get direct feedback on both the content of the group discussions and its process. Common age-specific issues that arise include illness, disability, losses of loved ones, changes in role, and increased dependency on others. Hearing other group members give voice to their own struggles provides some degree of normalization for issues that previously brought stigmatization and isolation. Group discussions afford the opportunity for individuals to provide support and constructive feedback to others, generating a sense of altruism and usefulness (Wyman et al., 2006). Ideally, such interactions can help to build self-esteem, interpersonal skills, social connections, and self-understanding (Leszcz, 2004). They can also stimulate and sharpen cognitive skills (Agronin, 2009a).

There are several different types of group therapy for older clients, varying by the structure of activities, the focus and form of therapy, and the cognitive level of group members. On one side of the spectrum are highly structured groups that provide orientation exercises and therapeutic activities for individuals with cognitive impairment. Such groups are often found in long-term care facilities and day care programs. On the other extreme are loosely structured groups that either focus on a particular issue or are open ended, and without a particular therapeutic bent. Support groups for caregivers, newly bereaved individuals, and those with a particular disease such as Parkinson's are examples. These groups might have at least one facilitator and are sometimes run by individual members. There are also highly structured groups with an insight-oriented or cognitive-behavioral bent that require members to be relatively cognitively intact. An example would be a dialectical behavioral therapy, or DBT, group developed for older individuals with depression (Lynch et al., 2003). The other group types are:

- Reality orientation (for individuals with cognitive impairment).
- Activity focused (e.g., music therapy, exercise, pet therapy).
- Educational (e.g., focusing on a specific disease management skill).
- Supportive (e.g., bereavement, caregivers, disease specific).
- Reminiscence or life review.
- Insight oriented or psychodynamic.
- Cognitive behavioral.

The selection of a particular type of group depends upon client factors such as the underlying psychiatric disorders or issues to be addressed, ego strength, motivation and cognitive ability, and practical factors such as the local availability of groups and the presence of transportation. Psychiatric diagnoses most amenable to group therapy include major depression and other mood disorders, anxiety disorders, adjustment disorders, and substance use disorders (Saiger, 2001). The presence of cognitive impairment does not preclude group participation but requires more structure and simplification of goals and activities. In addition, group participation requires adequate attention levels, verbal skills, and the absence of significant behavioral disturbances. Groups that focus on orientation and sensory stimulation (e.g., music and pet therapy) are best for the most severely impaired clients.

Older clients living with severe bipolar disorder or chronic psychotic disorders such as schizophrenia or schizoaffective disorder do best when the group is structured around their specific issues and needs (Agronin, 2009a). With respect to PDs, individuals with all three anxious cluster disorders (avoidant, dependent, and obsessive compulsive) as well as all dramatic cluster disorders (borderline, narcissistic, and histrionic), with the exception of antisocial PD, are generally good candidates for group therapy—but with sufficient group structure and a well-trained group leader, especially for DBT groups. The same goes for those with passive-aggressive and depressive PDs. Clients with odd cluster PDs (schizoid, schizotypal, and paranoid) as well as antisocial PD are likely to avoid or otherwise resist group therapy or may prove too disruptive to its structure.

In addition to the aforementioned diagnostic factors, other client factors that may preclude group participation include active suicidality, severe psychosis (e.g., disorganized thinking, thought blocking, inappropriate affect, clanging), agitation or aggression, motor restlessness, and intoxication. Group participation is also limited by medical or neurological symptoms that interfere with comprehendible, comfortable, or safe social interactions, such as excessive sleepiness or sedation, communicable respiratory or gastrointestinal diseases, pain, severe cough, aphasia, and severely dysarthric speech.

In terms of practical factors, group therapy programs can be found in a variety of inpatient and outpatient settings that are convenient for older clients, including day hospitals, assisted living facilities, and nursing homes (Schwartz, 2004, 2007). Support groups are often found in outpatient clinics and community settings, including educational and religious institutions. An intensive outpatient program is a structured form of group therapy similar to a partial hospitalization program, but with fewer hours, and involves formal screening and treatment planning as well as an eclectic mix of educational and supportive sessions to meet the goals of a mixed group (Agronin, Ryder, & Ford, 2008).

The practical message for any therapist is that it is important to have a menu of available group programs handy in order to provide a good match for the client and his or her needs. Group therapy can be an important augmentation to individual work, allowing individuals to put into practice certain tasks from therapy under the guidance of another professional. It can also fill in the gaps from individual work, such as when a grieving individual really needs to hear from others walking in his or her shoes in addition to the therapist.

Age-Specific Group Process

Group process with older clients actually begins before the first session, as the group leader or leaders must select its membership from a pool of potential clients. The goal is to match the client's needs and abilities with the purpose and structure of the group. With older individuals, it is important to have some degree of homogeneity in terms of both ego function and cognitive ability. This helps facilitate communication among members without immediately ostracizing someone who simply cannot participate at the same level. At the same time, inclusion criteria should not be applied too strictly, as there are always individuals who seem too impaired for the group process but end up doing quite well (Agronin, 2009a).

From the outset, group therapy with older individuals poses unique challenges that must be accommodated in order for the group to work. These challenges involve physical and psychological needs specific to late life such as assistance with transportation and toileting, snack breaks for adequate nutrition and hydration, sensory aids to accommodate visual and hearing loss, mobility in group (e.g., help with wheelchair), fears (e.g., the stigma of psychiatric diagnosis and treatment, fears of being around other old, depressed, or disabled persons; fears of incontinence, bodily odors, and physical appearance), and the presence of medical and psychiatric symptoms, including:

- Cognitive impairment
- Sensory deficits
- Pain
- Excessive sleepiness
- Medical illness
- Incontinence
- Dysphasia
- Dysarthria
- Physical disability
- Severe psychosis
- Agitation

Frieda's initial experience in the group highlights ways in which to meet these challenges.

Given her previous experiences with psychotherapy, Frieda was reluctant to attend a group but grudgingly agreed to try it out. However, she did not show up on the first day, telling the group leader later that she had a terrible head-ache and was too tired to come. The second day someone from the clinic went to actually pick up Frieda for group, but she appeared at the door still in her nightclothes and re-fused to go. On the third day, the outreach coordinator of the program went to Frieda's apartment 30 minutes prior to the group and helped get her dressed and fed then walked her over to the group. This same procedure was followed for about a week, until Frieda began showing up on her own accord.

Although such repeated attempts to get a person to attend the group might seem extreme, they are essential to maintain-ing any group with older individuals, especially in residential and long-term care settings, where physical symptoms, dis-ability, and difficulty with care needs such as dressing and feeding are real challenges and also serve as convenient forms of resistance. In Frieda's case, headache and fatigue were two core somatoform symptoms being addressed by the therapy, and so giving in to them would have defeated the very pur-pose of selecting her for the group in the first place.

The same challenges that interfere with group attendance also interfere with group participation. This is particularly true for individuals with hearing or visual loss, who may already be feeling socially isolated outside the group as a result of these deficits. The group leader should ensure ahead of time that these individuals have proper hearing aids or glasses and should always have on hand amplifying devices at the group site. The leader may also need to liaison with physicians to help attendees experiencing pain, incontinence, oversedation, or medication side effects that interfere with alertness and concentration during group sessions.

There are also certain interruptions that cannot be avoided but must be addressed in the scope of the group dynamics, such as interrupted group attendance because of doctor visits, medical procedures, and out-of-town visits by important friends or family, and leaves of absence due to transient illness, injury, or hospitalization. These interruptions can occur with younger group members, but typically not with the same frequency or carrying the same significance as they do in later life. A leader could certainly process with group members the meaning of missing a session due to a family meeting, but when this absence involves, for example, a semiannual visit by an out-of-town son or daughter, such processing runs the risk of offending or alienating members. As group leaders quickly learn, all these challenges and interruptions are part and parcel of group therapy with older clients and are often unrelated to either individual psychopathology or group dynamics.

The presence of cognitive impairment plays a unique role with many older participants and is not necessarily an obstacle to group process. For example, Saiger (2001) described a group in which most members did not know the names of the other participants, even with practice and prompting. This was not considered a problem, however, as over time, individuals still recognized each other and were able to participate and respond to others in meaningful ways. The group leader, however, must be able reorient cognitively impaired members, stimulate memory recall and verbalization, and redirect members into the group process without making them feel embarrassed or incompetent. With moderately impaired individuals, the group material may have to be presented in shorter segments with a lot of structure and cuing (Yost, Beutler, Corbishley, & Allender, 1986). Experiences with intensive outpatient programs have found that individuals who enter the group with mild to moderate cognitive impairment often experience improvement to both memory and the ability to express themselves, especially when there were aspects of depression and social isolation that previously made their impairment seem worse (Agronin et al., 2008).

Once the session begins, the actual material of group therapy in later life often revolves around several core themes: alterations in mood, such as depression or anxiety; loss of independence, self-esteem, and self-worth; shame; coping with life transitions; interpersonal conflict; memory impairment; and existential issues such as loss of meaning and purpose and the proximity of death (Saiger, 2001). Leszcz commented that the loss of self-esteem and the resultant hopelessness "are even more grievous for the elderly because the chance for restoration and substitution diminishes with aging. The greater the narcissistic caste to one's adult life, the greater the difficulty aging" (1987, p. 338). Saiger (2001) emphasized the role of shame among older group members, which results from the loss of defining attributes of the self. Over time, the self becomes viewed as incompetent or even bad.

The group process can prompt discussion of these fundamental losses in late life, allowing members to vent thoughts and feelings of inadequacy, collectively strategize about how to cope with them, and provide feedback and support to others facing similar losses (and hence, oneself). The developing sense of a common mission and connection among group members is called *group cohesion*. Let's return to Frieda:

Once she began attending on a regular basis, Frieda's intelligence and eagerness for attention allowed her to have a sense of control over the flow of the group. On some days she verbally challenged the labels that had brought members into the group, such as *aged, depressed,* and *mentally ill.* On other days she serenaded the group members with boisterous Russian and Yiddish folksongs from her past. The group members admired her for her spirit and energy, and many described feeling rejuvenated in her presence. Her role in the group culminated in a frenzied scene of song and motion one day when she interrupted the group leader toward the end of the session and called out; "Enough talk of depression—let's sing!" Frieda grabbed the hands of the group members to her right and left and began to boom out the words of the quintessential song of celebration: "Hava na-gila, Ha-va na-gila, ha-va na-gila ve-nis'mecha!" Suddenly all the members in the room joined hands and raised their arms in one motion. "Ha-va nagila!" they sang in unison. "Let's rejoice and be happy!" (Agronin, 2007c).

Although Frieda's behavior in the group may seem out of bounds, and a potential challenge to the group leader, she was building strong group cohesion and turning the group itself into an object of transference, representing what Saiger (2001) has described as the group's wish to experience itself as special. By extension, group members also began to idealize the group leader, valuing her for bringing someone as special as Frieda into the group.

Resistance to treatment among older individuals can take on unique forms. Sometimes it presents as a fear of getting worse by talking about depression or losses, or the fear or disdain of being around other old or impaired individuals—even when the member in question is close in age and has a similar disability. Many seemingly legitimate reasons for not showing up or not speaking in group sessions, such as sleepiness, somatic complaints, or memory deficits, can also represent unconsciously produced and sometimes intentionally feigned ways to resist talking about painful topics. These and other behaviors can lead to a specific group member being labeled the most impaired in the group, or scapegoated by other members as the reason that the group is not helping them. Of course, such attitudes can also be convenient ways to avoid facing issues in the group, especially when members seek to isolate or even eject certain individuals who seem to embody the issue at hand.

Noting how a group member's performance, disability, or complaints fluctuate based on the topic or activity in a session may be a clue to these forms of resistance. Group members may also take on excessive caretaking roles for other individuals as a way of avoiding talking about their own deficits (Saiger, 2001). With all these forms of resistance, the group leader has to carefully find supportive and constructive ways to address them, either in group or individual sessions, without alienating or embarrassing specific members.

At the same time, the group leader must recognize that some behaviors that appear to represent resistance, such as withholding information or spending significant time helping others in the group with various needs (such as wheeling them into the room, or passing them snacks), may be helping to empower critical ego functions such as autonomy, self-sufficiency (Saiger, 2001), self-worth, and personal identity. Frieda's singing in the group was certainly a way to divert attention from certain issues, but it was also a skill that made her feel valued by the group and in control. Such behaviors are thus double-edged swords, bringing gratification at the same time that they help to delay or avoid discussion of painful topics. Ultimately, however, a skillful group leader can steer the group in ways that allow such behaviors to meter the way in which individuals experience and work through critically important thoughts and feelings.

Group leaders must always take note of potential counter-transference reactions, as underlying attitudes or unconscious reactions toward aging, reminders of parents or grandparents, physical disability, and death can significantly affect group process. Sometimes the group leader is not consciously aware of his or her countertransference, but it is reflected through feelings of boredom, frustration, or sleepiness during group sessions. Such behaviors often reflect unconscious fears of or hostility toward specific group members or topics. Subtle feelings of fear or disgust on the part of the leader may be picked up on by group members, who can become more reluctant to participate as a result. The opposite extreme occurs when group leaders express excessive sympathy to the group or act in obsequious or paternalistic ways that rob members of opportunities to face difficult issues or to feel empowered and more independent. To head off some of these reactions, it is critical for group leaders to have both knowledge of the aging process and clinical experience with geriatric clients. Sometimes the presence of a co-leader can provide feedback allowing for recognition of countertransference and for the balancing out of these reactions.

Does Group Therapy Work in Late Life?

There is, in general, limited data on group therapy for any specific modality, but outcomes are generally positive compared to the outcomes for either individual psychotherapy or no treatment (Leszcz, 2004). Symptoms of depression are the most widely measured outcome and generally respond well, although severe depression has been found to respond better to pharmacotherapy (Gorey & Cryns, 1991). One particular study of 59 elderly nursing home residents in both task- and insight-oriented groups looked at a variety of self-reported outcome measures, including life satisfaction, sense of control, active coping, and striving for social approval. Compared to a control group, the task-oriented group improved significantly in all domains, and the insight-oriented group improved in areas of life satisfaction and control (Moran & Gatz, 1987).

Reminiscence therapy has been the most widely studied type of group therapy. Outcome measures have included psychiatric symptoms (e.g., depression, agitation, somatic complaints), cognition, function, activity levels, life satisfaction, well-being, and self-esteem. A number of studies have compared it with supportive group therapy and no-treatment controls in both individuals with and without dementia (Chin, 2007; Leszcz, 2004; Youssef, 1990). Several of these studies have shown improvements in depression (Chin, 2007; Youssef, 1990) but with diminishing or non-sustained gains in those with dementia (Goldwasser, Auberbach, & Harkins, 1987; Woods, Spector, Jones, Orrell, & Davies, 2005). Results with reminiscence groups were found comparable to both education and exercise groups (McMurdo & Rennie, 1991; Rattenbury & Stones, 1989).

Cognitive-behavioral group therapy for older individuals has been found to alleviate depression (Abraham, Onega, Reel, & Wofford, 1997; Zerhusen, Boyle, & Wilson, 1991) and improve self-concept and even cognitive function. DBT therapy, in particular, has demonstrated high rates of remission among depressed elderly participants (Lynch et al., 2003). Even individuals with moderate to mild dementia have benefited from various forms of group therapy, including CBT (Abraham, Neundorfer, & Currie, 1992), validation therapy (Toseland et al.,

1997), and a skills-training group focused on activities of daily living (Beck et al., 2002).

Many older individuals are reluctant to participate in group therapy because they do not understand its role and often feel that other similarly depressed or debilitated individuals will not be able to help or might even depress them further. What they often discover, however, is a rich and unique environment in which they can express themselves, feel acknowledged, and bond with others who know their dilemmas firsthand. In the preceding case vignette, Frieda finished up her last session by commandeering the group from the leader and leading them all in joyous singing. She got up after that, thanked the group, and then walked out, never to return. But in the ensuing months, she was noted to be less depressed and more active at the assisted living facility, an indication of a dramatic change in mood and overall well-being. No individual therapist or medication trial had been able to achieve what the group did. She probably felt cared for by others and was able to give back in return, leading to significant symptomatic improvement. This is a common reaction to successful group therapy and establishes it as an important therapeutic modality for the older client.

9

THE NINTH STAGE: THE THERAPIST'S ROLE IN THE LAST STAGE OF LIFE

As I walk the grounds of the long-term care campus where I work, I often imagine my older clients as the trees in the surrounding gardens, with deep roots, richly ringed trunks, and majestic canopies that stretch into the sky. The history, values, and wisdom provided by these clients are as life sustaining as the shade and fruits of the trees. I was struck, then, one day when I noticed that one of the trees in the center of the main yard was completely bare, stripped of both its foliage and many of its limbs. It appeared to have been abandoned to the elements, but I later discovered that it had just been pruned the day before by the gardening staff. Several months later the tree was again in full bloom, but with an even more sculpted and impressive green canopy. Similarly, many clients reach a point in life at which we see them as bereft and abandoned. We feel sadness and resignation and question whether there is anything we can do to help. The reality of aging, however, is more complex and holds more potential than we often realize. What we see as barrenness may actually represent a necessary pruning of activities; what we see as dying may actually be a stage of consolidation or even renewal. My point in this chapter is that this last season of life—what I am calling the *ninth stage*—still opens the door to opportunities for both therapist and client.

The last of Erikson's eight stages of human development centers around the task of developing a sense of integrity for one's life, characterized by the discovery of acceptance, meaning, and wholeness in the face of age-associated pressures and losses. Despair is the opposing ego-dystonic force postulated by Erikson, defined as expressing "the feeling that the time is now short, too short for the attempt to start another life and to try out alternate roads" (1950/1985, p. 113). Although cultivating a sense of integrity would seem to be the only ideal pursuit in later life, Erikson's framework is more supportive of a balance between syntonic and dystonic forces. This is not to suggest that a little despair is necessarily good, but rather that an unbridled sense of integrity without some realization of the limited horizon that lies ahead can be problematic. The achieved balance in perspective—a recognition and tolerance of competing life forces and of the reality of death—is what Erikson aptly labeled *wisdom*.

In their last book, titled *The Life Cycle Completed*, Erik and Joan Erikson proposed a ninth stage in the life cycle, representing individuals in their 80s and 90s who are facing "new demands, reevaluations, and daily difficulties" (1997, p. 105). Much of their description of the ninth stage is quite gloomy, as it depicts the unraveling of the life cycle resulting from bodily decline and the loss of autonomy, self-esteem, confidence, and ultimately hope itself, casting despair as the dominant force. They wrote that "there is much sorrow to cope with plus a clear announcement that death's door is open and not so far away" (Erikson & Erikson, 1997, p. 113). This description represents well how most individuals in the other eight stages visualize the last stage of life. It describes our greatest fears of aging, a projection of how miserable life must be in the absence of all the capabilities we cherish in earlier stages. To a great extent, the Eriksons' proposed ninth stage grew out of Joan Erikson's own struggles with aging. She discovered that the reality of aging threatens to nullify any developmental theory. Expectations for integrity or any other late-life goals—peace, contentedness, comfort, mutual relationships— may be dashed by perpetual illness and grief. Most individuals imagine the typical nursing home to be full of discarded individuals in this last stage, bereft of mind, body, and the last shreds of dignity.

The idea of a ninth stage of existence representing despair, abandonment, dementia, and depression is better formulated, however, with less negative and pathological attributes. Instead, consider a stage of life in which physical frailty or cognitive impairment has rendered an individual totally dependent on the care of others. Mobility is extremely limited; managing activities of daily living is difficult, if not impossible; and the ability to recognize, understand, and communicate may be limited. In this conception of a ninth stage we begin to reconsider whether it is even appropriate to speak of development. In addition, we ask an even more basic question posed by the ethicist Joanne Lynn: "Is it possible to live well while very sick and dying?" (2005, p. 515).

An exploration of this stage is so critical because many older clients referred for evaluations of depression, anxiety, panic attacks, agitation, and other mental health issues are in the ninth stage. The apparent precariousness of their existence, coupled with their seemingly limited ability to act independently and interact with us socially, prompts us to question whether treatment is futile. In addition, our views of the ninth stage may be immediately shaped by larger perspectives on aging that, for many, are distorted by youthful projections. Robert Butler described this attitude in his Pulitzer Prize–winning book *Why Survive?*

> Old age in America is often a tragedy. Few of us like to consider it because it reminds us of our own mortality. It demands our energy and resources, it frightens us with illness and deformity, it is an affront to a culture with a passion for youth and productive capacity. . . . At best, the living old are treated as if they were already half dead." (1975, p. xi)

The therapist is thus faced by a dilemma. How do we realistically approach these clients? What is both ethical and practical in terms of treatment? A therapist trying to conduct psychoanalysis with a client with severe dementia would be engaging in a futile, not to mention unethical, task. But what about supportive therapy with that same individual? Does that hold merit? And if an older individual is actively dying, what are the goals of therapy? Do therapists even have roles in the ninth stage, or are such roles not better suited for loved ones, clergy, or hospice workers?

The first step to answering these questions involves a broadening of perspective on the ninth stage. We often imagine that these clients are either unable or unwilling to engage with us. Disengagement theory suggests that there is an actual intrinsic drive in old age to withdraw from social and societal interests and interactions and turn inward in preparation for eventual death (Cumming & Henry, 1961). Other theories have countered this by proposing that what we view as disengagement is really a form of selective *engagement*. Like the analogy of the pruning of the tree, both selection, optimization, and compensation theory and socioemotional selectivity theory suggest that older individuals purposely try to be more selective in their choices in order to maximize their current resources and positive emotions (Baltes & Baltes, 1990; Carstensen et al., 2000). Tornstam (2005) has gone even further, proposing that many aged individuals experience "gerotranscendence," a feeling of closeness to certain elements beyond the normal confines of their lives, where time becomes less meaningful as a horizon and more meaningful as a moment. In this light, the ninth stage brings maturation, not just regression. Aspects of gerotranscendence proposed by Tornstam are:

- A feeling of cosmic communion with the universe and affinity with past and future generations.
- A redefinition of the perception of time, space, life, and death.
- A decreased fear of death.
- Decreased interest in material things and superfluous social interactions.
- Less focus on self-centeredness, more focus on time in meditative thought.

All three theories of engagement in late life are applicable to ninth-stage clients and suggest two main points relevant to the work of the therapist: (1) Even in severely debilitated cognitive or physical states, strengths are retained, sometimes masked by the predominant deficits and losses, and (2) it is possible to engage these strengths by identifying and then activating them through various activities and interactions. Some of the most activating therapeutic programs include music and pet therapy, arts and crafts, stretching, and time spent with nature or attending music, dance, or theater performances. Putting these strengths into practice in more formal methods of psychotherapy has been described in Chapters 6 through 8.

Therapeutic Tasks

Formal psychotherapy is sometimes the most appropriate treatment modality for individuals in the ninth stage. More often, however, therapists are called upon for discrete therapeutic tasks that require evaluation and short-term intervention. These interventions are typically aimed at helping clients, their families, or professional caregivers understand behaviors, engage in decision making, remove barriers to further treatment, or assist with death and dying. In all cases, the therapist's work is informed by key ethical principles of autonomy (the client's right to make his or her own decisions), beneficence (acting for the good of the client while doing no harm), justice (appropriate and fair allocation of resources), and confidentiality (protection of privacy).

Assessing Capacity

Therapists are often asked to determine whether a client has the ability to make certain decisions regarding medical or psychiatric care, financial matters, living situations, and personal affairs. The therapist might also be called to upon to help decide whether a client should be informed about a family crisis or loss or a terminal diagnosis. Consider the following case vignette.

> Pauline was an 85-year-old woman living with moderate dementia. She was oriented to person, but only partially to place and time, and lived in a nursing home. Her only child, Daniel, lived out of state and would call her every month

and visit her twice a year. She enjoyed this contact and would occasionally ask about him in between calls and visits. He was divorced and had a 5-year-old son, whom Pauline met on one occasion. The nursing staff was notified one day by Daniel's partner that he had died suddenly. That same day, Daniel's ex-wife contacted the social worker and informed her that she was now the next of kin and did not want Pauline notified about Daniel's death. She reasoned that it would be too painful for her to find out and that she wouldn't remember it anyway. She also made it clear that she was now Pauline's health care proxy and the manager of her estate, as designated several years earlier by Daniel. Nursing staff felt acutely uncomfortable about not telling Pauline that her son had died, and they were uncertain what to say if Pauline asked about her son. But they were obligated to follow the wishes of family. The therapist at the nursing home was asked whether they should tell Pauline the truth, and whether she could make her own health care decisions.

Although the therapist is being asked to play a Solomonic role here, it is really not his or her decision whether or not to inform Pauline about her son's death or who should serve as her health care proxy. These are issues to be worked out by the social worker and the family, perhaps in consultation with an ethics committee or in a legal setting. The therapist should simply confine the evaluation to the following questions:

- Does Pauline have the mental capacity to make her own decisions about personal matters (such as knowing what happened to her son) and health care matters (such as deciding about medical treatments and appointing a health care proxy)?

- If Pauline learns about the death of her son, what might be the impact? How should her potential reactions be addressed?

Note that in this discussion, the determination of *capacity* is a matter for the therapist, whereas *competency* is a legal state that can only be determined by a judge. Even if the therapist decides that Pauline has the mental capacity to make her own decisions, a judge could still find her incompetent. In practice, however, a determination of capacity often has the same practical consequences as a legal determination of competence (Grisso & Appelbaum, 1998).

The process of determining capacity follows the lines of evaluation outlined in Chapter 3. The key components are whether a client is able to understand and remember the information at hand, to appreciate the fact that there are choices, to consistently express a choice, and to understand the consequences of the decision (Beauchamp & Childress, 2001). In Pauline's case, she was unable to meet these basic standards for most decisions. Still, she retained a strong memory of her son and did ask about him on a regular basis, suggesting that although she did not have the capacity for general decision making, she was able to appreciate (and possibly remember over time) whether her son was alive or not. In this case, this important information was provided to Pauline's PCP and social worker, who brought it to the ethics committee for further review.

The second issue concerns potential reactions to bad news on the part of individuals like Pauline who are quite debilitated and disabled in various ways and might not have the psychic resources to process and cope with the loss of a loved one or a terminal diagnosis. Predicting an emotional reaction can be very difficult, as it varies based on many different factors, such as the baseline emotional state, the extent of under-standing, the ability to retain memory of the news, and the availability of psychological supports. In general, aside from individuals with severe receptive and expressive aphasia, many clients in the ninth stage are able to understand and cope with bad news. They are entitled to know the truth and to be given the opportunity to ask questions and grieve. If it becomes apparent that they do not remember the news after a period of time, it would be unwise or even cruel to submit them again to the experience of finding out. In that situation, the therapist might help staff deal with persistent questioning (e.g., "Where is my son? What is wrong with me? Why does this hurt?") and advise them how to comfort and redirect the client.

As noted at the beginning of the chapter, many clients are able to cope with bad news in novel ways that might surprise and even end up comforting grieving family members. Such reactions are facilitated by a greater understanding and accep-tance of death on their part. Consider what happened with Pauline.

Staff members at the nursing home were greatly troubled by the fact that Pauline was not notified by her family about her son's death. Finally, and after much discussion, the former daughter-in-law agreed to visit Pauline with her grandson to break the news. When they met, Pauline's first question was "Where's Daniel?" Her daughter-in-law ex-plained that he had died suddenly and began weeping. With tears in her eyes, Pauline hugged her grandson and her daughter-in-law and told them that Daniel was a great man and that they were lucky to have had him as a husband and father. "I lost my husband, too," she said, "but we have to go on." The therapist was present during the meeting to provide support and began meeting with Pauline on a regular basis afterward. On many days over the next month, Pauline seemed visibly sad and would speak about her son's death, and on other days she didn't seem to remember.

Determining a client's capacity is not an exact science, and always runs the risk of either unnecessarily stressing or traumatizing ninth-stage clients or depriving them of autonomy, privacy, and the right to know about their life circumstances. In all situations, the therapist must keep an open mind and be available for short-term counseling with both client and family.

Understanding and Treating the Seemingly Irrational

Therapists are called upon to evaluate and recommend treatment for a variety of seemingly irrational behaviors on the part of ninth-stage clients, including agitation; belligerence; repetitive verbalizations or motor habits; social isolation; excessive and inappropriate emotional outbursts; sexually disinhibited comments or behaviors; noncompliance with medical treatments; and refusal to eat, take medications, cooperate with caregiver requests, or be bathed, dressed, or moved. Sometimes these behaviors clearly arise from underlying symptoms or disorders such as depression, mania, anxiety, personality dysfunction, or even substance abuse. Just as often they arise suddenly and without any obvious source. Consider the following case vignette.

William was a 73-year-old man living in an assisted living facility. Other residents began complaining to staff that William was extremely malodorous and unkempt. When the director of nursing spoke to him, William insisted that he did shower and change his clothes daily, and he became irate about even being questioned about it. Several days later he was noted to have soiled pants, but he refused help with changing. The odor became so bad that staff confronted William and tried to coax him into the shower. He screamed at them and then locked himself in his room. The therapist was consulted to speak with William and help resolve the situation.

The therapist should keep in mind that these symptoms might have important meaning for the client. Some clients are able to describe why they are acting in a certain way, which may or may not be a sufficient explanation. In this case, William denied the problem, but in his mind his very autonomy and dignity were at stake. Even when the client has a plausible explanation, there is typically at least one precipitating factor. Several questions should guide the evaluation:

- Is there a psychiatric history? Recurring previous symptoms may look different in the ninth stage. See Table 9.1 for examples.
- Is there an underlying medical symptom, disorder, or medication effect that may be causing the behaviors? See Table 5.1 for examples. Individuals who cannot verbalize pain act it out.
- Have there been any recent personal or environmental stresses? Examples include the loss of a loved one or long-standing caregiver, a new residence, a new roommate, or a living situation that is frightening or uncomfortable.

The first step is to get a clear description of what is happening, as sometimes the reports are not accurate as a result of strong opinions or highly emotional reactions to the situation. This involves interviewing clients and allowing them time to

Table 9.1. Behavioral Manifestations of Psychiatric Symptoms in the Ninth Stage

Symptom	Behaviors
Depression	Sad facial expression, crying, irritability, motor retardation, impoverished speech, loss of tone in voice, disinterest in previously enjoyed activities, refusal to eat or allow caregiving, insomnia, weight loss.
Anxiety	Pained, anguished, or worried facial expressions; crying; shaking; tremor; hyperventilating; hypervigilance (looking around nervously); motor restlessness; screaming; moaning; repetitive verbalizations or vocalizations; agitation.
Mania	Motor hyperactivity, repetitive verbalizations or vocalizations, screaming, agitation, belligerence, inappropriate anger, assaultiveness (e.g., scratching, biting), inappropriate sexual comments or gestures, disrobing or masturbation in public, intrusive or impulsive comments or behaviors, pressured or hyperverbal speech.
Psychosis	Fearful or angry facial expressions, social isolation, hoarding food or other objects, refusal to accept help with dressing and hygiene, inappropriate or nonsensical verbalizations, misidentification of familiar individuals or strangers, belligerence, verbally abusive comments, talking to oneself or to the television, cursing, accusing others of trying to do one harm.
Obsessive-compulsive disorder	Hoarding, refusing to accept care or to allow others into one's space, repetitive habits, unusual placement of objects in one's rooms
Somatization	Constant complaints of pain without obvious signs of pain; negativity, disgusted facial expression, moaning.
Confusion	Closed eyes, agitation, motor restlessness, picking at oneself or at the air, moaning, reversed sleep-wake cycle.
Pain	Pained facial expression, irritability, motor agitation, wincing or screaming with movement, insomnia.

vent and feel supported, regardless of whether their reports are directly relevant to the problem. Multiple family members and other caregivers need to be interviewed as well.

The second step is to ensure that all relevant medical and psychiatric issues, such as depression or delirium, have been evaluated and treated. An adjunct to this step is to make certain that any unmet needs of the client with respect to diet, hygiene, safety, clothing, environment, and comfort are addressed. A client left in soiled clothing in an uncomfortable wheelchair may well be justified in being agitated. Similarly, environments that are too hot or cold or too noisy may be overstimulating to certain clients. Long-term care staff may administer daily care or regulate schedules in ways that are disruptive to someone. Educating caregivers and making simple changes based on the evaluation can sometimes lead to significant improvement or even resolution of the problem.

The therapist met with William several days after his outburst. It became clear that William was only partially oriented to place and time and was paranoid about staff. An underlying dementia had never even been diagnosed. In addition, liaison with William's PCP indicated that he had a history of prostate enlargement with frequent urinary tract infections. The therapist suggested that William was in urgent need of evaluations by both his PCP, who found an untreated urinary tract infection, and a geriatric psychiatrist, who diagnosed Alzheimer's disease with associated paranoid psychosis. After two weeks of treatment with an antibiotic and an antipsychotic medication, William was more cooperative with staff and was no longer having urinary incontinence. The therapist then began working individually with William to get to know him better and build up some trust. She educated staff about his background as a physician and suggested that he would respond best when staff treated him with respect and addressed him as "Doctor." On the basis of the therapist's suggestions, the family hired an aide, who got to know William and was able to help him shower on a regular basis. The therapist also referred William to a structured day program designed for individuals with early-stage dementia. Within months William's behavior and hygiene improved significantly.

The entire approach with William required the mental health expertise of the therapist, and once an outcome was reached, there was no longer a need for any ongoing therapy, just periodic consultations. Many similar behaviors yield to such an approach. Ultimately, many individuals with severe disability of any kind require highly structured settings in which hands-on care is provided in a timely, comfortable, and dignified manner.

Death and Dying

There are two sets of circumstances in which a therapist may be called upon to assist a dying client. The first is when the client him- or herself states an intent to die or even engages in suicidal or indirectly life-threatening behaviors. For some clients, this occurs very suddenly, and for others it represents the culmination of a lengthy process of pain and exhaustion that leads them to say, "Enough is enough." In both situations, family and caregivers may actively or silently agree with ninth-stage clients and even acquiesce to their requests or demands. The second situation is when the client has been diagnosed with a terminal illness or has reached the end stage of Alzheimer's disease or a chronic medical disease. In this situation, hospice workers often provide much of the care, including counseling for clients and family.

Unfortunately, medical professionals and hospice workers who tend to these individuals do not always see a role for the therapist. Perceptions of therapists as providing psychotherapy only for cognitively intact, motivated, and more robust individuals with a future may get in the way. Therapists may also feel that their role is limited once a terminal phase is reached, and this can lead to abandonment of the client. In her book *Jane Brody's Guide to the Great Beyond*, the long-standing *New York Times* columnist on personal health Jane Brody wrote about "doctors who disappear" in these moments, fearful of death and their own failures in the face of it (2009, p. 176). Similarly, as therapists, we sometimes are so focused on psychological growth and change that the very idea of death and dying seems anathema to our mission.

Therapists can and should, however, play key roles in evaluating and counseling clients and their caregivers in these situations. Their expertise is ideal for providing clarification, comfort, and actual therapy in the client's dying days. Consider the following case vignette.

Joseph was a 68-year-old homeless man with long-standing alcohol abuse and end-stage lung disease who was hospitalized for a severe bout of pneumonia. He survived the infection but was unable to be weaned off of the respirator and so a semipermanent tracheotomy tube was placed in his neck. After several weeks he was transferred to a nursing home. As result of the trach tube, his speech was quite poor and he could only communicate with nursing staff by using single words and hand gestures. Nurses reported that for several weeks Joseph had been repeatedly mouthing the

word "Die" and running his hand over his neck. On one occasion he pulled out his trach tube, and after it was replaced,
he had an angry facial expression and kept saying, "No!
No!" while pointing to it. In a meeting with his PCP, Joseph
was asked whether he wanted to continue living on the respirator and he angrily said, "No!" and grabbed the doctor's
hands. There was no family available except for a daughter,
whom the social worker was unable to contact. Plans were
made to respect Joseph's request and take him off of the
respirator. A therapist was consulted in order to certify Joseph's wishes.

In this case Joseph was severely disabled and unable to provide any care for himself. The remainder of his life span was
measured in months, even with the best of care. As in the case
of Pauline, the therapist was asked to make ethical decisions
that went above and beyond his or her role. The therapist's
role must be clarified: Is it to determine Joseph's capacity to
make a decision about his own health? Is it to help him cope
with his medical condition? Or is it to counsel him as he is
dying?

The therapist asked for clarification on the case. The PCP
replied that he was uncertain what to do with Joseph and
wanted the therapist to both determine his decision-making
capacity and help him cope with dying. The therapist evaluated Joseph and determined that although he did have mild
cognitive impairment, probably as a result of his chronic alcohol use, he did have intact judgment and insight into his
condition. At the same time, she felt that Joseph was anxious and depressed, and she spent time developing a way to
communicate with him by using words, gestures, and a
word-and-picture board in order to provide some counsel-

ing. Joseph knew he was dying and did not want to be in pain. The decision about taking Joseph off of the respirator was deferred while the PCP worked to reduce his pain and to provide antianxiety medication for the times when he struggled with the sensation of air blowing through the trach tube. These approaches helped enormously, and Joseph stopped asking to die. Contact was eventually made with his estranged daughter, who came to visit, and Joseph seemed relieved and more content after the meeting. Several weeks later he developed another bout of pneumonia and died.

The therapist's role with Joseph was a critical intervention, as it clarified his cognitive and emotional status, provided an enhanced means of communication, enabled better treatment for pain and anxiety, facilitated a final meeting with his daughter, and provided comfort during the dying process. These steps can apply to any situation with a dying client.

Providing actual therapy for an individual who is dying begins with a supportive presence. The goals and approaches of the various forms of therapy outlined in Chapter 7 may apply in certain situations when the client expresses a desire to accomplish something before death or seeks to understand the meaning of his or her life. More often these clients do not articulate their needs. Therapists should be careful not to impose their own religious, moral, or cultural beliefs in these situations, as it is the role of designated family or other caregivers to help make decisions based on the incapacitated client's known wishes or beliefs. Despite the many end-of-life ethical issues that arise at these points, ranging from artificial life support to tube feeding and the right to die, the actual care role of therapists transcends whatever their beliefs may be.

An open-ended approach is the best way to begin therapy in order to give the client the optimal opportunity to express thoughts, emotions, and needs. Impending death might not be known or understood, and the therapist needs to know what the client is capable of understanding and what the PCP or family has already told him or her before engaging in any discussion of it. Most often, death is not the topic of concern, but the therapist may be asked to help with appointments, family contacts, or pain control; liase with other specialists; or even provide direct care needs such as hydration. Although these tasks are usually the main responsibilities of nurses, family, social workers, and hospice workers, the therapist needs to be flexible and humane as he or she attends to an extremely debilitated individual—often right at the bedside. Small gestures like bringing a cup of ice chips to a thirsty client, adjusting the shades in the room, and finding a nurse to provide a pain pill are a natural part of therapy with the dying client. They send a powerful message of care and concern and engender a feeling of trust that may enable the dying client to feel comfortable exploring deeper issues.

A Final Word on the Client

Clients in the ninth stage provide some of the most vexing clinical dilemmas, as all the challenges of working with older individuals are amplified. In addition, there are pressing ethical concerns that threaten to distort and politicize the clinical mission. As therapists, we must keep in mind, however, that a caring and committed therapeutic relationship—whether lasting 1 hour or 1 year—is always at the heart of our work. And here I must again quote the author Jay Neugeboren. He interviewed hundreds of psychiatric clients who experienced recovery and asked them what the essential ingredient to their success was.

> What had made the difference? Some pointed to new medications, some to old; some said they had found God; some attributed their transformation to a particular program, but no matter what else they named, they all—every last one—said that a key element was a relationship with a human being . . . who said, in effect, "I believe in your ability to recover, and I am going to stay with you until you do. (Neugeboren, 2006, p. 17)

"I believe in your ability to recover." This statement defines hope. It begins with wonder and curiosity and requires a deeply caring attitude. And it takes courage and creativity to sustain. At all points it speaks to the essence of our work.

References

Abraham, I. L., Neundorfer, M. M., & Currie, L. J. (1992). Effects of group interventions on cognition and depression in nursing home residents. *Nursing Research, 41,* 196–202.

Abraham, I. L., Onega, L. L., Reel, S. J., & Wofford, A. (1997). Effects of cognitive group interventions on depressed frail nursing home residents. In R. L. Rubinstein & M. P. Lawton (Eds.), *Depression in long term and residential care: Advances in research and treatment* (pp. 154–168). New York: Springer.

Abrams, R. C., & Horowitz, S. V. (1996). Personality disorders after age 50: A meta-analysis. *Journal of Personality Disorders, 10*(3), 271–281.

Adams, K. B. (2001). Depressive symptoms, depletion, or developmental change? Withdrawal, apathy, and lack of vigor in the Geriatric Depression Scale. *Gerontologist, 41,* 768–777.

Agronin, M. E. (1994). Personality disorders in the elderly: An overview. *Journal of Geriatric Psychiatry, 27*(2), 151–192.

Agronin, M. E. (2006). Working with challenging caregivers. *CNS News, 8*(4), 4–5.

Agronin, M. E. (2007a, August). Caring for the dementia caregiver: Ways to identify and reduce burden. *Perspectives in Psychiatry: A Clinical Update* [Suppl. to *Psychiatric Times*], 2, 15–18.

Agronin, M. E. (2007b). Cherishing relics of all kinds. *CNS Senior Care, 6*(2), 3–4.

Agronin, M. E. (2007c). Let's rejoice. *CNS News, 9*(9), 18–19.

Agronin, M. E. (2007d). Sunshine. *CNS News, 9*(10), 24–25.

Agronin, M. E. (2007e). 39 doctors. *CNS News, 9*(7), 12–13.

Agronin, M. E. (2008). *Alzheimer disease and other dementias* (2nd ed.). Philadelphia, PA: Lippincott Williams & Wilkins.

Agronin, M. E. (2009a). Group therapy in older adults. *Current Psychiatry Reports, 11*(1), 27–32.

Agronin, M. E. (2009b). Personality disorders. In W. E. Reichman & P. R. Katz (Eds.), *Psychiatry in long-term care* (2nd ed., pp. 217–233). New York: Oxford University Press.

Agronin, M. E. (2009c). Somatoform disorders. In D. G. Blazer & D. C. Steffens (Eds.), *The American Psychiatric Publishing textbook of geriatric psychiatry* (4th ed., pp. 347–356). Washington, DC: American Psychiatric Publishing.

Agronin, M. E., & Maletta, G. J. (2000). Personality disorders in late life: Understanding and overcoming the gap in research. *American Journal of Geriatric Psychiatry, 8,* 4–18.

Agronin, M. E., Ryder, D., & Ford, S. (2008, March). *Group therapy in the elderly: Experiences with a structured outpatient program (SOP)*. Presented at the 21st Annual Meeting of the American Association for Geriatric Psychiatry, Orlando, FL.

Aldrich, S., Eccleston, C., & Crombez, G. (2000). Worrying about chronic pain: Vigilance to threat and misdirected problem solving. *Behaviour Research and Therapy, 38,* 457–470.

Alessi, C. A., & Cassel, C. K. (2004). Medical evaluation and common medical problems of the geriatric psychiatry patient. In J. Sadavoy, L. F. Jarvik, G. T. Grossberg, & B. S. Meyers (Eds.), *Comprehensive textbook of geriatric psychiatry* (3rd ed., pp. 281–313). New York: Norton.

Alexopoulos, G. S. (1996). Geriatric depression in primary care. *International Journal of Geriatric Psychiatry, 11,* 397–400.

Alexopoulos, G. S., Meyers, B. S., Young, R. C., Kakuma, T., Silbersweig, D., & Charlson, M. (1997). Clinically defined vascular depression. *American Journal of Psychiatry, 154,* 562–565.

Alexopoulos, G. S., Meyers, B. S., Young, R. C., Mattis, S., & Kakuma, T. (1993). The course of geriatric depression with "reversible dementia": A controlled study. *American Journal of Psychiatry, 150,* 1693–1699.

Allport, G. W. (1937). *Personality: A psychological interpretation.* New York: Holt.

Allport, G. W. (1943). The productive paradoxes of William James. *Psychological Review, 50*(1), 95–120.

Alzheimer's Association. (2008). Take care of yourself: 10 ways to be a healthier caregiver. PDF under Caregiving / caregiver stress. Retrieved

December 28, 2009 from: www.alz.org/alzheimers_disease_publica tions_care_topics.asp

American Association of Suicidology. (2009). *Elderly suicide fact sheet.* Retrieved October 25, 2009, from http://www.suicidology.org/web/ guest/stats-and-tools/fact-sheets

American Geriatrics Society Panel on Chronic Pain in Older Persons. (2002). The management of persistent pain in older persons. *Journal of the American Geriatrics Society, 50*(6), S205–S244.

American Psychiatric Association. (2000). *Diagnostic and statistical manual of mental disorders* (4th ed., text rev.). Washington, DC: American Psychiatric Publishing.

Ardelt, M., & Oh, H. (2010). Wisdom: Definition, assessment, and relation to successful cognitive and emotional aging. In C. A. Depp & D. V. Jeste (Eds.), *Successful cognitive and emotional aging* (pp. 87–114). Washington, DC: American Psychiatric Publishing.

Areán, P. A. (2009). Problem-solving therapy. *Psychiatric Annals, 39*(9), 854–862.

Areán, P. A., Perri, M. G., Nezu, A. M., Schein, R. L., Christopher, F., & Joseph, T. X. (1993). Comparative effectiveness of social problem-solving therapy and reminiscence therapy as treatments for depression in older adults. *Journal of Consulting and Clinical Psychology, 61*(6), 1003–1010.

Arking, R. (2006). *The biology of aging: Observations and principles* (3rd ed.). New York: Oxford University Press.

Ball, K., Berch, D. B., Helmers, K. F., Jobe, J. B., Leveck, M. D., Marsiske, M., Morris, J. N., Rebok, G. W., Smith, D. M., Tennstedt, S. L., Unverzagt, F. W., & Willis, S. L. (2002). Effects of cognitive training interventions with older adults: A randomized controlled trial. *Journal of the American Medical Association, 288*(18), 2271–2281.

Ballard, C., Brown, R., Fossey, J., Douglas, S., Bradley, P., Hancock, J., . . . Howard, R. (2009). Brief psychosocial therapy for the treatment of agitation in Alzheimer disease (the CALM-AD trial). *American Journal of Geriatric Psychiatry, 17*(9), 726–733.

Balsis, S., Woods, C. M., Gleason, M. E. J., & Oltmanns, T. F. (2007). Overdiagnosis and underdiagnosis of personality disorders in older adults. *American Journal of Geriatric Psychiatry, 15*, 742–753.

Baltes, P. B., & Baltes, M. M. (1990). Psychological perspectives on successful aging: The model of selective optimization with compensation. In P. B. Baltes & M. M. Baltes (Eds.), *Successful aging: Perspectives from the behavioral sciences* (pp. 1–34). New York: Cambridge University Press.

Barry, K. L., & Blow, F. C. (1999). Screening and assessment of alcohol problems in older adults. In P. A. Lichtenburg (Eb.), *Handbook of assessment in clinical gerontology* (pp. 243–269). New York: Wiley.

Barsky, A. J. (2001). The patient with hypochondriasis. *New England Journal of Medicine, 345*(19), 1395–1399.

Basseches, M. (1984). *Dialectical thinking and adult development.* Norwood, NJ: Ablex.

Beauchamp, T. L., & Childress, J. F. (2001). *Principles of biomedical ethics* (5th ed.). New York: Oxford University Press.

Beck, C. K., Vogelpohl, T. S., Rasin, J. H., Uriri, J. T., O'Sullivan, P., Walls, R., . . . Baldwin, B. (2002). Effects of behavioral interventions on disruptive behavior and affect in demented nursing home residents. *Nursing Research, 51,* 219–228.

Berrios, G. E., & Brook, P. (1982). The Charles Bonnet syndrome and the problems of visual perceptual disorder in the elderly. *Age and Ageing, 11,* 17–23.

Biglan, K. M. (2008). Neurologic manifestations of systemic disease: Disturbances of the kidneys, electrolytes, water balance, rheumatology, hematology/oncology, alcohol, and iatrogenic conditions. In J. I. Sirven & B. L. Malamut (Eds.), *Clinical neurology of the older adult* (2nd ed., pp. 499–528). Philadelphia, PA: Lippincott Williams & Wilkins.

Black, D. W., Baumgard, C. H., & Bell, S. E. (1995). A 16- to 45-year follow-up of 71 men with antisocial personality disorder. *Comprehensive Psychiatry, 36*(2), 130–140.

Blazer, D. G., Steffens, D. C., & Koenig, H. G. (2009). Mood disorders. In D. G. Blazer & D. C. Steffens (Eds.), *The American Psychiatric Publishing textbook of geriatric psychiatry* (4th ed., pp. 275–299). Washington, DC: American Psychiatric Publishing.

Blazer, D. G., & Williams, C. D. (1980). The epidemiology of dysphoria and depression in an elderly population. *American Journal of Psychiatry, 137,* 439–444.

Blow, F. (1998). *Substance abuse among older adults.* Treatment Improvement Protocol Series No. 26. Rockville, MD: U.S. Department of Health & Human Services, Public Health Service, Substance Abuse and Mental Health Services, Center for Substance Abuse Treatment.

Blum, N. S. (1991). The management of stigma by Alzheimer family caregivers. *Journal of Contemporary Ethnography, 20,* 263–284.

Book, H. E. (1988). Empathy: Misconceptions and misuses in psychotherapy. *American Journal of Psychiatry, 145*(4), 420–424.

Borson, S., Scanlan, J., Brush, M., Vitaliano, P., & Dokmak, A. (2000). The Mini-Cog: A cognitive "vital signs" measure for dementia screening in multi-lingual elderly. *International Journal of Geriatric Psychiatry, 15,* 1021–1027.

Boyd, R. (1980). Materialism without reductionism: What physicalism does not entail. In N. Block (Ed.), *Readings in philosophy of psychology* (Vol. 1, pp. 67–106). Cambridge, MA: Harvard University Press.

Breuer, J., & Freud, S. (1964). Studies on hysteria. In J. Strachey (Ed. & Trans.) *The standard edition of the complete psychological works of Sigmund Freud* (Vol. 2, pp. xxix–251). London: Hogarth. (Originally published 1895)

Brody, J. (2009). *Jane Brody's guide to the great beyond.* New York: Random House.

Bush, K., Kivlahan, D. R., McDonell, M. B., Fihn, S. D., & Bradley, K. A. (1998). The AUDIT alcohol consumption questions (AUDIT-C): An effective brief screening test for problem drinking. *Archives of Internal Medicine, 158,* 1789–1795.

Butler, R. N. (1963). The life review: An interpretation of reminiscence in the aged. *Psychiatry, 26,* 65–75.

Butler, R. N. (1975). *Why survive? Being old in America.* New York: Harper & Row.

Butler, R. N. (2008). *The longevity revolution: The benefits and challenges of living a long life.* New York: Public Affairs.

Carstensen, L. L., Pasupathi, M., Mayr, U., & Nesselroade, J. R. (2000). Emotional experience in everyday life across the adult life span. *Journal of Personality and Social Psychology, 79*(4), 644–655.

Cath, S. H. (1984). A psychoanalytic hour: A late-life awakening. In L. W. Lazarus (Ed.), *Clinical approaches to psychotherapy with the elderly* (pp. 2–14). Washington, DC: American Psychiatric Publishing.

Centers for Disease Control and Prevention. (2005). *Web-based injury statistics query and reporting system (WISQARS).* Retrieved December 1, 2009 from: www.cdc.gov/ncipc/wisqars/default.htm

Charles, S. T., & Carstensen, L. L. (2008). Unpleasant situations elicit different emotional responses in younger and older adults. *Psychology and Aging, 23*(3), 495–550.

Charles, S. T., & Horwitz, B. N. (2010). Positive emotions and health: What we know about aging. In C. A. Depp & D. V. Jeste (Eds.), *Success-*

ful cognitive and emotional aging (pp. 56–72). Washington, DC: American Psychiatric Publishing.

Chin, A. M. H. (2007). Clinical effects of reminiscence therapy in older adults: A meta-analysis of controlled trials. *Hong Kong Journal of Occupational Therapy, 17*(1), 10–22.

Clark, D. A., Hollifield, M., Leahy, R., & Beck, J. S. (2009). Theory of cognitive therapy. In G. O. Gabbard (Ed.), *Textbook of psychotherapeutic treatments* (pp. 165–200). Washington, DC: American Psychiatric Publishing.

Clipp, E. C., & George, L. K. (1990). Psychotropic drug use among caregivers of patients with dementia. *Journal American Geriatrics Society, 38,* 227–235.

Cohen, C. I. (1993). Age-related correlations in patient symptom management strategies in schizophrenia: An exploratory study. *International Journal of Geriatric Psychiatry, 8,* 211–213.

Cohen, G. D. (2000). *The creative age: Awakening human potential in the second half of life.* New York: HarperCollins.

Cohen, G. D. (2005). *The mature mind: The positive power of the aging brain.* New York: Basic Books.

Commons, M. L., & Richards, F. A. (1984). A general model of stage theory. In M. L. Commons, F. A. Richards, & S. Armon (Eds.), *Beyond formal operations Vol. 1: Late adolescent and adult cognitive development* (pp. 120–140). New York: Praeger.

Connell, C. M., Janevic, M. R., & Gallant, M. P. (2001). The costs of caring: Impact of dementia on family caregivers. *Journal of Geriatric Psychiatry & Neurology, 14*(4), 179–187.

Conwell, Y., Duberstein, P. R., & Caine, E. D. (2002). Risk factors for suicide in later life. *Biological Psychiatry, 52,* 193–204.

Costa, P. T., Jr., & McCrae, R. R. (1992). *Revised NEO Personality Inventory (NEO-PI-R) and NEO Five-Factor Inventory (NEO-FFI) professional manual.* Odessa, FL: Psychological Assessment Resources.

Costa, P. T., Jr., & McCrae, R. R. (1994). Set like plaster? Evidence for the stability of adult personality. In T. F. Heatherton & J. L. Weinberger (Eds.), *Can personality change?* (pp. 21–40). Washington, DC: American Psychological Association.

Costa, P. T., Jr., & Widiger, T. A. (1994). Introduction: Personality disorders and the five-factor model of personality. In P. T. Costa Jr. & T. A. Widiger (Eds.), *Personality disorders and the five-factor model of personality* (pp. 1–12). Washington, DC: American Psychological Association.

Crook, T., Bartus, R., Ferris, S., Whitehouse, P., Cohen, G. D., & Gershon, S. (1986). Age-associated memory impairment: Proposed diagnostic criteria and measures of clinical change—report of a National Institute of Mental Health work group. *Developmental Neuropsychology, 2,* 261–276.

Cullum, S., Huppert, F. A., McGee, M., Dening T. O. M., Ahmed, A., Paykel, E. S., & Brayne, C. (2000). Decline across different domains of cognitive function in normal aging: Results of a longitudinal population-based study using CAMCOG. *International Journal of Geriatric Psychiatry, 15,* 853–862.

Cumming, E., & Henry, W. (1961). *Growing old: The process of disengagement.* New York: Basic Books.

de las Cuevas, C., Sanz, E. J., de la Fuente, J. A., Padilla, J., & Berenguer, J. C. (2000). The Severity of Dependence Scale (SDS) as a screening test for benzodiazepine dependence: SDS validation study. *Addiction, 95,* 245–250.

Dewan, M., Weerasekera, P., & Stormon, L. (2009). Techniques of brief psychodynamic psychotherapy. In G. O. Gabbard (Ed.), *Textbook of psychotherapeutic treatments* (pp. 69–96). Washington, DC: American Psychiatric Publishing.

Diagnosis and treatment of depression in late life: Consensus statement. (1991). *NIH Consensus Development Conference, 9*(3), 1–27.

Dobbs, D., Eckert, J. K., Rubenstein, B., Keimig, L., Clark, L., Frankowski, A. C., & Zimmerman, S. (2008). An ethnographic study of stigma and ageism in residential care or assisted living. *Gerontologist, 48*(4), 517–526.

Doraiswamy, P. M., & Agronin, M. E. (2009, April 28). Brain games: Do they work? *Scientific American Mind.* Retrieved September 25, 2009, from http://www.scientificamerican.com/article.cfm?id=brain-games-do-they-really

Duberstein, P. R., Heisel, M. J., & Conwell, Y. (2006). Suicide in older adults. In M. E. Agronin & G. J. Maletta (Eds.), *Principles and practice of geriatric psychiatry* (pp. 393–405). Philadelphia, PA: Lippincott Williams & Wilkins.

Dunkin, J. J., & Amano, S. S. (2005). Psychological changes with normal aging. In B. J. Sadock & V. A. Sadock (Eds.), *Kaplan & Sadock's comprehensive textbook of psychiatry* (8th ed., pp. 3624–3631). Philadelphia, PA: Lippincott Williams & Wilkins.

Dunkin, J. J., & Anderson-Hanley, C. (1998). Dementia caregiver bur-

References

den: A review of the literature and guidelines for assessment and intervention. *Neurology, 51*(Suppl. 1), S53–S60.

Dyer, A. R. (1988). *Ethics and psychiatry: Toward professional definition.* Washington, DC: American Psychiatric Publishing.

Erikson, E. H. (1985). *Childhood and society.* New York: Norton. (Originally published 1950)

Erikson, E. H., & Erikson, J. M. (1997). *The life cycle completed: Extended version with new chapters on the ninth stage of development.* New York: Norton.

Erikson, E. H., Erikson, J. M., & Kivnick, H. Q. (1986). *Vital involvement in old age.* New York: Norton.

Ernst, R. L., & Hay, J. W. (1994). The US economic and social costs of Alzheimer's disease revisited. *American Journal of Public Health, 84*(8), 1261–1264.

Evans, D. (2004). *Placebo: Mind over matter in modern medicine.* New York: Oxford University Press.

Fishbain, D. A., Cutler, R., Rosomoff, H. L., & Rosomoff, R. S. (1997). Chronic pain–associated depression: Antecedent or consequence of chronic pain? A review. *Clinical Journal of Pain, 13,* 116–137.

Folstein, M. F., Folstein, S. E., & McHugh, P. R. (1975). "Mini–Mental State": A practical method for grading the cognitive state of patients for the clinician. *Journal of Psychiatric Research, 12*(3), 189–198.

Fonagy, P., & Target, M. (2009). Theoretical models of psychodynamic psychotherapy. In G. O. Gabbard (Ed.), *Textbook of psychotherapeutic treatments* (pp. 3–42). Washington, DC: American Psychiatric Publishing.

Forester, B., Antognini, F. C., & Stoll, A. (2006). Geriatric bipolar disorder. In M. E. Agronin & G. J. Maletta (Eds.), *Principles and practice of geriatric psychiatry* (pp. 367–391). Philadelphia, PA: Lippincott Williams & Wilkins.

Freud, S. (1964a). The dynamics of transference. In J. Strachey (Ed. & Trans.), *The standard edition of the complete psychological works of Sigmund Freud* (Vol. 12, pp. 97–108). London: Hogarth. (Originally published 1912)

Freud, S. (1964b). On psychotherapy. In J. Strachey (Ed. & Trans.), *The standard edition of the complete psychological works of Sigmund Freud* (Vol. 7, pp. 255–268). London: Hogarth. (Originally published 1905)

Fries, J. F. (1980). Aging, natural death, and the compression of morbidity. *New England Journal of Medicine, 303,* 130–135.

Gabbard, G. O. (2005). *Psychodynamic psychiatry in clinical practice* (4th ed.). Washington, DC: American Psychiatric Publishing.

Gabbard, G. O. (2009). Techniques of psychodynamic psychotherapy. In G. O. Gabbard (Ed.), *Textbook of psychotherapeutic treatments* (pp. 43–67). Washington, DC: American Psychiatric Publishing.

Gallagher-Thompson, D., & Steffen, A. (1994). Comparative effects of cognitive-behavioral and brief psychodynamic therapies for depressed family caregivers. *Journal of Consulting and Clinical Psychology, 62,* 543–549.

Gallagher-Thompson, D., & Thompson, L. W. (1996). Applying cognitive-behavioral therapy to the psychological problems of later life. In S. H. Zarit & B. G. Knight (Eds.), *A guide to psychotherapy and aging* (pp. 61–82). Washington, DC: American Psychological Association.

Gallo, J. J., Anthony, J. C., & Muthen, B. O. (1994). Age differences in the symptoms of depression: A latent trait analysis. *Journal of Gerontolgy: Psychological Sciences, 49,* P251–P264.

Geda, Y. E., Negash, S., & Peterson, R. C. (2006). Memory disorders. In M. E. Agronin & G. J. Maletta (Eds.), *Principles and practice of geriatric psychiatry* (pp. 273–282). Philadelphia, PA: Lippincott Williams & Wilkins.

Gilbertson, M. W., Shenton, M. E., Ciszewski, A., Kasai, K., & Lasko, N. B. (2002). Smaller hippocampal volume predicts pathologic vulnerability to psychological trauma. *Nature Neuroscience, 5,* 1242–1247.

Goldberg, E. (2005). *The wisdom paradox.* New York: Gotham Books.

Goldwasser, A. N., Auerbach, S. M., & Harkins, S. W. (1987). Cognitive, affective, and behavioral effects of reminiscence group therapy on demented elderly. *International Journal of Aging and Human Development, 25,* 209–222.

Gorey, K. M., & Cryns, A. G. (1991). Group work as interventive modality with the older depressed client: A meta-analytic review. *Journal of Gerontological Social Work, 16,* 137–157.

Grad, R., Tamblyn, R., Holbrook, A. M., Hurley, J., Feightner, J., & Gayton, D. (1999). Risk of a new benzodiazepine prescription in relation to recent hospitalization. *Journal of American Geriatrics Society, 47,* 184–188.

Grant, B. F., Dawson, D. A., Stinson, F. S., Chou, S. P., Dufour, M. C., & Pickering, R. P. (2004). The 12-month prevalence and trends in DSM-IV alcohol abuse and dependence: United States, 1991–1992 and 2001–2002. *Drug and Alcohol Dependence, 74,* 223–234.

References

Grant, B. F., Hasin, D. S., & Stinson, F. S. (2004). Prevalence, correlates, and disability of personality disorders in the United States: Results from the National Epidemiologic Survey on Alcohol and Related Conditions. *Journal of Clinical Psychiatry, 65*(7), 948–958.

Green, M. F., Kern, R. S., & Heaton, R. K. (2004). Longitudinal studies of cognition and functional outcome in schizophrenia: Implications for MATRICS. *Schizophrenia Research, 72,* 41–51.

Grisso, T., & Appelbaum, P. S. (1998). *Assessing competence to consent to treatment: A guide for physicians and other health care professionals.* New York: Oxford University Press.

Gross, J. J., Carstensen, L. L., Pasupathi, M., Tsai, J., Skorpen, C. G., & Hsu, A. Y. (1997). Emotion and aging: Experience, expression, and control. *Psychology and Aging, 12,* 590–598.

Gutheil, T., & Gabbard, G. O. (1998). Misuses and misunderstandings of boundary theory in clinical and regulatory settings. *American Journal of Psychiatry, 155,* 409–414.

Hall, C. S., & Lindzey, G. (1958). *Theories of personality.* New York: Wiley.

Halpern, J. (2001). *From detached concern to empathy: Humanizing medical practice.* Oxford, UK: Oxford University Press.

Harris, M. J., & Jeste, D. V. (1988). Late-onset schizophrenia: An overview. *Schizophrenia Bulletin, 14,* 39–55.

Harvey, P. D., Silverman, J. M., Mohs, R. C., Parrella, M., White, L., Powchik, P., . . . Davis, K. L. (1999). Cognitive decline in late-life schizophrenia: A longitudinal study of geriatric chronically hospitalized patients. *Biological Psychiatry, 45,* 32–40.

Harwood, D. G., Barker, W. W., Cantillon, M., Loewenstein, D. A., Ownby, R., & Duara, R. (1998). Depressive symptomatology in first-degree family caregivers of Alzheimer disease patients: A cross-ethnic comparison. *Alzheimer Disease and Associated Disorders, 12*(4), 340–346.

Hausdorf, F. F. J., Levy, B., & Wei, J. (1999). The power of ageism on physical function of older persons: Reversibility of age-related gait changes. *Journal of the American Geriatrics Society, 47,* 1346–1349.

Hayflick, L. (1994). *How and why we age.* New York: Ballantine.

Heaton, R. K., Gladso, J. A., Palmer, B. W., Kuck, J., Marcotte, T. D., & Jeste, D. V. (2001). Stability and course of neuropsychological deficits in schizophrenia. *Archives of General Psychiatry, 58,* 24–32.

Hill, R. D. (2005). *Positive aging: A guide for mental health professionals and consumers.* New York: Norton.

Himes, C. L. (2001). *Elderly Americans*. Washington, DC: Population Reference Bureau.

Hinrichsen, G. A. (1997). Interpersonal psychotherapy for depressed older adults. *Journal of Geriatric Psychiatry, 30,* 239–257.

Hinrichsen, G. A. (2009). Interpersonal psychotherapy: A treatment for late-life depression. *Psychiatric Annals, 39*(9), 838–843.

Hinrichsen, G. A., & Clougherty, K. F. (2006). *Interpersonal psychotherapy for depressed older adults*. Washington, DC: American Psychological Association.

Hoffman, M. L. (2000). *Empathy and moral development: Implications for caring and justice*. Cambridge, UK: Cambridge University Press.

Holroyd, S., & Duryee, J. J. (1997). Substance use disorders in a geriatric psychiatry outpatient clinic: Prevalence and epidemiologic characteristics. *Journal of Nervous and Mental Disease, 185,* 627–632.

Horowitz, M. J. (1997). *Formulation as a basis for planning psychotherapy treatment*. Washington, DC: American Psychiatric Publishing.

Hsieh, H. F., & Wang, J. J. (2003). Effect of reminiscence therapy on depression in older adults: A systematic review. *International Journal of Nursing Studies, 40,* 335–345.

Jacobowitz, J., & Newton, N. (1990). Time, context, and character: A life-span view of psychopathology during the second half of life. In R. A. Nemiroff & C. A. Colarusso (Eds.), *New dimensions in adult development* (pp. 306–329). New York: Basic Books.

Jacobson, S. (1995, April). Overselling depression to the old folks. *Atlantic Monthly,* pp. 46–51.

James, W. (1890). *The principles of psychology*. New York: Holt.

Jeste, D. V., Gladsjo, J. A., Lindamer, J. A., & Lacro, J. P. (1996). Medical comorbidity in schizophrenia. *Schizophrenia Bulletin, 22,* 413–430.

Jeste, D. V., Symonds, L. L., Harris, M. J., Paulsen, J. S., Palmer, B. W., & Heaton, R. K. (1997). Nondementia nonpraecox dementia praecox? Late-onset schizophrenia. *American Journal of Geriatric Psychiatry, 5,* 302–317.

Karim, S., & Burns, A. (2006). Psychosis in the elderly. In M. E. Agronin & G. J. Maletta (Eds.), *Principles and practice of geriatric psychiatry* (pp. 407–419). Philadelphia, PA: Lippincott Williams & Wilkins.

Karp, J. F., & Weiner, D. K. (2006). Psychiatric care of the older adult with persistent pain. In M. E. Agronin & G. J. Maletta (Eds.), *Principles and practice of geriatric psychiatry* (pp. 657–676). Philadelphia, PA: Lippincott Williams & Wilkins.

References

Keefe, R. S. E., & Eesley, C. E. (2009). Neurocognition in schizophrenia. In B. J. Sadock, V. A. Sadock, & P. Ruiz (Eds.), *Kaplan & Sadock's comprehensive textbook of psychiatry* (9th ed., pp. 1531–1541). Philadelphia, PA: Lippincott Williams & Wilkins.

Kernberg, O. F. (1965). Notes on countertransference. *Journal of the American Psychoanalytic Association, 13,* 38–56.

Kivnick, H. Q. (1993). Everyday mental health: A guide to assessing strengths. *Generations, 17*(1), 13–20.

Klerman, G. L., Weismann, M. M., Rounsaville, B. J., & Chevron, E. S. (1984). *Interpersonal psychotherapy of depression.* Northvale, NJ: Jason Aronson.

Knight, B. G. (1996). *Psychotherapy with older adults* (2nd ed.). Thousand Oaks, CA: Sage.

Knopman, D. (2006). Alzheimer's disease. In M. E. Agronin & G. J. Maletta (Eds.), *Principles and practice of geriatric psychiatry* (pp. 283–300). Philadelphia, PA: Lippincott Williams & Wilkins.

Kraepelin, E. (1893). *Psychiatrie: Ein Lehrbuch für Studierende und Ärzte.* Vol. 4. Leipzig, Germany: Barth.

Kral, V. (1962). Senescent forgetfulness: Benign and malignant. *Canadian Medical Association Journal, 86,* 257–260.

LaBouvie-Vief, G. (1982). Growth and aging in life-span perspective. *Human Development, 25,* 65–78.

Lantz, M. (2006). Adjustment disorders. In M. E. Agronin & G. J. Maletta (Eds.), *Principles and practice of geriatric psychiatry* (pp. 429–448). Philadelphia, PA: Lippincott Williams & Wilkins.

Lauderdale, S. A., Kelly, K., & Sheikh, J. I. (2006). Anxiety disorders in the elderly. In M. E. Agronin & G. J. Maletta (Eds.), *Principles and practice of geriatric psychiatry* (pp. 421–427). Philadelphia, PA: Lippincott Williams & Wilkins.

Lazarus, L. W., Groves, L., Gutmann, D., Ripeckyi, A., Frankel, R., Newton, N., . . . Havasy-Galloway, S. (1987). Brief psychotherapy with the elderly: A study of process and outcome. In J. Sadavoy & M. Leszcz (Eds.), *Treating the elderly with psychotherapy: The scope for change in late life* (pp. 265–293). Madison, CT: International Universities Press.

Leszcz, M. (1987). Group psychotherapy with the elderly. In J. Sadavoy & M. Leszcz (Eds.), *Treating the elderly with psychotherapy: The scope for change in late life* (pp. 325–349). Madison, CT: International Universities Press.

Leszcz, M. (2004). Group therapy. In J. Sadavoy, L. F. Jarvik, G. T. Grossberg, & B. S. Meyers (Eds.), *Comprehensive textbook of geriatric psychiatry* (3rd ed., pp. 1023–1054). New York: Norton.

Leuchter, A. F., & Spar, J. E. (1985). The late-onset psychoses. *Journal of Nervous and Mental Disease, 173,* 488–494.

Leventhal, E. A., & Burns, E. A. (2004). The biology of aging. In J. Sadavoy, L. F. Jarvik, G. T. Grossberg, & B. S. Meyers (Eds.), *Comprehensive textbook of geriatric psychiatry* (3rd ed., pp. 105–130). New York: Norton.

Lipsitz, J. D. (2009). Theory of interpersonal psychotherapy. In G. O. Gabbard (Ed.), *Textbook of psychotherapeutic treatments* (pp. 289–308). Washington, DC: American Psychiatric Publishing.

Lipton, J. (1977). *An exaltation of larks* (2nd ed.). New York: Grossman.

Lively, W. J. (2002). Treating the emotional dysregulation cluster of traits. *Psychiatric Annals, 32*(10), 601–607.

Llorente, M. D., Oslin, D. W., & Malphurs, J. (2006). Substance use disorders in the elderly. In M. E. Agronin & G. J. Maletta (Eds.), *Principles and practice of geriatric psychiatry* (pp. 471–488). Philadelphia, PA: Lippincott Williams & Wilkins.

Loewenstein, D. A., Acevedo, A., Czaja, S. J., & Duara, R. (2004). Cognitive rehabilitation of mildly impaired Alzheimer disease patients on cholinesterase inhibitors. *American Journal of Geriatric Psychiatry, 12*(4), 395–402.

Lynch, T. R., Morse, J. Q., Mendelson, T., & Robins, C. J. (2003). Dialectical behavior therapy for depressed older adults: A randomized pilot study. *American Journal of Geriatric Psychiatry, 11,* 33–45.

Lynn, J. (2005). Living long in fragile health: The new demographics shape end of life care. *Improving end of life care: Why has it been so difficult? Hasting Center Report Special Report, 35*(6), S14–S18.

Mahncke, H. W., Bronstone, A., & Merzenich, M. M. (2006). Brain plasticity and functional losses in the aged: Scientific bases for a novel intervention. *Progress in Brain Research, 157,* 81–109.

Mahncke, H. W., Connor, B. B., Appelman, J., & Merzenich, M. M. (2006). Memory enhancement in healthy older adults using a brain plasticity–based training program: A randomized, controlled study. *Proceedings of the National Academy of Sciences, 103*(33), 12523–12528.

Maltsberger, J. T., & Buie, D. H. (1974). Countertransference hate in the treatment of suicidal patients. *Archives of General Psychiatry, 30,* 625–633.

May, R. (1977). *The meaning of anxiety.* New York: Norton. (Originally published 1950)

References

McCrae, R. R., & Costa, P. T., Jr. (1990). *Personality in adulthood*. New York: Guilford.

McEwan, E. G. (1987). The whole grandfather: An intergenerational approach to family therapy. In J. Sadavoy & M. Leszcz (Eds.), *Treating the elderly with psychotherapy: The scope for change in late life* (pp. 295–324). Madison, CT: International Universities Press.

McGlashan, T. H. (1986). The Chestnut Lodge follow-up study: III. Long-term outcome of borderline personalities. *Archives of General Psychiatry, 43*, 20–30.

McGoldrick, M., Gerson, R., & Petry, S. (2008). *Genograms: assessment and intervention*. New York: Norton.

McGurk, S. R., Twamley, E. W., Sitzer, D. I., McHugo, G. J., & Mueser, K. T. (2007). A meta-analysis of cognitive remediation in schizophrenia. *American Journal of Psychiatry, 164*(12), 1791–1802.

McMurdo, M. E. T., & Rennie, L. (1991). A controlled trial of exercise by residents of old people's homes. *Age and Ageing, 22*, 11–15.

Meakins, J. C. (1936). *The practice of medicine*. St. Louis, MO: C. V. Mosby.

Moene, F. C., Landberg, E. H., Hoogduin, K. A., Spinhoven, P., Hertzberger, L. I., Kleyweg, R. P., & Weeda, J. (2000). Organic syndromes diagnosed as conversion disorder: Identification and frequency in a study of 85 patients. *Journal of Psychosomatic Research, 49*(1), 7–12.

Moran, J. A., & Gatz, M. (1987). Group therapies for nursing home adults: An evaluation of two treatment approaches. *Gerontologist, 27*, 588–591.

Moss, K. S., & Scogin, F. R. (2008). Behavioral and cognitive treatments for geriatric depression: An evidence-based perspective. In D. Gallagher-Thompson, A. M. Steffen, & L. W. Thompson (Eds.), *Handbook of behavioral and cognitive therapies in older adults* (pp. 1–17). New York: Springer.

Mouradian, M. S., Rodgers, J., Kashmere, J., Jickling, G., McCombe, J., Emery, D. J., . . . & Shuaib, A. (2004). Can rt-PA be administered to the wrong patient? Two patients with somatoform disorder. *Canadian Journal of Neurological Sciences, 31*(1), 99–101.

Murray, H. A. (1981). This I believe. In E. S. Shneidman (Ed.), *Endeavors in psychology: Selections from the personology of Henry A. Murray* (pp. 613–614). New York: Harper & Row. (Originally published 1954)

Murray, H. A., & Kluckhohn, C. (1953). Outline of a conception of personality. In C. Kluckhohn, H. A. Murray, & D. Schneider (Eds.), *Person-*

ality in nature, society, and culture (2nd ed., pp. 3–52). New York: Knopf.

Myers, J. K., Weissman, M. M., Tischler, G. L., Tischler, G. L., Holzer, C. E., III, Leaf, P. J.,. . . Stoltzman, R. (1984). Six-month prevalence of psychiatric disorders in three communities. *Archives of General Psychiatry, 41,* 959–970.

Nagy, I., & Spark, G. M. (1973). *Invisible loyalties: Reciprocity in intergenerational family therapy.* Hagerstown, MD: Harper & Row.

Nasreddine, Z. S., Chertkow, H., Phillips, N., Whitehead, V., Collin, I., & Cummings, J. L. (2004). The Montreal Cognitive Assessment (MoCA): A brief cognitive screening tool for detection of mild cognitive impairment. *Neurology, 62*(7, Suppl. 5), A132.

Nemiroff, R. A., & Colarusso, C. A. (1990). Frontiers of adult development in theory and practice. In R. A. Nemiroff & C. A. Colarusso (Eds.), *New dimensions in adult development* (pp. 97–124). New York: Basic Books.

Neugeboren, J. (1997). *Imagining Robert: My brother, madness, and survival: A memior.* New York: William Morrow.

Neugeboren, J. (1999). *Transforming madness: New lives for people living with mental illness.* New York: William Morrow.

Neugeboren, J. (2006, February 6). Meds alone couldn't bring Robert back. *Newsweek,* p. 17.

Newmann, J. P., Klein, M. H., Jensen, J. E., & Essex, M. J. (1996). Depressive symptom experiences among older women: A comparison of alternative measurement approaches. *Psychology and Aging, 11,* 112–126.

Nezu, A. M., Nezu, C. M., & Perri, M. G. (1989). *Problem-solving therapy for depression: Theory, research, and clinical guidelines.* New York: Wiley.

Nielsen, L., Knuton, B., & Carstensen, L. L. (2008). Affect dynamics, affective forecasting, and aging. *Emotion, 8*(3), 318–330.

Office of Applied Studies. (2007). *Results from the 2006 National Survey on Drug Use and Health: National findings* (DHHS Publication No. SMA 07-4293, NSDUH Series H-32). Rockville, MD: Substance Abuse and Mental Health Services Administration.

Ong, A. D., & Bergeman, C. S. (2007). Psychosocial theories. In K. S. Markides (Ed.), *Encyclopedia of health and aging* (pp. 480–483). Thousand Oaks, CA: Sage.

Osler, W. (1919). *A way of life. An address delivered to Yale students on the evening, April 20th, 1913.* Springfield, IL: C. C. Thomas.

Oslin, D. W., Katz, I. R., & Edel, W. S. (2000). Effects of alcohol consumption on the treatment of depression among elderly patients. *American Journal of Geriatric Psychiatry, 8,* 215–220.

Oslin, D. W., & Mavandadi, S. (2009). Alcohol and drug problems. In D. G. Blazer & D. C. Steffens (Eds.), *The American Psychiatric Publishing textbook of geriatric psychiatry* (4th ed., pp. 409–428). Washington, DC: American Psychiatric Publishing.

Pap, K. V., Walsh, S. J., & Snyder, P. J. (2009). Immediate and delayed effects of cognitive interventions in healthy elderly: A review of current literature and future directions. *Alzheimer's & Dementia, 5,* 50–60.

Paris, J., Brown, R., & Nowlis, D. (1987). Long-term follow-up of borderline patients in a general hospital. *Comprehensive Psychiatry, 2,* 530–535.

Parker, R. G. (1995). Reminiscence: A continuity theory framework. *Gerontologist, 35*(4), 515–525.

Parks, S. M. (2000). A practical guide to caring for caregivers. *American Family Physician, 62*(12), 2613–2622.

Parmalee, P. A., Katz, I. R., & Lawton, M. P. (1989). Depression among institutionalized aged: Assessment and prevalence estimation. *Journal of Gerontology, 44*(1), M22–M29.

Parsons, T. (1951). *The social system.* New York: Free Press.

Peterson, C., & Seligman, M. E. P. (2004). *Character strengths and virtues: A handbook and classification.* New York: Oxford University Press.

Pickholtz, J. L., & Malamut, B. L. (2008). Cognitive changes associated with normal aging. In J. I. Sirven & B. L. Malamut (Eds.), *Clinical neurology of the older adult* (2nd ed., pp. 64–76). Philadelphia, PA: Lippincott Williams & Wilkins.

Pollack, G. H. (1987). The mourning-liberation process: Ideas on the inner life of the older adult. In J. Sadavoy & M. Leszcz (Eds.), *Treating the elderly with psychotherapy: The scope for change in late life* (pp. 3–30). Madison, CT: International Universities Press.

Rabinowitz, T., Hirdes, J. P., & Desjardins, I. (2006). Somatoform disorders in late life. In M. E. Agronin & G. Maletta (Eds.), *Principles and practice of geriatric psychiatry* (pp. 489–503). Philadelphia, PA: Lippincott Williams & Wilkins.

Rattenbury, C., & Stones, M. J. (1989). A controlled evaluation of reminiscence and current topic discussion groups in a nursing home context. *Gerontologist, 29,* 768–771.

Reminiscence. (2009). In *American Heritage dictionary of the English lan-*

guage (4th ed.). New York: Houghton Mifflin. Retrieved October 1, 2009, from http://dictionary.reference.com/browse/reminiscence

Reynolds, C. F., III, Frank, E., Perel, J. M., Imber, S. D., Cornes, C., Miller, M. D., . . . Kupfer, D. J. (1999). Nortriptyline and interpersonal psychotherapy as maintenance therapies for recurrent major depression: A randomized controlled trial in patients older than 59 years old. *Journal of the American Medical Association, 281*(1), 39–45.

Robins, L. N., Helzer, J. E., Weissman, M. M., Orvaschel, H., Gruenberg, E., Burke, J. D., Jr., & Regier, D. A. (1984). Lifetime prevalence of specific psychiatric disorders in three sites. *Archives of General Psychiatry, 41,* 949–958.

Robinson, R. G., Starr, L. B., Kubos, K. L., & Price, T. R. (1983). A two-year longitudinal study of post-stroke mood disorders: Findings during the initial evaluation. *Stroke, 14,* 736–741.

Rolland, J. S., & Walsh, F. (2009). Family systems theory and practice. In G. O. Gabbard (Ed.), *Textbook of psychotherapeutic treatments* (pp. 499–531). Washington, DC: American Psychiatric Publishing.

Rosenthal, R.N. (2009). Techniques of individual supportive psychotherapy. In G. O. Gabbard (Ed.), *Textbook of psychotherapeutic treatments* (pp. 417–446). Washington, DC: American Psychiatric Publishing.

Rosenzweig, A., Prigerson, H., Miller, M. D., & Reynolds, C. F., III. (1997). Bereavement and late-life depression: Grief and its complications in the elderly. *Annual Review of Medicine, 48,* 421–428.

Rowe, J. W., & Kahn, R. L. (1998). *Successful aging.* New York: Pantheon Books.

Rupert, M. P., Loewenstein, D. A., & Eisdorfer, C. (2004). Normal aging: Changes in cognitive abilities. In J. Sadavoy, L. F. Jarvik, G. T. Grossberg, & B. S. Meyers (Eds.), *Comprehensive textbook of geriatric psychiatry* (3rd ed., pp. 131–146). New York: Norton.

Saiger, G. M. (2001). Group psychotherapy with older adults. *Psychiatry, 64*(2), 132–145.

Sapolsky, R. M., Krey, L. C., & McEwen, B. S. (1986). The neuroendocrinology of stress and aging: The glucocorticoid cascade hypothesis. *Endocrinology Review, 7*(3), 284–301.

Schaie, K. W. (2005). *Developmental influences on adult intelligence: The Seattle Longitudinal Study.* New York: Oxford University Press.

Schaie, K. W., & Willis, S. L. (1993). Age difference patterns of psychometric intelligence in adulthood: Generalizability within and across ability domains. *Psychological Aging, 8,* 44–55.

Schonfeld, L. (2007). Elder abuse and neglect. In K. S. Markides (Ed.), *Encyclopedia of health and aging* (pp. 188–190). Thousand Oaks, CA: Sage.

Schuckit, M. A. (2009). Alcohol-related disorders. In B. J. Sadock, V. A. Sadock, & P. Ruiz (Eds.), *Kaplan & Sadock's comprehensive textbook of psychiatry* (9th ed., pp. 1268–1288). Philadelphia, PA: Lippincott Williams & Wilkins.

Schulz, R., & Beach, S. R. (1999). Caregiving as a risk factor for mortality: The Caregiver Health Effects Study. *Journal of the American Medical Association, 282*(23), 2215–2219.

Schulz, R., O'Brien, A. T., Bookwala, J., & Fleissner, K. (1995). Psychiatric and physical morbidity effects of dementia caregiving: Prevalence, correlates, and causes. *Gerontologist, 35*(6), 771–791.

Schwartz, K. (2004). Concurrent group and individual psychotherapy in a psychiatric day hospital for depressed elderly. *International Journal of Group Psychotherapy, 54*, 177–201.

Schwartz, K. (2007). Remembering the forgotten: Psychotherapy groups for the nursing home resident. *International Journal of Group Psychotherapy, 57*(4), 491–514.

Searle, J. (1984). *Minds, brains, and science.* Cambridge, MA: Harvard University Press.

Sheehan, B., Bass, C., Briggs, R., & Jacoby, R. (2003). Somatization among older primary care attendees. *Psychological Medicine, 33*(5), 867–877.

Siegler, I. C., Poon, L. W., Madden, D. J., Dilworth-Anderson, P., Schaie, K. W., Willis, S. W., & Martin, P. (2009). Psychological aspects of normal aging. In D. G. Blazer & D. C. Steffens (Eds.), *The American Psychiatric Publishing textbook of geriatric psychiatry* (4th ed., pp. 137–155). Washington, DC: American Psychiatric Publishing.

Sims, A. (1995). *Symptoms in the mind: An introduction to descriptive psychopathology* (2nd ed.). Philadelphia, PA: W. B. Saunders.

Smith, G. E., Housen, P., Yaffe, K., Ruff, R., Kennison, R. F., Mahncke, H. W., & Zelinski, E. M. (2009). A cognitive training program based on principles of brain plasticity: Results from the Improvement in Memory With Plasticity-Based Adaptive Cognitive Training (IMPACT) study. *Journal of the American Geriatrics Society, 57*(4), 594–603.

Stevens-Long, J. (1990). Adult development: Theories past and future. In R. A. Nemiroff & C. A. Colarusso (Eds.), *New dimensions in adult development* (pp. 125–169). New York: Basic Books.

Styron, W. (1989, December). Darkness visible. *Vanity Fair,* pp. 212–286.

Sugar, J. A., & McDowd, J. M. (1992). Memory, learning, and attention. In J. E. Birren, R. B. Sloane, & G. D. Cohen (Eds.), *Handbook of mental health and aging* (2nd ed., pp. 307–337). New York: Academic Press.

Sullivan, H. S. (1953). *The interpersonal theory of psychiatry.* New York: Norton.

Swan, G. E., & Carmelli, D. (1996). Curiosity and mortality in aging adults: A 5-year follow-up of the Western Collaborative Group Study. *Psychology and Aging, 11,* 449–453.

Swartz, H. A., & Markowitz, J. C. (2009). Techniques of interpersonal therapy. In G. O. Gabbard (Ed.), *Textbook of psychotherapeutic treatments* (pp. 309–338). Washington, DC: American Psychiatric Publishing.

Swift, J. (2003). *Gulliver's travels.* New York: Barnes & Noble Classics. (Originally published 1735)

Tariq, S. H., Tumosa, N., Chibnall, J. T., Perry, M. H., III, & Morley, J. E. (2006). Comparison of the Saint Louis University Mental Status Examination and the Mini–Mental State Examination for detecting dementia and mild neurocognitive disorder: A pilot study. *American Journal of Geriatric Psychiatry, 14*(11), 900–910.

Thompson, L. W., Spira, A. P., Depp, C. A., McGee, J. S., & Gallagher-Thompson, D. (2006). The geriatric caregiver. In M. E. Agronin & G. J. Maletta (Eds.), *Principles and practice of geriatric psychiatry* (pp. 37–48). Philadelphia, PA: Lippincott Williams & Wilkins.

Tice, C. J., & Perkins, K. (1996). *Mental health issues & aging: Building on the strengths of older persons.* Pacific Grove, CA: Brooks/Cole.

Timiras, P. S. (1994). Aging of the nervous system: Structural and biochemical changes. In P. S. Timiras (Ed.), *Physiological basis of aging and geriatrics* (pp.). Boca Raton, FL: CRC Press.

Tornstam, L. (2005). *Gerotranscendence: A developmental theory of positive aging.* New York: Springer.

Toseland, R. W., Diehl, M., Freeman, K., Manzanares, T., Naleppa, M., & McCallion, P. (1997). The impact of validation group therapy on nursing home residents with dementia. *Journal of Applied Gerontology, 61,* 31–50.

U.S. Census Bureau. (1999). *Centenarians in the United States (1990).* Retrieved December 1, 2009 from www.census.gov/population/www/socdemo/age/general-age.html

U.S. Department of Health & Human Services. (2009). *A patient's guide to* the HIPAA Privacy Rule: When health care providers may communicate about you with your family, friends, or others involved in your care. Retrieved December 1, 2009 from www.hhs.gov/ocr/privacy/hipaa/understanding/consumers/consumer_ffg.pdf

Vaillant, G. E. (1977). *Adaptation to life.* Boston: Little, Brown.

Vaillant, G. E. (2002). *Aging well.* Boston: Little, Brown.

Vaillant, G. E. (2007). Aging well. *American Journal of Geriatric Psychiatry, 15*(3), 181–183.

Victoroff, J. (2005). Central nervous system changes with normal aging. In B. J. Sadock & V. A. Sadock (Eds.), *Kaplan & Sadock's comprehensive textbook of psychiatry* (8th ed., pp. 3610–3624). Philadelphia, PA: Lippincott Williams & Wilkins.

Watt, L. M., & Cappeliez, P. (1995). Reminiscence interventions for the treatment of depression in older adults. In B. Haight & J. D. Webster (Eds.), *The art and science of reminiscing: Theory, research, methods, and applications* (pp. 221–232). Washington, DC: Taylor & Francis.

Waxman, H. M., McCreary, G., Weinrit, R. M., & Carner, E. A. (1995). A comparison of somatic complaints among depressed and nondepressed older persons. *Gerontologist, 25*(5), 501–507.

Weissmann, M. M. (1995). *Mastering depression through interpersonal psychotherapy and monitoring forms.* San Antonio, TX: Psychological Corporation.

Weissman, M. M., Bruce, M. L., Leaf, P. J., Florio, L. P., & Holzer, C., III. (1991). Affective disorders. In L. N. Robins & D. A. Regier (Eds.), *Psychiatric disorders in America: The Epidemiologic Catchment Area Study* (pp. 53–80). New York: Free Press.

Weissman, M. M., Leaf, P. J., Tischler, G. L., Blazer, D. G., Karno, M., Bruce, M. L., & Florio, L. P. (1988). Affective disorders in five United States communities. *Psychological Medicine, 18*(1), 141–153.

Weissman, M. M., Markowitz, J. C., & Klerman, G. L. (2000). *Comprehensive guide to interpersonal psychotherapy.* New York: Basic Books.

Widlitz, M., & Marin, D. (2002). Substance abuse in older adults: An overview. *Geriatrics, 57,* 29–34.

Williams, W. C. (1984). *The doctor stories.* New York: New Directions. (Originally published 1958)

Willis, S. E., Tennstedt, S. I., Marsiske, M., Ball, K., Elias, J., Koepke, K. M., . . . Wright, E. (2006). Long-term effects of cognitive training on everyday functional outcomes in older adults. *Journal of the American Medical Association, 296,* 2805–2814.

Won, A. B., Lapane, K. L., Vallow, S., Schein, J., Morris, J. N., & Lipsitz, L. A. (2004). Persistent nonmalignant pain and analgesic prescribing patterns in elderly nursing home residents. *Journal of the American Geriatrics Society, 52*(6), 867–874.

Woods, B., Spector, A., Jones, C., Orrell, M., & Davies, S. (2005). Reminiscence therapy for dementia. *Cochrane Database of Systematic Reviews*, Issue 2. Art. No. CD001120. doi: 10.1002/14651858.CD001120.pub2

Wyman, M. F., Gum, A., & Areán, P. A. (2006). Psychotherapy with older adults. In M. E. Agronin & G. J. Maletta (Eds.), *Principles and practice of geriatric psychiatry* (pp. 177–197). Philadelphia, PA: Lippincott Williams & Wilkins.

Yassa, R., Dastoor, D., Nastase, C., Camille, Y., & Belzile, L. (1993). The prevalence of late-onset schizophrenia in a psychogeriatric population. *Journal of Geriatric Psychiatry and Neurology, 6,* 120–125.

Yassa, R., Nair, N. P., & Iskander, H. (1988). Late-onset bipolar disorder. *Psychiatric Clinics of North America, 11*(1), 117–131.

Yost, E. B., Beutler, L. E., Corbishley, M. A., & Allender, J. R. (1986). *Group cognitive therapy: A treatment approach for depressed older adults.* New York: Pergamon.

Young, R. C., & Klerman, G. L. (1992). Mania in late life: Focus on age of onset. *American Journal of Psychiatry, 149,* 867–876.

Youssef, F. A. (1990). The impact of group reminiscence counseling on a depressed elderly population. *Nurse Practitioner, 15,* 32–38.

Zerhusen, J. D., Boyle, K., & Wilson, W. (1991). Out of the darkhouse: Group cognitive therapy for depressed elderly. *Journal of Psychosocial Nursing and Mental Health Services, 29,* 16–21.

Zweig, R., & Agronin, M. E. (2006). Personality disorders in late life. In M. E. Agronin & G. J. Maletta (Eds.), *Principles and practice of geriatric psychiatry* (pp. 449–470). Philadelphia, PA: Lippincott Williams & Wilkins.

Index

Index

Index